Biotechnology, Gestation, and the Law

Biotechnology, Gestation, and the Law

ELIZABETH CHLOE ROMANIS
*Associate Professor in Biolaw, Durham Law School,
University of Durham, UK*

OXFORD
UNIVERSITY PRESS

OXFORD
UNIVERSITY PRESS

Great Clarendon Street, Oxford, OX2 6DP,
United Kingdom

Oxford University Press is a department of the University of Oxford.
It furthers the University's objective of excellence in research, scholarship,
and education by publishing worldwide. Oxford is a registered trade mark of
Oxford University Press in the UK and in certain other countries

Published in the United States of America by Oxford University Press
198 Madison Avenue, New York, NY 10016, United States of America

British Library Cataloguing in Publication Data

Data available

Library of Congress Control Number: 2024946527

ISBN 9780198873785

DOI: 10.1093/9780191986574.001.0001

Printed and bound by
CPI Group (UK) Ltd, Croydon, CR0 4YY

MIX
Paper | Supporting responsible forestry
FSC® C013604

The manufacturer's authorised representative in the EU for product safety is Oxford University Press España S.A. of el Parque Empresarial San Fernando de Henares, Avenida de Castilla, 2 – 28830 Madrid (www.oup.es/en).

For
Elizabeth Juliet Romanis
Elizabeth Patricia Wilson
Elizabeth Blanche Romanis

ACKNOWLEDGEMENTS

The writing of this book was supported by two fellowships: (1) a fellowship-in-residence at the Edmond and Lily Safra Center for Ethics and the Petrie-Flom Center for Health Law Policy, Biotechnology, and Bioethics at Harvard Law School at Harvard University and (2) a visiting fellowship with Lancaster University's Wellcome-funded Future of Human Reproduction Programme. I am thankful to the Edmond and Lily Safra Center for Ethics for hosting a seminar in which we discussed the ideas in Chapter 5, and especially to Dr Louise King who was a commentator on the paper. Equally, I am grateful to the Future of Human Reproduction Project for the numerous seminars they organised in which I could present and receive feedback on the ideas in Chapters 5, 6, and 7. Special thanks to Dr Laura O'Donovan, Professor Alison Stone, and Dr Nicola Williams for acting as commentators at these events.

I extend particular thanks to colleagues who at various points read a chapter of this book: Dr Dunja Begović, Nathan Chalk, Dr Sabrina Germain, Dr Richard Gibson, Dr Victoria Hooton, Dr Alice King, Dr Dafni Lima, Dr Zaina Mahmoud, Dr Anna Nelson, Dr Jordan Parsons, and Dr Zoe Tongue. Feedback at various informal gatherings in the E&L Safra Center for Ethics at Harvard were also really helpful; so I am also thankful to my fellows-in-residence for regular discussion. Finally, a thank you to all who attended the work-in-progress session hosted by Gender and Law at Durham. I am grateful to those who listened and gave feedback at the embodiment stream of the Socio-Legal Studies Conference 2024 and the Future of Human Reproduction-funded 'Normative Implications of the Metaphysics of Extra-Corporeal Gestation' conference at the University of Liverpool (especially to Professor Mary O'Donnelly for acting as commentator). A thank you also to Dr Victoria Adkins for our Teams writing days.

The gestation of this book took rather longer than anticipated due to unforeseen circumstances (among a number of things). I wish to thank all of the family and friends who supported in practical ways when things were at their most difficult. There are too many to name, but you know who you are. Thanks are also due to Matthew Williams at Oxford University Press for his patience.

Finally, my biggest thanks are always for Nathan Chalk and Nora. Thank you for your endless patience, love, kindness, and encouragement when I thought writing this book would never end.

CONTENTS

TABLE OF CASES

IRELAND

GERMANY

EUROPEAN COURT OF HUMAN RIGHTS

EUROPEAN COURT OF JUSTICE (EUROPEAN UNION)

TABLE OF LEGISLATION

CANADA

FRANCE

SPAIN

INTERNATIONAL INSTRUMENTS

1
INTRODUCTION

Gestation, the process of becoming before birth,[1] is the process of which each of us are the result. The very nature of human gestation, however, has shifted and will continue to shift because of technology. Biotechnologies, in all sorts of forms, have 'dramatically altered humankind', most notably in how they have expanded choices for individuals about 'what they do with their bodies and how they relate to their bodies'.[2] Gestation is no exception: technologies that could enable new modalities of gestation (as part of and beyond bodies) are within our imagined future. Uterus transplantation (UTx), the transplant of a functioning uterus into the body of a person absent a uterus, enables a person who was previously unable to sustain a pregnancy to do so. Gestation as we have known it has been confined to the uterus of a person born assigned female at birth (AFAB). UTx makes imaginable pregnancies in bodies that were not AFAB. Thus, it has the capacity to 'unsex' pregnancy and introduce the possibility of gestation beyond the confines of reproductive biosex.[3] Ectogestation, the partial or complete facilitation of gestation in an artificial device (outside the body), more drastically alters the nature of gestation as we know it: by enabling gestation without pregnancy, that is, gestation beyond the body. These novel technological interventions enabling gestation in different modalities, and the process of gestation itself, are the focus of this book.

There has been relatively little ethico-legal academic interest in pregnancy itself (rather than the fetus),[4] and there has been even less in *gestation*.[5] My goal

[1] Elizabeth Chloe Romanis and Victoria Adkins, 'Artificial Placentas, Pregnancy Loss and Loss-sensitive Care' (2024) 50 Journal of Medical Ethics 299–307, 302.

[2] Margaret Brazier, Anne-Maree Farrell, and Danielle Griffiths, 'Translational Bodies: Exploring the Socio-legal Contours of Human Bodies Past Present and Future' (2015) 7 Law, Innovation, and Technology 151–60, 153.

[3] Elizabeth Chloe Romanis and Alan Brown, 'Legal Parenthood, Novel Reproductive Practices, and the Disruption of Reproductive Biosex' (2024) Modern Law Review <doi.org/10.1111/1468-2230.12914> accessed 1 September 2024; see Chapter 5.

[4] Suki Finn, 'Being-from-Birth: Pregnancy and Philosophy' (2023) 19 European Journal of Analytic Philosophy S17–S32, S19.

[5] This is because often where scholars claim to be examining 'gestation' they are examining 'pregnancy' perpetuating a category mistake (see discussion in Chapter 2) eg Andrea Mulligan, 'Surrogacy and the Significance of Gestation: Implications for Law and Policy' (2024) Bioethics <doi.org/10.1111/bioe.13302> accessed 1 September 2024.

Biotechnology, Gestation, and the Law. Elizabeth Chloe Romanis, Oxford University Press.
 DOI: 10.1093/9780191986574.003.0001

in this work is to bring both pregnancy and gestation into the foreground of an analysis of procreative futures. Gestation, pregnancy, and birthing are, in a social sense, central organizing concepts in how we think about the classification of bodies, how we construct individual and parental identity, and how we recognize (or do not recognize) families. In this book, I critically interrogate gestation in the law (what it is and what its implications are) in relation to procreative choice-making, abortion rights, sex and gender, and parenthood. To identify the pertinent questions, I focus on the significance of gestation and of pregnancy across different contexts. My approach is unique and significant in bringing insights from metaphysics and phenomenology, as well as classification, to provide conceptual clarity to an area of law in which category mistakes are common and the implications are ever greater as new technologies come to the fore. The implications are not, as illustrated, confined to one issue or one area of the law.

Procreative technologies, as Rosser describes them, are neither innately good nor bad, rather 'it is the way that they are used that determines their potential for benefit or harm'.[6] I argue that it is not only how technologies enabling gestation are used but the social and legal *context* in which they are used that can determine whether their consequences are a net harm or benefit. As I illustrate throughout this book, without radical social and legal reform, the potential of novel technologies enabling gestation cannot be realized, most especially for people whose procreative journeys and experiences are often the subject of the most stringent social and legal obstacles.

Technologies Enabling Gestation

For successful procreation, there must be gestation. This process transforms a conceptus into an entity that can (usually) survive in the external environment.[7] As a matter of evolutionary biology, human gestation is sustained by pregnancy facilitated by the uterus[8] of a person AFAB. Where individuals want to become parents by creating new life but do not have the capacity (for biological, psychosocial, or social reasons) to become pregnant, they must seek assistance with gestation. Assistance with gestation has historically been

[6] Sue Rosser, *Teaching Science and Health from a Feminist Perspective* (Pergamon Press 1986) 40.
[7] Romanis and Adkins (n 1); see Chapter 2.
[8] An adaptive hypothesis of human gestation holds that human gestation is a process confined to mature bodies as a protective strategy (it provides the safest environment): Michael Power and Jay Schulkin, *The Evolution of the Human Placenta* (Johns Hopkins University Press 2012) 51.

talked about narrowly—in being necessary to support people experiencing subfertility/involuntary childlessness because of the, as Ber put it, 'womb factor'.[9] Ber describes this as affecting people AFAB who biotypically would have a functional uterus, but who do not due to a primary/secondary anatomical malformation meaning that it is non-functional, or the individual is lacking a uterus because of a congenital condition or surgical removal.[10] However, it is not only people AFAB who are in need of assistance with gestation but also, for example, people assigned male at birth (AMAB) who are single or in a same-sex relationship will need gestational support to procreate. For some time, surrogacies,[11] in which a person other than the intended parent sustains the pregnancy facilitating gestation and births the resulting child,[12] have been the available form of assistance. Gestational surrogacies, in which the person undertaking pregnancy is not genetically related to the gestating entity,[13] is more prevalent than the alternative (full surrogacies) in which the surrogate is also the egg donor,[14] because it allows an intended parent to provide the egg and be biologically related to the resulting child (where it is possible for them to do so).[15] Consequently, it is predominantly gestational surrogacies that are discussed throughout this book. However, gestational surrogacies as a descriptor still encompasses a number of different procreative arrangements, for example, those termed 'commercial' and those deemed 'altruistic', though it should be noted that the boundary between commercial and altruistic arrangements is not always clear.[16]

While surrogacies have existed in some forms almost as long as human procreation, it has a much shorter legal history. The UK was the first jurisdiction to introduce legal regulation of surrogacies in the 1980s.[17] Today surrogacies are prohibited in many jurisdictions (eg Spain, Germany, Italy, and France), and in

[9] Rosalie Ber, 'Ethical Issues in Gestational Surrogacy' (2000) 21 Theoretical Medicine and Bioethics 153–69, 154.

[10] ibid.

[11] I use the plural term 'surrogacies' in recognition of the fact that surrogacy is not a singular monolithic technology/practice but takes multiple forms, per Anika König and others, 'Shifting Surrogacies: Comparative Ethnographies' (2022) 63 International Journal of Comparative Sociology 235–46, 237.

[12] F Shenfield and others, 'ESHRE Task Force on Ethics and Law 10: Surrogacy' (2005) 20 Human Reproduction 2705–07, 2705.

[13] ibid.

[14] Kirsty Horsey, 'The Future of Surrogacy: A Review of Current Global Trends and National Landscapes' (2024) 48 Reproductive Biomedicine Online <doi.org/10.1016/j.rbmo.2023.1037642> accessed 1 September 2024.

[15] Benjamin Jones and others, 'Options for Acquiring Motherhood in Absolute Uterine Factor Infertility: Adoption, Surrogacy and Uterine Transplantation' (2021) 21 The Obstetrician & Gynaecologist 138–47, 140.

[16] Horsey, 'The Future of Surrogacy' (n 14).

[17] ibid.

many others, surrogacies are heavily/proscriptively regulated (eg UK, Canada, and some US states) or aspects of it are regulated (eg Denmark, Russia, and the Netherlands).[18] As Lima highlights, the regulatory framework of surrogacies in the UK, in its current form, is complex: it 'sits somewhere between prohibition and recognition'[19] in the sense that 'altruistic' arrangements are not prohibited,[20] but are also not actively facilitated.[21] Surrogacy arrangements are unenforceable,[22] the surrogate (and if married, their spouse) are the legal parents at birth,[23] and transfer of legal parenthood to intended parents after birth is a complex process in which a number of criteria must be satisfied.[24] Although in practice parental orders are often granted where criteria are not met in the interests of born children,[25] this does not detract from the complexity of the process for both surrogate and intended parents.

As Horsey and others have argued, there are many prevailing stereotypes about surrogates, and misconceptions about persons who seek out surrogacies, that taint perceptions of the practice—namely by overlooking how surrogates in domestic arrangements do not perceive themselves as vulnerable while the intended parents do have some specific (and less considered) vulnerabilities.[26] Often those who pursue procreation as intended parents through surrogacies have faced considerable difficulty in their pursuit of parenthood (which is incredibly meaningful to them)—whether this be marked by the social stigma of biological 'subfertility', the impact on their self-esteem, or the discrimination that can be experienced by people who are 'socially' infertile (eg in a same-sex relationship).[27] Acknowledging the vulnerabilities of intended parents is not to deny that surrogates *can* be exploited (even by people with their own vulnerabilities). The position I take in this book is that surrogacies are a reality because there are always people who need assistance with gestation, and there are always people willing to undertake that generative work as

[18] ibid.

[19] Dafni Lima, 'Legal Parenthood in Surrogacy: Shifting the Focus to the Surrogate's Negative Intention' (2024) 46 Journal of Social Welfare and the Law 245–66, 250.

[20] Commercial surrogacy is prohibited per Surrogacy Arrangements Act 1985, ss 2 and 3.

[21] Lima (n 19) 250.

[22] Surrogacy Arrangements Act 1985, s 1A.

[23] Human Fertilisation and Embryology Act 2008, s 33(1).

[24] ibid ss 54 and 54A.

[25] Kirsty Horsey, 'Fraying at the Edges: UK Surrogacy Law in 2015' (2016) 24 Medical Law Review 608–21; Amel Alghrani and Danielle Griffiths, 'The Regulation of Surrogacy in the United Kingdom: The Case for Reform' (2017) 29 Child & Family Law Quarterly 165–86.

[26] Kirsty Horsey and others, 'UK Intended Parents' Characteristics, Experiences, and Views on Surrogacy Law Reform' (2023) 37 International Journal of Law, Policy, and the Family ebad004 <doi.org/10.1093/lawfam/ebad004> 3, accessed 1 September 2024.

[27] ibid.

a form of assistance, even where it is unlawful.[28] Surrogacies are not *innately* exploitative.[29] Surrogacies could be free from exploitation, for example, where they are not underpinned by biological and procreative essentialism and are facilitated in ways designed by surrogates and intended parents to recognize the intentions of all involved (the positive intention of the intended parents to become parents, and the negative intention of the surrogate not to become a parent).[30] Moreover, to avoid exploitation, arrangements must be cognizant of the nature of the work involved: that pregnancy is *fleshy*, *generative*, *transformative* work (whether that is performed for one's own parental goals or someone else),[31] and rights to bodily integrity must be upheld.

While surrogacies are important in supporting procreation where individuals/couples are unable to gestate (for biological, social, and/or psychosocial reasons), different modalities of gestation may be preferable, for intended parents and persons willing to help facilitate gestation,[32] if they were available. For example, for persons who feel strongly that they want to experience pregnancy themselves, surrogacies may be able to facilitate their desire to become a parent, but not *how* to become a parent. Moreover, surrogacies are complex processes—socially, emotionally, and legally, and so an alternative may be valued not only for affording the experience of pregnancy, but also for its ability to circumvent these complexities.[33] The development of uterus transplantation, in which a uterus (including cervix) is transplanted into a body absent a uterus, installs/restores procreative anatomy assigned female,[34] and thus, it has been welcomed as an important development in affording people the opportunity to sustain pregnancies and birth.[35]

[28] ibid.

[29] Though there are circumstances in which surrogacies are or become exploitative. See Dunja Begović, 'Upholding Women's Autonomy in Pregnancy: Responding to the Challenges of New Reproductive Technologies' (PhD thesis, University of Manchester 2021) 138.

[30] See Lima (n 19).

[31] This means affording surrogates the respect that should be afforded to all pregnant people (eg respect for their bodily boundaries).

[32] The perspective of a person who wants to assist another (eg by undertaking surrogacy or donating their womb) is often neglected in these reflections: Alexandra Mullock and others, 'Surrogacy and Uterus Transplantation Using Live Donors: Examining the Options from the Perspective of "Womb-Givers"' (2021) 25 Bioethics 820–28, 820.

[33] ibid 821; Jones and others (n 15) 140; Laura O'Donovan and others, 'Ethical and Policy Issues Raised by Uterus Transplants' (2019) 131 British Medical Bulletin 19–28, 19.

[34] Jones and others (n 15) 142.

[35] Laura O'Donovan, 'Pushing the Boundaries: Uterine Transplantation and the Limits of Reproductive Autonomy' (2018) 32 Bioethics 489–98.

Uterus Transplantation (UTx)

Where uterus transplantation is successful, it enables the uterus recipient to sustain a pregnancy (and thus, themselves, sustain a gestation). In the procedure the donor's uterus (excluding ovaries/oviduct) is isolated for removal,[36] a process that is complex because of the careful isolation of uterus from the internal iliac veins and arteries (that drain blood in the lower body).[37] The uterus can be obtained from either a live or deceased donor.[38] The organ is then flushed for transplantation. Simultaneous to these processes, surgery is undertaken to prepare the recipient for the organ by dissecting the iliac vessels for connection. The uterus is brought into the pelvis and the donor uterine veins are connected to the external iliac veins.[39] The recipient then must take immunosuppressive drugs to prevent rejection of the uterus.[40] Embryo transfer into the uterus[41] can then take place to establish a pregnancy after a period of time (about six months to one year). Birth must be by caesarean section.[42] UTx is conceptualized as an 'ephemeral' transplant[43] and a procreative technology since '[s]uccess of UTx is determined by a clear endpoint: childbirth'.[44] The United States Uterus Transplant Consortium defined success by reference to seven stages: (1) technical success (viability three months post-surgery), (2) menstruation, (3) embryo implantation, (4) pregnancy, (5) delivery, (6) graft removal, and (7) longer-term follow-up.[45] Surgeons recommend, unsurprisingly since UTx has been conceptualized as an ephemeral procreative

[36] While most surgeries to date have been open laparotomies, some research teams are investigating the use of robotic-assisted laparoscopy (and some procedures successfully performed): Mats Brännström and others, 'Uterus Transplantation: From Research, through Human Trials and into the Future' (2023) 29 Human Reproduction Update 521–44, 539.

[37] Mats Brännström and others, 'Livebirth after Uterus Transplantation' (2015) 385 The Lancet 607–16, 608.

[38] For debate on the relative permissibility of deceased and living donation see Nicola Williams, 'Should Deceased Donation be Morally Preferred in Uterine Transplantation' (2016) 30 Bioethics 415–24.

[39] Brännström and others (n 37) 609.

[40] Guiseppe D'Amico and others, 'Immunosuppression in Uterus Transplantation: From Transplant to Delivery' (2023) 29 Expert Opinion on Pharmacotherapy 29–35.

[41] Egg retrieval is often undertaken before uterus transplantation. One group explains that this is because they only undertake the procedure where the recipient has their own viable eggs. See Brännström and others (n 37).

[42] Elliott Richards and others, 'Uterus Transplant: State of the Art in 2021' (2021) 38 Journal of Assisted Reproduction and Genetics 2251–59, 2256.

[43] Brännström and others (n 37).

[44] Ledibabari Ngaage and others, 'The Changing Paradigm of Ethics in Uterus Transplantation: A Systematic Review' (2020) 33 Transplant International 260–69, 264. Liza Johannesson and others, 'Guidelines for Standardized Nomenclature and Reporting in Uterus Transplantation: An Opinion from the United States Uterus Transplant Consortium' (2020) 20 American Journal of Transplantation 3319–25, 3321.

[45] Johannesson and others (n 44) 3321.

technology,[46] that the uterus is removed after the recipient has undertaken one or two pregnancies resulting in live birth.[47] This recommendation is premised on the notion that two pregnancies[48] allow people to build their families over a period of time, but means that there is not prolonged exposure to immunosuppressive drugs. In this conceptualization of UTx, involuntary childlessness from an inability to sustain a pregnancy is construed as a 'medical need' and a means of 'treating a particular kind of infertility' which has significant implications.[49]

UTx is in the process of transitioning from clinical research to being considered clinical treatment[50] following a considerable number of successful surgeries (and live births resulting from the transplants) worldwide.[51] Advancements in the development of UTx since first proof of concept in humans in the early 2000s have been described as 'rapid', since there was less than fifteen years between first proof of concept (though a failed attempt)[52] and a live birth.[53] This live birth was the result of over a decade of animal research into uterus transplantation undertaken by several groups across the world.[54] Advancements since the first birth have also been rapid. The first baby was born from a transplanted uterus (donated by a sixty-one-year-old family friend unrelated to the recipient) in Sweden in 2014,[55] and since it has been estimated that there have been over forty-five live births from UTx across the globe.[56] UTx is now very much a global endeavour, with the transplant having been

[46] That this is the case has significant normative implications, including where its use is considered appropriate. As one example, where its use is procreative, its use is for pregnancy, and there may be other uses (eg to experience menstruation) that would not be considered sufficient for transplant. See Elizabeth Chloe Romanis and Evie Kendal, 'Subjective Experience, Gestational Preferences and Justice: Valuing Both Uterus Transplantation and Ectogestation' in Natasha Hammond-Browning and Nicola Williams (eds), *International Legal and Ethical Perspectives on Uterus Transplantation* (Edward Elgar 2024) 118.

[47] Richards and others (n 42) 2256.

[48] Romanis and Kendal (n 46) 118.

[49] Ruby Catsanos, Wendy Rogers, and Mianna Lotz, 'The Ethics of Uterus Transplantation' (2013) 27 Bioethics 65–73, 67.

[50] Natasha Hammond-Browning, 'Regulating Uterus Transplantation: The United Kingdom' in Natasha Hammond-Browning and Nicola Williams (eds), *International Legal and Ethical Perspectives on Uterus Transplantation* (Edward Elgar 2024) 275.

[51] Mats Brännström and others, 'Registry of the International Society of Uterus Transplantation: First Report' (2023) 107 Transplantation 10–17.

[52] Although scholars often reference an attempt in 2000 in Saudi Arabia as the first attempt, it is more accurate to note that UTx was first attempted in the early 1930s in Germany (though this was not thought to establish 'proof of concept'). See Natasha Hammond-Browning and Nicola Williams, 'Introduction' in Natasha Hammond-Browning and Nicola Williams (eds), *International Legal and Ethical Perspectives on Uterus Transplantation* (Edward Elgar 2024) 2.

[53] Ledibabari Ngaage and others (n 44) 264.

[54] Brännström and others (n 36) 523–26.

[55] Brännström and others (n 37) 607.

[56] Hakan Ongun and others, 'Miracles of Science: Birth after Uterus Transplantation' (2024) 50 Journal of Obstetrics and Gynaecology Research 4–14, 8.

performed over 100 times worldwide in at least fourteen countries.[57] A uterus transplant was first performed in the UK during the gestation of this book in 2023.[58]

What is fascinating about UTx is how pioneering surgeons describe the idea as having come from their patients: patients who might want to become pregnant in the future. Brännström, the leading surgeon behind the world's first live birth from UTx, describes how he had never contemplated UTx as a concept until a patient facing a hysterectomy informed him that she had a solution to her (soon-to-be) absence of a uterus: a transplant with her mother as the donor.[59] As noted, UTx has been framed 'as solely a treatment for [cis-]women's infertility',[60] and, consequently, it is unsurprising that the procedure has, to date, only been performed on people AFAB without a functional uterus.[61] The international community of research surgeons developing the procedure have, over the years, developed ethical frameworks for UTx, including 'the Montreal Criteria',[62] which outlined what experts considered to be an ethical framework for decisions about eligibility for UTx. The authors list the first criterion of the recipient as being that they are 'a genetic female of reproductive age with no medical contraindications to transplantation'.[63] As Balayla and others note, this suggested criterion 'inherently disqualifies transgender, some non-binary, gender-diverse, and cis-gender women who have a non-XX karyotype'.[64] The criterion was suggested not as a matter of moral comment on the possibility of UTx for people AMAB in future, rather as a reflection on the additional complexities of the procedure in a person with physiology assigned male.[65]

In recent years there has been suggestion that UTx should be taken seriously as a therapeutic option for fertility preservation for transgender women or nonbinary people AMAB.[66] These individuals similarly suffer from absolute

[57] Hammond-Browning and Williams (n 52) 5.

[58] Coincidentally, this transplant took place in the department at the Churchill where I worked as a healthcare assistant in transplant surgery for a short time shortly after leaving secondary school. See NHS Imperial College Healthcare Trust, 'First Womb Transplant Performed in the UK' (2023) <https://www.imperial.nhs.uk/about-us/news/first-womb-transplant-performed-in-the-uk> accessed 25 June 2024.

[59] Mats Brännström, 'The Swedish Uterus Transplantation Project: The Story Behind the Swedish Uterus Transplantation Project' (2015) 94 Acta Obstetricia et Gynecologica Scandinavica 675–79, 676.

[60] Romanis and Kendal (n 46) 118.

[61] Jacques Balayla and others, 'The Montreal Criteria and Uterine Transplants in Transgender Women' (2021) 35 Bioethics 326–30, 327.

[62] Ariel Lefkowitz, Marcel Edwards, and Jacques Balayla, 'The Montreal Criteria for the Ethical Feasibility of Uterine Transplantation' (2012) 25 Transplant International 439–47.

[63] ibid 444.

[64] Balayla and others (n 61) 327.

[65] ibid.

[66] Erna Bayar and others, 'Fertility Preservation and Realignment in Transgender Women' (2023) 26 Human Fertility 463–82, 473–74.

uterine factor infertility, which causes the same psychological distress observed in some cis-gendered women absent a uterus who want to experience pregnancy.[67] There has not yet been an attempt to transplant a uterus into a person who was not assigned female at birth, but a group of gynaecological surgeons based in the UK conclude that, 'despite a number of anatomical, hormonal, fertility and obstetric considerations that require consideration, there is no overwhelming clinical argument against performing UTx as part of [gender reassignment]'.[68] Balayla and others list some of the anatomical challenges as space in the abdomen, suitable vascularization of the uterus, and variance in the hormonal profile of the recipient.[69] In addition, Jahromi and others cite the lack of ligamentous support for the uterus.[70] Nevertheless, these are only *technical* difficulties, not insurmountable challenges.[71] Jones and others note that there is considerable interest amongst transgender women in the possibility of receiving a transplanted uterus, often for reproducing.[72] There has also been the suggestion that cis-gendered men might also be interested in the possibility of receiving a transplanted uterus in order to undertake pregnancy.[73] While the challenges in these cases may be greater still, we should not consider them impossible to overcome.

Future directions in UTx do not concern only who obtains a uterus, but also what uterus that person obtains. There is the potential in future that the development of a bioengineered uterus (using the person wanting a uterus's own stem cells to generate the necessary material and a scaffold) might be able to reduce the complexities (both ethical and surgical) of uterus donation.[74] A bioengineered uterus would enable individuals to obtain a uterus (for procreative or other purposes) without the need for a donor, and there would be a decreased risk of organ rejection (since the organ comprises the person's own genetic material).[75] Bioengineered uterine segments, though not complete

[67] Benjamin Jones and others, 'Uterine Transplantation in Transgender Women' (2019) 126 British Journal of Obstetrics & Gynaecology 152, 152.

[68] ibid 156.

[69] Balayla and others (n 61) 329.

[70] Alireza Hamidian Jahromi and others, 'Uterine Transplantation and Donation in Transgender Individuals: Proof of Concept' (2021) 22 International Journal of Transgender Health 349–59, 351.

[71] ibid; Balayla and others (n 61) 329.

[72] Benjamin Jones and others, 'Perceptions and Motivations for Uterus Transplant in Transgender Women' (2021) 4 JAMA Network Open e2034561.

[73] Robert Sparrow, 'Is it Every Man's Right to Have Babies if He Wants Them? Male Pregnancy and the Limits of Procreative Liberty' (2008) 18 Kennedy Institute of Ethics Journal 275–99.; Tim Murphy, 'Assisted Gestation and Transgender Women' (2014) 20 Bioethics 389–97, 391.

[74] Brännström and others (n 36) 539.

[75] Andrea Etrusco and others, 'The Reproductive Potential of Uterus Transplantation: Future Prospects' (2022) 93 Acta Biomed e2022138; Mats Brännström, 'Uterus Transplantation and Beyond' (2017) 28 Journal of Materials Science: Materials in Medicine <doi.org/10.1007/s10856-017-5872-0> accessed 1 September 2024.

functioning organs, have been successfully tested in animals.[76] Brännström and others thus predict that it might be at least a decade until a technique for bioengineered uteri is refined enough in animal models for human testing.[77] It makes for an exciting future prospect for those absent a uterus who wish to become pregnant. However, for those with or without a uterus who specifically wish to avoid a pregnancy, uterus transplants, with donor material or bioengineered material, do not meet their procreative needs.

Ectogestation

There has been sustained interest in the possibility of the 'artificial womb' and of babies gestated from conception to birth outside the body for a century, since the idea was first suggested by JBS Haldane in the 1920s.[78] This process when imagined was referred to as 'ectogenesis'.[79] This term, from its etymological roots 'ecto' (outside) and 'genesis', 'literally means "development outside"'.[80] As Kingma and Finn note, however, there is considerable development that human entities undergo after their birth (post-gestation). When we refer to machines that can perform gestation (where there is no person facilitating a pregnancy), we are not referring to 'development outside the body', but a very specific process of development outside the body,[81] that is, gestation, the process of transformation from conceptus to mature fetus (this process is described in more detail in Chapter 2). Gestation ex utero, they explain, is better termed 'ectogestation' (literally meaning 'outside' gestation).[82] There have been some attempts made by scientists to enable gestation outside of pregnancy (ie gestation beyond person-facilitated gestation) in the past; however, interest has intensified since successful animal studies of model artificial placentas facilitating *partial* ectogestation were published in 2017. In contrast to

[76] Mats Hellström and others, 'Bioengineered Uterine Tissue Supports Pregnancy in a Rat Model' (2016) 106 Fertility and Sterility 487–95e.1.

[77] Brännström and others (n 36) 539.

[78] JBS Haldane, *Daedalus or Science and the Future: A Paper Read to the Heretics, Cambridge on February 4th, 1923* (EP Dutton & Company 1924). See discussion Progress Educational Trust, '100 years of "Daedalus": The Birth of Assisted Reproductive Technology' <https://www.progress.org.uk/100-years-of-daedalus-the-birth-of-assisted-reproductive-technology/> accessed 25 June 2024.

[79] ibid.

[80] Elselijn Kingma and Suki Finn, 'Neonatal Incubator or Artificial Womb? Distinguishing Ectogestation and Ectogenesis using the Metaphysics of Pregnancy' (2020) 34 Bioethics 354–63, 356; Suki Finn and Sasha Isaac, 'Evaluating Ectogenesis via the Metaphysics of Pregnancy' in Robbie Davis-Floyd, *Birthing Techno-Sapiens: Human Evolution and the Future of Reproduction* (Routledge 2021) 136.

[81] Kingma and Finn (n 80) 356.

[82] ibid 360.

complete ectogestation (the facilitation of gestation from conception to birth by machine), *partial* ectogestation describes a process in which a fetus is partially gestated by a pregnancy but then the process is continued by a machine. Both complete and partial ectogestation are technologies enabling gestation offering different procreative futures. Partial ectogestation, it must be noted, is the more immediate possibility.[83]

In 2017 a team of fetal scientists and surgeons in Philadelphia revealed an artificial placenta prototype that had yielded promising results in animal testing.[84] Their design, named the Biobag/EXTEND therapy, is carefully designed to extend gestation after pregnancy by mimicking the uterine environment and functions of the placenta in a mammalian pregnancy. EXTEND seals its animal subject in artificial amniotic fluid, to which essential nutrients are supplied through cannulae emulating an umbilical cord. Circulation is maintained, exactly as in utero, by the subject's heartbeat supported by an oxygenator.[85] EXTEND has been successfully used to gestate lambs extracted preterm from ewe uteri for a period of 110 days, during which time there was clear evidence of continued 'creation' (growth and organ maturation). The lambs developed as if they had remained in utero, and there were no incidences of the common complications associated with preterm birth (infection, respiratory distress, and heart failure).[86] Another research team, based in Western Australia, has reported similar results from testing their prototype artificial placenta, the EVE platform.[87] Their design is similar in composition and function to EXTEND, and has also yielded positive results in animal testing (though there are greater incidences of complications).[88] Further teams in the USA[89] and Canada[90] have reported animal testing of their model devices on fetal pigs (which they claim make have better 'translational relevance'[91] as

[83] Elizabeth Chloe Romanis, 'Partial Ectogenesis: Freedom, Equality, and Political Perspective' (2020) 46 Journal of Medical Ethics 89–90, 89.

[84] Emily Partridge and others, 'An Extra-uterine System to Physiologically Support the Extreme Preterm Lamb' (2017) 8 Nature Communications 15112.

[85] See ibid 2–4 for a detailed description of how EXTEND functions.

[86] ibid, 2; ibid, 6.

[87] Harou Usuda, Shimpei Watanabe, Yuichiro Miura, and others, 'Successful Maintenance of Key Physiological Parameters in Preterm Lambs Treated with Ex Vivo Uterine Environment Therapy for a Period of 1 Week' (2017) 217 American Journal of Obstetrics and Gynecology 457.e1–457.e13; Harou Usuda, Shimpei Watanabe, Masatoshi Saito, and others, 'Successful Use of an Artificial Placenta to Support Extremely Preterm Ovine Fetuses at the Border of Viability (2019) 221 American Journal of Obstetrics and Gynecology 69.

[88] ibid.

[89] Ayssa Abrao Trad and others, 'Report of an Experiment with a Fetal Ex-Utero Support System in Piglets' (2023) 15 Cureus e38223.

[90] Alex Charest-Pekeski and others, 'Achieving Sustained Extrauterine Life: Challenges of an Artificial Placenta in Fetal Pigs as a Model of the Preterm Human Fetus' (2021) 9 Physiological Reports e14742.

[91] Abrao Trad and others (n 89).

there are greater similarities in umbilical cord anatomy and weight between the pig and human fetus than between the lamb and human fetus).[92] Another research team in the Netherlands is presently planning to test early versions of their model on fetal manikins (with a digital twin).[93]

These devices are being pursued as an alternative to neonatal intensive care because of the inherent limitations of current technologies, including the constraints of fetal maturity and the common complications of conventional interventions.[94] Artificial placentas are thought potentially capable of circumventing the current viability limit of twenty-two weeks,[95] because, unlike mechanical ventilation, artificial placentas do not require their subject to have fully formed lungs. Moreover, it is thought that common complications from intensive care, such as lung damage, infection, and heart failure, which often prove fatal, could be entirely avoided,[96] where the process of gestation is continued post-pregnancy, rather than a premature human entity (that is physiologically immature) being supported with the life functions it must perform in order to survive in the external environment (eg breathing air).[97] Gestation ex utero (ectogestation) facilitates continued organ maturation, as the 'central principle underlying the iterative development of [these devices] . . . is to treat extremely preterm infants as fetuses, rather than as small babies . . . to avoid the use of pulmonary gas exchange'.[98] These devices, as they are designed to facilitate partial ectogestation, begin with a pregnancy that must be ended, and thus there is some intervention to remove the fetus and transfer it to an artificial placenta device.[99] This is a form of surgical delivery (inevitably) because it allows more control over fetal physiology in the transfer of the entity; the fetus must be prevented from making the transition from fetal to neonatal physiology.[100] Because of the focus on the state of the fetus in the delivery, and because of the

[92] Charest-Pekeski and others (n 90).

[93] Bettine van Willigen and others, 'A Review Study of Fetal Circulatory Models to Develop a Digital Twin of a Fetus in a Perinatal Life Support System' (2022) 10 Frontiers in Pediatrics 915846.

[94] Elizabeth Chloe Romanis, 'Artificial Womb Technology and the Frontiers of Human Reproduction: Conceptual Differences and Potential Implications' (2018) 44 Journal of Medical Ethics 751, 752.

[95] This point is identified because it is the approximate gestational age of the youngest premature neonate that has survived.

[96] Partridge and others (n 84).

[97] Emily Partridge and Alan Flake, 'The Artificial Womb' in Mark Kilby, Antony Johnson, and Dick Oepkes, *Fetal Therapy: Scientific Basis and Critical Appraisal of Clinical Benefits* (CUP 2020) 83.

[98] Harou Usuda and others (n 88).

[99] E Joanne Verweij and Elselijn Kingma, 'Artificial Placenta – Imminent Ethical Considerations for Research Trials and Clinical Translation' (2023) 23 The American Journal of Bioethics 87–89, 87.

[100] Alan Flake, 'A Supportive Physiologic Environment for the Extreme Premature Infant: Improving Life Outside the Womb' (2022) 57 Journal of Pediatric Surgery 167–71, 169.

timing/conditions of delivery, surgical delivery for transfer to an artificial placenta is far more complex than a caesarean section.[101]

All the research teams currently developing artificial placenta prototypes are optimistic about the prospects of the technology as treatment for preterm neonates in the not-so-distant future. The EVE team note that their findings 'demonstrate the clinical utility of a further refined EVE therapy system to improve outcomes for extremely preterm infants'.[102] The EXTEND team have consistently reiterated that their device will soon be ready for testing on human subjects.[103] In 2019, the lead investigator predicted that only a decade from now conventional neonatal intensive care will have been replaced by artificial placenta devices.[104] The EXTEND team have obtained sufficient equity financing for human testing.[105] The US Food and Drug Administration (FDA), agreeing with the EXTEND team's assessment that movement from lamb testing to first-in-human use is appropriate,[106] has designated EXTEND a 'breakthrough device', meaning it will receive expedited FDA assessment and priority review for premarket approval.[107] The FDA Pediatric Advisory Committee dedicated its September 2023 meeting to discussion of 'the appropriate development plans for establishing safety and effectiveness of artificial womb technology (AWT) devices, including regulatory and ethical considerations for first in human (FIH studies)' limited to its use in place of conventional neonatal intensive care for extremely preterm neonates.[108] While the FDA did not give the immediate go ahead to testing in humans, their answer was not 'no' but a 'not now'. Substantial progress has been made in the development of these technologies in the time I have been researching them; however, it is clear that some challenges remain ahead of clinical translation, for example, design of

[101] I am grateful to Dr E Joanne Verweij for discussion of this process.

[102] Usuda and others (n 88).

[103] Partridge and others (n 84).

[104] Children's Hospital of Philadelphia, 'Unique Womb-Like Device Could Reduce Mortality and Disability for Extremely Premature Babies' (2017) *Medical Xpress* <https://medicalxpress.com/news/2017-04-unique-womb-like-device-mortality-disability.html> accessed 22 October 2019.

[105] John George, 'Vitara Biomedical Raises $25M to Advance its Artificial Womb Technology for Premature Babies' (2022) <https://www.bizjournals.com/philadelphia/news/2022/08/09/vitara-biomedical-philadelphia-artificial-womb.html> accessed 25 June 2024.

[106] Alan Flake, 'A Supportive Physiologic Environment for the Extreme Premature Infant: Improving Life Outside the Womb' (2022) 57 Journal of Pediatric Surgery 167–71, 169.

[107] US Food and Drug Administration, 'Breakthrough Devices Program' (nd) <https://www.fda.gov/medical-devices/how-study-and-market-your-device/breakthrough-devices-program> accessed 25 June 2024.

[108] US Food and Drug Administration, 'Pediatric Advisory Committee Meeting Announcement' (2023) <https://www.fda.gov/advisory-committees/advisory-committee-calendar/pediatric-advisory-committee-meeting-announcement-09192023> accessed 25 June 2024.

the device,[109] and the collection of sufficient animal data both about the period of time animals are in the device and their condition post-ex utero gestation.[110] That said, partial ectogestation is, in all likelihood, in the not-so-distant future.

All the model artificial placenta devices mentioned are capable of only facilitating *partial ectogestation* since they are reliant on the subject having fetal physiology (organs are formed but immature).[111] There are a number of regulatory and scientific barriers to the development of complete ectogestation. In many jurisdictions, including those in the UK,[112] the 'keeping or using [of] an embryo after the appearance of the primitive streak',[113] which is taken to appear at 'the end of the period of 14 days', is unlawful.[114] The fourteen-day rule is described as 'one of the most internationally agreed rules in reproductive science and medicine to date'[115] because it is widely enshrined in domestic provisions worldwide and/or domestic guidance that determines funding. Canada has adopted legislation very similar to that in England but makes a more explicit reference to the sexed body; 'no person shall knowingly . . . maintain an embryo outside the body of a female person after the fourteenth day of its development'.[116] Therefore, complete ectogestation is unlawful.[117] Even if it were not, however, we are a long way from understanding the science of early gestation, and from figuring out how to facilitate it.[118] Flake, the leader of the EXTEND team in Philadelphia, in emphasizing that the device is capable of assisting neonates from around 22 weeks' gestation, notes that 'we have no technology (nor are we even close to developing a technology) that spans the gap between embryo culture (with oxygen delivery by diffusion) and extracorporeal circuit

[109] For some ethical reflections on design see Elizabeth Chloe Romanis, Seppe Segers, and Ben de Jong, 'Value Sensitive Design and the Artificial Placenta' (2024) <https://doi.org/10.1136/jme-2024-110066> accessed 18 September 2024.

[110] Felix De Bie and others, 'Artificial Placenta and Womb Technology: Past, Current and Future Challenges Towards Clinical Translation' (2020) 41 Prenatal Diagnosis 145–58. For reflection on the ethical challenges in clinical translation see Alice Cavolo and Daniel Pizzolato, 'Expanding the Ethical Debate on Human Artificial Placenta Trials' (2024) Research Ethics <https://doi.org/10.1177/17470161241259127> accessed 6 September 2024; Elizabeth Chloe Romanis, 'Artificial Womb Technology and Clinical Translation: Innovative Treatment or Medical Research?' (2020) 34 Bioethics 392–402.

[111] Elizabeth Chloe Romanis, *Regulating the 'Brave New World:' Ethico-Legal Implications of the Quest for Partial Ectogenesis* (PhD Thesis, University of Manchester 2020) 201; Flake (n 106) 171.

[112] Human Fertilisation and Embryology Act 1990, s 3(3)(a).

[113] ibid.

[114] ibid, s 3(4).

[115] Insoo Hyun and others, 'Embryology Policy: Revisit the 14-day Rule' (2016) 533 Nature 169–71, 169.

[116] Assisted Human Reproduction Act 2004 (Canada) s 5(1)(d).

[117] Amel Alghrani, 'The Legal and Ethical Ramifications of Ectogenesis' (2007) 2 Asian Journal of WTO & International Health Law and Policy 189–212, 193; Romanis (n 111) 29–32; Elizabeth Chloe Romanis and Claire Horn, 'Artificial Wombs and the Ectogenesis Conversation: A Misplaced Focus? Technology, Abortion, and Reproductive Freedom' (2020) 13 International Journal of Feminist Approaches to Bioethics 174–94, 176–77.

[118] Romanis (n 111) 30–32.

support via the umbilical cord'.[119] It is critical to acknowledge these scientific realities because they enable us to understand that the state of the art is that partial ectogestation is likely within our futures, whereas we cannot make this statement about complete ectogestation. However, I do not take the position that we should not speculate about different devices in the future that may be able to facilitate a complete gestation from conception to mature fetal physiology (this is explored in the next section).

There is some debate about how we should refer to devices that facilitate gestation ex utero. The devices have been called 'artificial wombs', 'artificial placentas', and 'artificial amniotic sac and placenta technology' (AAPT).[120] In scientific literature, the terms 'artificial womb' and 'artificial placenta' have come to be used to differentiate between different models.[121] De Bie and others explain that artificial womb and artificial placenta models 'differ in the extent to which they attempt to recreate fetal and utero-placental physiology'[122] (an artificial womb being a closer attempt then the artificial placenta). Spencer and Mychaliska note the principal difference as the artificial womb being a pump-less system, and the artificial placenta being a pump-driven system.[123] De Bie and others note that artificial wombs, unlike artificial placentas, keep the subject of the device (termed the 'gestateling'[124] or 'fetonate'[125])[126] insulated in a 'warm fluid environment'.[127] While the use of these terms are deemed the most appropriate by research scientists, this is disputed in the philosophical literature. As Kingma and Finn explain, the device that facilitates ectogestation is best not described as a 'womb' because it is:

> the provision of engineered replacements for parts of the fetus/gestateling's body. Just as a kidney dialysis machine replaces, or takes over, the function of kidneys . . . the reported technology replaces the placenta and amniotic sac. The womb itself is not replaced; the 'lamb-in-a-sack' is most like a free-floating fetus in its artificial amnion. Hence a more apt label would be: artificial amnion and placenta technology (AAPT).[128]

119 Flake (n 106) 171.
120 Kingma and Finn (n 80) PN.
121 Brianna Spencer and George Mychaliska, 'Updates in Neonatal Extracorporeal Membrane Oxygenation and the Artificial Placenta' (2022) 49 Clinics in Perinatology 873–91, 881.
122 De Bie and others (n 110) 151.
123 Spencer and Mychaliska (n 121) 881.
124 Romanis (n 94) 751.
125 Felix De Bie and others, 'Ethics Considerations Regarding Artificial Womb Technology for the Fetonate' (2023) 23 The American Journal of Bioethics 67–78.
126 Elizabeth Chloe Romanis, 'The Ethical and Legal Status of "fetonates" or "gestatelings"' (2023) 23 The American Journal of Bioethics 90–92.
127 De Bie and others (n 110) 151.
128 Kingma and Finn (n 80) 361.

Other scholars have agreed, noting that a device capable of ectogestation 'may be alternative form of the process of gestation, but it is not an alternative womb (organ of the female body) or pregnancy'.[129] Language that positions ectogestative devices as alternative 'wombs' could fuel some of the more dangerous normative implications of these devices (even where they are only used for partial ectogestation), for example, the policing of choices in pregnancy because an alternative form of gestation, in which there is no pregnant person whose behaviour could constitute a 'threat' to the fetus, is constructed as an alternative.[130] There are obviously differences in the way different models work, and in their risk profiles, and these will be material in determining which models work best/are ready for first-in-human use. However, we can recognize the difference between models and recognize that neither are artificial wombs.[131] Consequently, because artificial amnion and placenta technology (AAPT) is a more accurate descriptor, and because the language used has significant implications, I will adopt this terminology throughout this book.

Procreation and Speculative Thinking

The technologies enabling gestation I have described range from practices that are not rare in occurrence today (gestational surrogacies) to those that remain, at present, confined to the realms of science fiction (complete ectogestation). This begs the question of when, why, and how we should engage in speculation about procreative futures. Given my focus is gestation, how its boundaries are, can, and could be shifted by biotechnologies, and the social, ethical, and legal implications of those technologies, thinking speculatively is inevitably built into the approach I am taking.

Legal scholars have long reiterated the need for anticipatory reflection regarding novel technologies. Alghrani explains that 'the rapid rate at which reproductive technologies unfolds mean they leave in their trail a complex web of legal, ethical, social and regulatory questions which the government has no option but to address, often in haste and trying to catch up with a fait accompli'.[132] While not all the legal issues on which I reflect are speculative,

[129] Elizabeth Chloe Romanis and others, 'Reviewing the Womb' (2021) 47 Journal of Medical Ethics 820–29, 825.

[130] ibid 825.

[131] Alan Flake and others, 'The Artificial Placenta and EXTEND Technologies: One of These Things is not Like the Other' (2023) 32 Journal of Perinatology 1343–48.

[132] Amel Alghrani, *Regulating Assisted Reproductive Technologies: New Horizons* (CUP 2018) 16.

for example, because surrogacies are a not-wholly-uncommon practice in England and Wales, in applying them to new contexts (UTx in people AMAB and ectogestation), I am undertaking a speculative analysis. Given that the development of UTx has transpired within a decade of animal studies, and animal testing of ectogestation is illustrative of proof of concept, progress is being made toward new modalities of human gestation. As such, we need a body of speculative literature considering the potential legal, social, political, and ethical implications.[133] Law in particular requires anticipatory consideration because, as I have recognized with Horn elsewhere,

> Lawmakers – both legislatures and courts – are often at a disadvantage when striving to understand and respond to legal, ethical, and social implications of new technologies. It is also often the case that such situations highlight gaps in the law that were not noticeable before the technological possibility made it so.[134]

Anticipatory reflection is necessary to ensure that there is adequate time and space to consider complicated and intersecting issues spanning a number of different aspects of law and social policy.[135] The exact trajectory of technological development—as well as the social response to developments—cannot be precisely predicted.[136] Speculative reflection, therefore, should make space for contradictory accounts of the implications of technology.

Some scholars have gone further than advocating for speculative reflection on novel procreative technologies and stipulated that 'the law relating to reproductive technologies should, as far as possible, be proactive rather than constantly reactive'.[137] While in some places throughout this book I advocate for legal reform, I do not specify the exact content of a new legislative scheme for technologies enabling gestation. Much of the reform for which I advocate relates to existing law and its problematic application in a speculative *and* a contemporary context. In other instances, I highlight normative questions that

[133] Romanis (n 117) 25.

[134] Claire Horn and Elizabeth Chloe Romanis, 'Establishing Boundaries for Speculation about Artificial Wombs, Ectogenesis, Gender, and the Gestating Body' in Chris Dietz, Mitchell Travis, and Michael Thomson (eds), *A Jurisprudence of the Body* (Palgrave 2020) 233.

[135] Elizabeth Chloe Romanis, '"The Law is Very, Very Outdated and Not Keeping Up with the Technology": Novel Forms of Assisted Gestation, Legal Challenges, and Perspectives of Reproductive Rights Advocates in England and Wales' (2023) 10 Journal of Law and the Biosciences <doi.org/10.1093/jlb/lsad027> accessed 1 September 2024.

[136] Ari Schick, 'Whereto Speculative Bioethics? Technological Visions and Future Simulations in a Science Fictional Culture' (2016) 42 Medical Humanities 225, 229.

[137] Alghrani (n 132) 16.

are raised by novel technologies enabling gestation that need consideration. This approach results from considerable reflection on the merits of proactive regulation but also the specific harms that it can have, especially in the context of procreation. Being mindful of how restrictive regulation can limit who can procreate and in what ways, there may also be some merit in an approach of 'letting things get messy'[138]—in considering *how* people want to use technologies, or how they might help people realize their procreative aspirations, before we determine what is or is not permissible or what implications are beneficial or harmful. There is a balance to be reached here, of course, in that proactive regulation and 'letting things get messy' are not necessarily mutually exclusive. There may be some legal issues that arise from technologies enabling gestation that need to be addressed *before* they are used (for the first time or in a novel context or for a novel purpose), whereas there may be others that cannot be anticipated, or that we cannot know *how* to address, before a period of use.[139]

In this book, I engage in speculation not only as a form of anticipatory reflection, but also to examine what speculative procreative futures reveal about the values that underpin concepts in and surrounding the generative work in procreation that are underexplored. With Horn elsewhere, I warned against speculation that was silent about the scientific realities of the technologies that are the subject of speculation and this does carry the risk of engaging in technological determinism and of collapsing future possibilities into the present.[140] While I take the position that 'speculation without caveat is misleading' and that there is the need for a more robust literature examining the ethical and the legal challenges of more urgent uses of technology, I still believe speculation to be valuable. As such, I am engaging in speculative thinking as a theoretical lens throughout this work. Johnson and I have argued that 'thinking about novel technologies [or novel uses of technologies]—that do not yet exist [or have not been attempted in a particular context] in a contemporary context can also contribute to increasing visibility of contemporary problems'.[141] Segers and Accoe note that speculation can help signal concerns about the ethical (and political) values underscoring procreation.[142] Similarly, Kendal has explained that speculation 'serves as a useful tool for interrogating social and political attitudes toward procreation and childrearing, adopting a similar

138 Romanis (n 135).
139 ibid.
140 Horn and Romanis (n 134) 232.
141 Tess Johnson and Elizabeth Chloe Romanis, 'The Relationship between Speculation and Translation in Bioethics: Methods and Methodologies' (2023) 41 Monash Bioethics Review 1–19.
142 Seppe Segers and Dorian Accoe, 'Telling "Science" from "Science-Fiction": The Ethics of Ectogestative Technology' (2023) 177 JAMA Pediatrics 1110.

degree of abstraction as a philosophical thought experiment'.[143] Speculating can tell us much about problems in the present by magnifying contemporary issues. Thinking about novel technologies enabling gestation can help us uncover more of the (less visible) assumptions that undergird legal and social regulation of pregnancy and gestation in the present. This best works where speculation is informed by the scientific basis for developing technologies and social realities[144] because this better ensures that there is no discussion about what *could* be without consideration of *what is* and what follows from that.[145]

The Nature and Sociality of Procreation

Throughout this book, examining the technologies I have just introduced, I will explore what gestation and pregnancy are in ontological terms, the shifting nature of gestation, and the implications in a number of legal contexts. It is impossible to undertake such critical reflection on gestation, without thinking about the broader process that gestation is a constituent part of—procreation. The act of procreating, of creating a new human entity that comes into being, is inevitably social activity: something becomes someone that is situated in the web of relations that were imagined for it by the people involved. Procreation does not need to be a deliberate endeavour for this to be the case. Procreation is also social activity in a broader sense, in how we live our lives as individuals and how we perceive ourselves in relation to others (some of which we may have created), and also in how we as a society (and as a species) define and redefine our existence and continuance. As such, while procreation is a private matter, and the choice to procreate or not and how will have great significance for individuals, it is also very much a public matter.[146] Procreation is never without social context and 'can be conscious, rational, moral, and political'.[147] All of these dimensions of the activity in procreation must be afforded due attention. The stakes for all in procreation, and the extent to which it is shaped by and shapes social institutions, are high.[148]

[143] Evie Kendal, 'Utopian Literature and Bioethics: Exploring Reproductive Difference and Gender Equality' (2018) 36 Literature and Medicine 56–84, 56.
[144] Horn and Romanis (n 134) 233.
[145] Jordan A Parsons and others, 'Translational or Translationable? A Call for Ethno-immersion in (Empirical) Bioethics Research' (2024) 38 Bioethics 252–61, 260.
[146] Nancy Riley and Nilanjana Chatterjee, *Controlling Reproduction: Women, Society, and State Power* (Polity Press 2023) 24.
[147] Carmel Shalev, *Birth Power: The Case for Surrogacy* (Yale University Press 1989) 120.
[148] Riley and Chatterjee (n 146) 2.

Human procreation is more often described as 'reproduction'. However, as many theorists have elucidated, such framing of the making of new life as 're-productive'—rather than generative,[149] productive, or procreative—obscures much of what is undertaken in the process of making new life. Nelson explains that 'really there is no such thing as reproduction, only acts of production'.[150] Ruddick explains that 'the vocabulary of reproduction, with its heavy emphasis on repetition and its indebtedness to the material production of inanimate goods, misses altogether the originality of birth'.[151] Chadwick provides even greater elucidation of the mechanism of harm in the vocabulary in arguing that conceptualizing the work involved in procreation as 'reproductive' inherits and reiterates biocapitalist conceptual baggage that affects how procreative bodies, and the work that people and bodies perform in procreation and beyond it, are thought of.[152] The language of 'reproduction' 'does things (erases, straightens, naturalizes, individualizes, and medicalises)'.[153] As she explains:

> creative and generative procreative labors are reframed as matters of repetition, replication, or copying. Any sense of such activities as creative, conscious, psychofleshy, and collaborative engagements with natural forces—as productive labor, as 'truly human, that is, conscious, social activity' (Mies 1986, 53)—is lost. Reproduction becomes naturalized and thinkable only as a narrow and essentialized 'biological' process.[154]

It is through this biocapitalist lens, constructing procreation as the same making more of the same in the same ways, that 'the biological' becomes a form of narrative oppression. What is considered not to be 'naturally' possible in procreative terms is so otherized. As Drouillard describes, however, 'we are creative procreative people'[155] and individuals, with or without the aid of procreative technologies, are always seeking to build their families in different ways—some of which attempt to circumvent the 'biological' or social constructions of 'the biological'.

149 Donna Harroway, 'The Promises of Monsters: A Regenerative Politics for Inappropriate/d Others' in Lawrence Grossberg, Cary Nelson, and Paula Treichler, *Cultural Studies* (Routledge 1991) 299.

150 Maggie Nelson, *The Argonauts* (Greywolf Press 2015) 178.

151 Sara Ruddick, *Maternal Thinking: Towards a Politics of Peace* (Beacon Press 1989) 49.

152 Rachelle Chadwick, 'Visceral Acts: Gestationality as Feminist Figuration' (2022) *Signs* 229–55, 233.

153 ibid.

154 ibid.

155 Jill Drouillard, 'The King was Pregnant: Reproductive Ethics and Transgender Pregnancy' (2021) 14 *International Journal of Feminist Approaches to Bioethics* 120, 134.

In thinking of procreation as reproduction, and embedding this conceptualization of procreation in medical and legal frameworks, material harms result—not least in the way pregnant people are treated (in that they are often treated as passive agents and reduced to the pregnancy they are carrying),[156] but also in who has access to technologies enabling procreation (in how the 'biological' or 'natural' comes to frame what should be made possible). In this book, I endeavour to explore gestation, as a constituent element of procreation, beyond biological essentialism (the belief that the procreation is a matter of biology and cannot change) and biological romanticism (the belief that 'natural' procreative processes are preferable). To do so, I invoke Chadwick's notion of 'gestationality as feminist figuration',[157] which is a concept developed to describe procreation as grounded in the realities of embodied gestation facilitated by pregnancy) to centre 'fleshy inheritances, racialized histories, and concrete realities of life-making work in a way that "reproduction" [as a concept] does not'.[158] Though Chadwick does not distinguish between gestation (a process, sometimes facilitated by psychofleshy-embodied work) and pregnancy (a state of being) as I do in this book,[159] her approach remains instructive not least in that the approach is concerned with both ontologies and politics. In this book, I examine what gestation *is*, its modalities when facilitated by pregnancy and beyond it, and how it has been historico-legally constructed, to then understand how gestation has come to have significance in various aspects of the law and consequently our social lives.

Being cognizant of social context means that the law must analysed contextually alongside social, political, and cultural phenomena.[160] This is critically important given the social and political nature of procreation—a matter which is innately 'sociomaterial, intersectional, and [connected to] environmental struggles'.[161] Historically, legal scholarship that reflected on procreative rights focused on procreative liberty—that is a focus on choice, the individual, and non-state interference.[162] However, these approaches, Roberts explains, are insufficient in recognizing the social dimensions of procreation. In reality, '[r]eproductive freedom is a matter of social justice'.[163] It is

[156] Virginia Held, 'Birth and Death' (1989) 99 Ethics 362–88, 373.
[157] Chadwick (n 152) 232.
[158] ibid.
[159] Romanis and Adkins (n 1); See Chapter 2.
[160] Margaret Davies and Vanessa Munro, 'Editors' Introduction' in Margaret Davies and Vanessa Munro (eds), *The Ashgate Research Companion to Feminist Legal Theory* (Ashgate Publishing 2013).
[161] Chadwick (n 152) 250.
[162] Dorothy Roberts, *Killing the Black Body: Race, Reproduction, and the Meaning of Liberty* (20th anniversary edition, Vintage Books 2017) 6.
[163] ibid.

an oversimplification to discuss, therefore, procreation as if only individual choice is at stake. Procreative laws and policies, that determine who can reproduce and how, affect the (social) status of entire groups.[164] Procreative politics are social politics; procreation is tinged with all of the same power relations and oppressive forces that constrain groups and individuals alike across other domains of their social lives. Across disciplines, feminist scholars have developed conceptual frameworks (building on intersectionality)[165] that better centre pertinent broader context, and recognize procreation as a 'sociopolitical, intersectional, and power-laden site rather than simply a set of "natural" processes that are biologically determined'.[166] Colen, in outlining the concept of 'stratified reproduction', stresses that both the physical (biological) and the social (encompassing physical, mental, and emotional labour) tasks in procreation are 'accomplished differently according to inequalities based on hierarchies of class, race, ethnicity, and gender' as well as economic and migrant status.[167] Reproductive justice, a conceptual framework born from the work of Black feminist activists in the US,[168] positions procreation as a matter of social justice, but also emphasizes that procreation cannot be conceptualized narrowly. Being attentive to social justice issues stresses the importance of the right to procreate, the right not to procreate, *and* the right to parent in a safe and healthy environment.[169] Such an approach ensures that the procreative life span is not reduced to single issues (eg abortion),[170] and affords recognition of the fact that procreative decision-making occurs in broader context. The framework enables reflection on the conditions that affect procreation beyond ensuring there is no state interference: it allows reflection on the spaces and places where state action, and inaction in other contexts, constitutes interference with procreative decision-making to the same/similar degree.

[164] ibid.

[165] Kimberlé Crenshaw, 'Demarginalizing the Intersection of Race and Sex: a Black Feminist Critique of Antidiscrimination Doctrine, Feminist Theory and Antiracist Politics' (1989) 1 University of Chicago Legal Forum 139. Though Crenshaw coined the term for the concept that . . . The idea is explored in earlier feminist theory, eg Angela Davis, *Women, Race and Class* (Women's Press 1982); bell hooks, *Feminist Theory: From Margin to Center* (South End Press 1984).

[166] Chadwick (n 152) 235.

[167] Shellee Colen, '"Like a Mother to Them": Stratified Reproduction and West Indian Childcare Workers and Employers in New York' in Faye Ginsburg and Rayna Rapp, *Conceiving the New World Order: The Global Politics of Reproduction* (University of California Press 1995) 78.

[168] For information about the group that led this movement—Sistersong—and their motivations for a campaign for reproductive justice see Loretta Ross and Rickie Solinger, *Reproductive Justice: An Introduction* (University of California Press 2017) 55–57.

[169] ibid 9.

[170] Loretta Ross, 'Understanding Reproductive Justice' in Carole McCann and others, *Feminist Theory Reader: Local and Global Perspectives* (5th edn, Routledge 2020) 77.

For example, access to community resources like housing, healthcare, and 'a safety net for when things fail'.[171] Any individual person's ability to pursue their chosen procreative path 'is directly linked to the conditions in her community and these conditions are not just a matter of individual choice and access' to services and technologies but broader group/community oppression wielded by the state (and beyond it) such as economic injustice, environmental injustice, and criminal injustice.[172]

There has been a turn in feminist legal scholarship away from a focus on procreative liberty and procreative rights towards the use of these frameworks to afford proper attention to the socio-material and intersectional considerations of procreation and its social politics. Horn has noted the importance of thinking with reproductive justice in the context of AAPT as the literature often is 'constructed around an implicitly neutral classless, raceless, subject who is understood to have access to reproductive care and to the conditions under which reproductive choice can be exercised'.[173] Taking this approach is not to deny the importance of the exercise of autonomy for individuals making procreative decisions[174] (readers will notice I feel strongly that choices about gestation are material to individuals), but rather to recognize that our procreative choices, and the decisions we can and cannot make, are always socially situated and the product of the social, legal, and physical environments in which we live. These reflections are a means of grounding the speculation I am undertaking in thinking about gestation, technologies enabling gestation, procreative futures and the law, and in helping illustrate that social injustices (whether legally or extra-legally facilitated) are as much barriers to what might be considered desirable procreative futures as the law is.

Approach

In this book I reflect on the place of gestation in the law and the implications of novel technologies enabling gestation for law, which is important because law

[171] Ross and Solinger (n 168) 9.
[172] Ross (n 170) 77–78.
[173] Claire Horn, 'Ectogenesis, Inequality, and Coercion: A Reproductive Justice-informed Analysis of the Impact of Artificial Wombs' (2023) 18 Biosocieties 523–44, 526.
[174] Roberts (n 162) 6.

literally can dictate (or enable the dictation of) what procreative experiences are permissible. Moreover, law makes explicit, in contexts where the legibility of social convention is rare, 'the rules of action and behavior that human societies accept as controlling'.[175] Thus, what the law (which does operate as an authoritative normative domain within cultures) can often tell us something about societal norms at the time that it was made. While procreative technologies are a global endeavour, where I focus on specifics of the law I primarily refer to England and Wales, because this is the jurisdiction in which I am trained. However, the conceptual arguments I make in every chapter are of broader significance in highlighting normative questions and challenges that do and will matter in other legal systems. My focus on the law is an inevitability of my training as a legal scholar, and is a result of the fact that law both reflects and shapes societal conventions, and thus, law and social norms about procreation are often co-constituting and sometimes difficult to disentangle (even where social norms are evolving beyond existing law). Most importantly, the way law frames procreative technologies materially impacts on the conditions in which they can be used, and thus the experiences of individuals and groups. The law can be a powerful instrument either hindering or supporting change because of its intrusive quality and its capacity for signalling. The approach I take to the exploration of gestation and the law in this book is transdisciplinary (moving across and between different disciplines).[176] This is inevitable in that considerations of novel technologies, particularly those changing the nature of procreative practices, are *necessarily* interdisciplinary[177] (and multidisciplinary) because we must utilize the sources of knowledge and methods that can be offered by different disciplines. Not least in the sense that with new technologies 'even the most basic concepts require reexamination'.[178] This is why, throughout this book, there is heavy emphasis on concept analysis, drawing from the biological sciences, philosophy (metaphysics, feminist phenomenology, and feminist theory) and anthropology to understand and interpret what is happening in procreation, what the law says about it, what assumptions underpin it, and why.

[175] Sheila Jasanoff, 'Rewriting Life, Reframing Rights' in Sheila Jasanoff (eds), *Reframing Rights: Bioconstitutionalism in the Genetic Age* (MIT Press 2011) 1.

[176] See Peter Osborne, 'Problematizing Disciplinarity, Transdisciplinary Problematics' (2015) 32 Theory, Culture, & Society 3–35.

[177] Laura Shanner, 'Procreation' in Alison Jaggar and Iris Marion Young (eds), *A Companion to Feminist Philosophy* (Blackwell Publishing 2017) 429.

[178] ibid.

Structure of the Book

In Chapters 2 and 3 of this book, I provide some conceptual background to the ethical and legal analysis of novel technologies enabling gestation. In Chapter 2, I argue there is considerable ontological confusion about what pregnancy, gestation, and birth are in philosophical and legal terms. I adopt a parthood model of pregnancy, using the work of Kingma,[179] to argue that the fetus is a part of the pregnant person. This makes visible the distinction between pregnancy (a state of being) and gestation (a generative process of formation). I argue that the law adopts unstable premises in the model of pregnancy it adopts—sometimes it recognizes that a fetus is part of a pregnant person but more often it treats pregnant people as containers. Understanding pregnancy, gestation, and birth, and also what the law takes these concepts to be, is a critical prerequisite to the examination in this book of how novel technologies will change our perceptions of modes of being and the generative work in procreation. In Chapter 3, I defend the utility of considering technologies enabling gestation as a 'genus' of technologies assisting with procreation (that critically must be distinguished from technologies assisting with conception). I note that the failure of the law to properly account for the possibilities arising from technologies enabling gestation (and inadequate regulation of surrogacy) is inevitable since the legal framework is focused on assisted conception. I argue that technologies enabling gestation should not just be encapsulated within a legal framework that was envisaged to regulate a wholly different procreative enterprise. Analysis that is attentive to the similarities and differences between surrogacies, UTx, and ectogestation enable us to see how technologies alter the modalities of gestation in different ways, and the ways in which different technologies meet different procreative needs. The first two chapters, therefore, construct the necessary theoretical background for exploration of a number of ethico-legal issues raised by technologies enabling gestation that are explored in the following chapters.

In Chapter 4, I explore ethico-legal, and associated socio-political, issues in access to technologies enabling gestation. I argue that without significant legal—and social—reform to decouple notions of the procreative from the 'biological', current legal frameworks will consistently limit the transformative potential of technologies enabling gestation by limiting their use to circumstances mimicking 'natural' procreation. In Chapter 5, I explore the implications of technologies enabling gestation for the concepts of sex and gender and

179 Elselijn Kingma, 'Were You a Part of Your Mother?' (2019) 128 Mind 609–46.

the arguments that these technologies may be necessary (even if not sufficient) for equality. I argue that considering technologies enabling gestation as mechanisms for sex and gender equality overstate their capacities, even though they are important and equality-enhancing interventions for marginalized individuals (including gender minorities). The biggest obstacle to some of the transformative potential of technologies enabling gestation result from the legal and social obstacles to their gender-rupturing potential.

Gestation is the anchor by which legal parents are identified.[180] In Chapter 6, I explore why we use gestation to attribute parenthood, the origins of this approach, and consider whether the use of gestation to attribute legal parenthood works where gestation is facilitated in new modalities as a result of novel technologies. With gestation taken as *necessary* for recognition of a person as a legal mother, there are difficult and complex questions raised by novel technologies enabling gestation. I argue that these technologies raise conceptual questions that should prompt us to re-evaluate gestation as the anchor criterion that it is. Finally in Chapter 7, I advocate for the importance of abortion and illustrate that technologies enabling gestation have no bearing on the morality of abortion, especially when we centre the harms of unwanted pregnancy. However, as is illustrated by the fact that the literature surrounding ectogestation is dominated by claims about abortion, technologies that change the nature of gestation inevitably mean that there are likely to be politically motivated challenges to abortion provision. In each chapter I illustrate how social and legal reform is necessary in order to support technologies enabling gestation to achieve the transformative potential they do have, whilst also ensuring that existing biological essentialism is not propagated and that disparities in procreative and pregnancy outcomes are not worsened.

[180] Romanis and Brown (n 3).

2
ONTOLOGIES OF GESTATION

Pregnancy, gestation, and birth are facts of life. We are all born from flesh.[1] And yet, there is so much ambiguity, in social, cultural, philosophical, and legal terms, about what each of these significant aspects of the beginning of life *are*, their boundaries, and what they mean. In this chapter, I explore these facts of life and how they are conceptualized in the law. This is an important prerequisite to the examination in the later chapters of novel technologies that will change the way we perceive the generative work and modes of being at the beginning of life. Building on the work of Kingma[2] and Finn,[3] I draw on the metaphysics of pregnancy to interrogate what gestation, pregnancy, and birth *are* and how they are understood in the law.

Pregnancy, gestation, and birth as phenomena in and of themselves have received very little attention in either philosophical or legal scholarship until recently. This might seem like a strange claim given the volume of literature exploring abortion and birthing. However, as Finn explains, '[i]f pregnancy or birth *itself* were of philosophical value, then we would see the topics treated on their own terms, without relating solely and directly with ethical issues to do with the foetus'.[4] Typically, the focus is on '*events*' that take place while a person is pregnant: whether to have an abortion, to undergo various types of prenatal screening and testing, or how to give birth. This speaks to the lack of academic interest in pregnancy as a *mode of being*, instead there is interest in the fetus. There is a growing volume of work on the metaphysics of pregnancy[5] and the phenomenology of pregnancy[6] engaging with both the

[1] Adrienne Rich, *Of Woman Born: Motherhood as Experience and Institution* (WW Norton & Company 1995).
[2] Elselijn Kingma, 'Were You a Part of Your Mother?' (2019) 128 Mind 609–46.
[3] Elselijn Kingma and Suki Finn, 'Neonatal Incubator or Artificial Womb? Distinguishing Ectogestation and Ectogenesis Using the Metaphysics of Pregnancy' (2020) 34 Bioethics 354–63.
[4] Suki Finn, 'Being-from-Birth: Pregnancy and Philosophy' (2023) 19 European Journal of Analytic Philosophy S17–S32, S19.
[5] eg Kingma, 'Were You a Part of Your Mother?' (n 2); Suki Finn, 'The Philosophy of Reproduction' (2021) 20 Think 49–62.
[6] eg Nicole Miglio, *Gestational Phenomenology* (forthcoming). I am thankful to Dr Miglio for sharing her draft of this, as of yet, unpublished manuscript.

Biotechnology, Gestation, and the Law. Elizabeth Chloe Romanis, Oxford University Press.
 DOI: 10.1093/9780191986574.003.0002

circumstance and experience of pregnancy in itself. This work, however, has taken place within the disciplinary boundaries of philosophy. There has yet to be a critical exploration of how the law constructs pregnancy as a mode of being: what the law says about the ontology of pregnancy (rather than what it says about things that can happen during a pregnancy, for example, the permissible conditions for termination of pregnancy). This is indicative of the ways in which legal sense-making 'tends to accept the separation between law-work and science-work, seeing the former as normative and the latter as epistemic'.[7] Such an approach neglects the extent to which scientific knowledge has built-in social and cultural norms.[8] More importantly, while law has non-epistemological dimensions (in having to regulate where truth-seeking is difficult or impossible),[9] it nevertheless reflects, and equally can dictate, social norms and knowledge.

> It matters what matters we use to think other matters with; it matters what stories we tell to tell other stories with; it matters what knots knot knots, what thoughts think thoughts, what descriptions describe descriptions, what ties tie ties.[10]

How we think about pregnancy—and what state of being we take pregnancy to be—has significant normative implications. While no moral conclusions can be drawn directly from our metaphysical understanding of pregnancy, this understanding (combined with certain social constructions) changes *what we take to be the relevant ethical, legal, and political questions* about pregnancy.[11] Thus, it is critical, ahead of the socio-legal exploration of pregnancy and technologies enabling gestation in this book, to elucidate both what I take pregnancy to be, and what *the law* takes pregnancy to be. In making visible how the law understands and constructs pregnancy we can tease out the values in its depiction that, because of the way that the law is the tool by which social lives are organized, govern and condition behaviour.

[7] Sheila Jasanoff, 'Introduction: Rewriting Life, Rewriting Rights' in Sheila Jasanoff (eds), *Reframing Rights: Bioconstitutionalism in the Genetic Age* (MIT Press 2011) 13.

[8] ibid.

[9] Marvin Backes, 'Epistemology and the Law: Why There is No Epistemic Mileage in Legal Cases' (2020) 177 Philosophical Studies 2759–78.

[10] Donna Haraway, *Staying with the Trouble: Making Kin in the Chthulucene* (Duke University Press 2016) 12.

[11] Finn, 'The Philosophy of Reproduction' (n 5) 58.

Distinguishing Pregnancy and Gestation

In earlier work, I asserted the importance of ensuring careful 'conceptual separation of gestation from pregnancy' in our thinking about novel technologies in order to 'prevent excessive social and legal regulation of pregnant people'.[12] Gestation and pregnancy are terms that are often used interchangeably to describe generative work in bringing new life into existence. Mangione, for example, argues that 'Gestation, that is pregnancy, is here considered a physiological state of an individual during which an entity develops inside her body'.[13] However, using these terms interchangeably makes/perpetuates a category mistake. Though gestation and pregnancy both describe activity at the beginning of life, and are closely interconnected, they are, in fact, distinct phenomena. De Beauvoir posits that pregnancy is a process rather than an act/activity.[14] However, I argue that it is gestation, rather than pregnancy, that is a *process*, while pregnancy is a *state of being*.[15]

Gestation describes the 'generative process between conception and birth'.[16] A process I take to be the occurrence of a series of chemical and mechanical operations on something that changes its nature; that transforms something into something *else*. Arni describes to the process of prenatal development (used as a synonym gestation) as 'a process of change in a structure during which different forms emerge, fade, and succeed each other until the organism has attained a definitive arrangement of limbs and organs'.[17] In gestation the entity in the process of becoming has several forms, all distinct from one another—'the embryo is no longer germ and not yet fetus, the fetus is no longer embryo and not yet nursling'.[18] Gestation is, thus, clearly a process—a series of events and physical and chemical happenings in which a conceptus (a blastocyst) transforms from a ball of cells with a unique genetic profile into an entity with mature fetal physiology that *could* make the transition to physiology able to withstand the external environment when the process of gestation ends. The becoming of a new human entity is not something singular—it happens as a series of knitted-together occurrences over time. By contrast, pregnancy

[12] Elizabeth Chloe Romanis, 'Assisted Gestative Technologies' (2022) 48 Journal of Medical Ethics 439–46.

[13] Emanuele Mangione, 'Carrying the Same Pregnancy: A Bioethical Overview on Reciprocal Effortless IVF and Similar Techniques' (2023) 18 Clinical Ethics 271–79, 272.

[14] See Miglio (n 6) 151.

[15] Elizabeth Chloe Romanis and Victoria Adkins, 'Artificial Placentas, Pregnancy Loss and Loss-sensitive Care' (2024) 50 Journal of Medical Ethics 299–307, 300.

[16] ibid.

[17] Caroline Arni, *Of Human Born: Fetal Lives 1800–1950* (Zone Books 2024) 39.

[18] ibid 40.

is a mode of being. Pregnancy is a state which a person is in. Pregnancy is the condition a person is in to enable their body to facilitate generative work (the process of gestation). De Beauvoir's description of pregnancy as a process conflates pregnancy with gestation, but I still believe she was correct to identify that pregnancy is not an act or an activity. Pregnancy is not something simply 'done' or 'undertaken' in a removed sense. Rather, it is something that an individual has *been*. Pregnancy is something that the individual *is* or *was* in how it transcends their boundaries of self. Individuals are more than pregnancy, but there is no pregnancy where there is no individual.

Pregnancy is neither a 'static' nor a *passive* state of being. There is a tendency, both in scholarship and in socio-cultural depictions of pregnancy, to refer to the pregnant person as 'expecting'. The inference is that pregnancy is a period of 'uneventful waiting' 'as though this new life were flying in from another planet and she [the pregnant person] sat in her rocking chair by the window, occasionally moving the curtain aside to see whether the ship is coming'.[19] Young explains that this discourse emerges from the failure to centre the embodied subjective experience of the pregnant person, since for those thinking outside the body 'pregnancy is primarily a time of waiting and watching' but for the pregnant person 'pregnancy has a temporality of movement, growth, and change'.[20] The account of a pregnancy as passive, according to Miglio, substantially *invisibilizes* the epistemic and political agency of the pregnant person, ignoring their lived sense of embodied temporality.[21] Pregnancy is a state of doing *generative* work.[22] In this way, pregnancy is more than the generative work itself. This new literal part of the pregnant person demands substantial physical effort of the pregnant person to facilitate: 'it is an active biological undertaking even if not conscious'.[23] Pregnant persons experience themselves as 'source and participant in the creative process. Though she does not plan and direct it, neither does it merely wash over her; rather she *is* this process, this change'.[24] I use the term 'work' deliberately to describe the pregnant state—it is a working state. There is a tendency for the language of 'labour' to be used to describe being pregnant (eg performing 'gestational labour'). While this might seem a matter of semantics, there are meaningful ways in which the language used here does a lot of heavy lifting in how we think about the value of

[19] Iris Marion Young, *Throwing Like a Girl and Other Essays in Feminist Philosophy and Social Theory* (Indiana University Press 1990) 167.
[20] ibid.
[21] Miglio (n 6) 65.
[22] Romanis and Adkins (n 15) 300.
[23] ibid 302.
[24] Young (n 19) 167.

the labour/work. Arendt describes 'labour' as activity that sustains survival but nothing more, contrasting this with 'work' that creates value beyond survival (eg heritage).[25] We degrade pregnancy to something that does not recognize its creative and transcendent power[26] in using the language of labour.

The distinction between gestation and pregnancy is clearest in those instances where there is one without the other; where there is the state of being without the process, or where there is the process without the state of being. Ectogestation (whether complete or partial) is the most obvious example of gestation without pregnancy, since the process is facilitated by a machine, rather than supported by a pregnant person.[27] Pregnancy without gestation is more common; it occurs in the natural state of things, for example (most) ectopic pregnancies, in which the fertilized ovum implants somewhere other than the uterus for example the abdominal cavity or fallopian tube, or molar pregnancies (a form of gestational trophoblastic disease) involving the implantation of a non-viable fertilized egg into the uterus. In these cases, a person becomes pregnant, but there is no gestation because embryogenesis and fetal maturation are impossible.[28] Carpenter and others, in response and agreement, describe a further illustrative example: fetal death in utero. In this case, there was both pregnancy and gestation, however, gestation ceases at the point at which the fetus dies (as something is no longer undergoing the process of becoming), but pregnancy does not end until the fetus and placenta is expelled from the body.[29] Placental retention is another example in which a state of pregnancy may be maintained without gestation being facilitated.

The significance of the distinction might seem small—instances of the state without the process are rare, and instances of the process without the state of being are, at the time of writing, speculative. This likely explains the tendency, in socio-cultural terms, to speak of gestation and pregnancy interchangeably because the distinction is not readily visible. As Middlemiss explains (writing about second-trimester pregnancy loss) pregnancy is, in law, 'understood in relation to its teleological outcome of a living, viable, healthy baby' rather than the embodied experience that it is (and the multiple endings it can have).[30] The law does not distinguish between pregnancy and gestation. In a 2019 provision,

[25] See Hann ah Arendt, *The Human Condition* (2nd edn, Chicago University Press 2018).
[26] See Virgina Held, 'Birth and Death' (1989) 99 Ethics 362–88, 376.
[27] Romanis and Adkins (n 15) 302.
[28] ibid.
[29] Hannah Carpenter and others, 'Procreative Loss without Pregnancy Loss: The Limitations of Fetal-centric Conceptions of Pregnancy' (2024) 50 Journal of Medical Ethics 310–11.
[30] Aimee Middlemiss, *Invisible Labours: The Reproductive Politics of Second Trimester Pregnancy Loss in England* (Berghahn Books 2024) 4.

pregnancy loss was legally defined as occurring 'when a person's pregnancy ends and, after being parted from the pregnant person, the foetus does not breathe or show any other signs of life'.[31] In this provision the ending of a pregnancy and the ending of gestation are conflated (which excludes the experiences of persons who experience pregnancy loss without procreative loss).

This lack of distinction is also made visible in the case of abortion. In cases where the fetus has died in utero and is not (fully) expelled, the medical determination can be made that it is necessary to induce the ending of the pregnancy. In England and Wales, the unlawful procurement of miscarriage is a criminal offence.[32] Miscarriage has been legally defined as 'the expulsion of the contents of a pregnant uterus' at any point in pregnancy.[33] Miscarriage is not *unlawful* miscarriage when performed in permitted circumstances, such as on socio-medical grounds before twenty-four weeks of pregnancy[34] or where it is necessary to save the pregnant person's life.[35] The law is clear that an abortion is the *ending of a pregnancy*, not the ending of gestation. This is material in how it comes to limit and frame access to reproductive health care in that there must be a legal justification for any ending of a pregnancy (including that which might constitute managed preterm birth where medically indicated).[36] Or, in more speculative cases, the law limits choice where a person seeks to end their pregnancy without ending the process of gestation[37] (discussed in Chapter 4).

Pregnancy as a State of Being: (Usually) Having a Gestating Part

When it comes to understanding what and who is involved in a pregnancy, what is termed the 'fetal container model' has been, philosophically and culturally, assumed. This account takes it that there are two separate and distinct organisms involved in a pregnancy, the pregnant person and the fetus. The fetus, as a separate organism, is *merely contained* within the pregnant person (as opposed to being understood as a part of the pregnant person). In defending this understanding of pregnancy, Brogaard and Smith describe the fetus-pregnant

[31] Civil Partnerships, Marriages and Deaths (Registration etc) Act 2019, s 3(2).
[32] Offences Against the Person Act 1861, s 58.
[33] *R (On the Application of Smeaton) v Secretary of State for Health* [2002] EWHC 610 (admin).
[34] Abortion Act 1967, s 1(1)(a).
[35] Vivienne Harpwood, *Legal Issues in Obstetrics* (1st edn Dartmouth 1996) 216; *Smeaton* (n 33).
[36] Elizabeth Chloe Romanis, 'Artificial Womb Technology and the Choice to Gestate Ex Utero: Is Partial Ectogenesis the Business of the Criminal Law?' (2020) 28 Medical Law Review 342–74, 359.
[37] ibid.

person connection as analogous to 'a palm kernel that is lodged within your digestive tract'[38] or like a pot of yoghurt in the fridge.[39] A common Western cultural reference often used to articulate the same sentiment is 'a bun in the oven'. Describing pregnancy in this way, imagines the fetus as an object (be it a yoghurt or a bun) that is not a part of another object (whether fridge or oven) while still contained within that second object. This way of thinking constructs pregnancy as a 'state of the developing fetus, for which the woman [/pregnant person] is a container'.[40] Thus, the pregnancy 'does not belong' to the pregnant person themselves.[41] Pregnancy, through this account, is the supporting of entities imagined as 'already separate, individuated, "babies"'.[42] That socioculturally it is taken as given that pregnancy involves two individuals imagined as individuated does not tell us that a pregnancy does actually involve two individuals—rather, it tells us something about the epistemic frame that has come to dominate conceptions of pregnancy.

In contrast to this prevailing view, Kingma offers the parthood view of pregnancy.[43] She suggests that the fetus is not merely contained by the pregnant person, rather it is a *proper part of* the pregnant person. This is not just a matter of its geography, but, of homeostasis and physiological autonomy, metabolic and functional integration, topological continuity, and immunological tolerance.[44] The fetus is spatially integrated within the pregnant person—implanted within the deciduous tissue of the uterine wall.[45] Indeed, there is no physical discontinuity between the fetus and pregnant person and the fetus does not have 'its own' external boundary.[46] The internal conditions of the fetus *are* those of the pregnant person whose entire being is maintained as one 'internal environment within the narrow range of parameters that are compatible with life'.[47] Moreover, the fetus is 'functionally and metabolically integrated, and interdependent with (other) parts of the' pregnant person.[48] While the fetus has a distinct genetic makeup from the pregnant person—it is wholly possible for functionally integrated parts of persons to have a distinct genetic makeup

[38] Barry Smith and Berit Brogaard, 'Sixteen Days' (2003) 1 Journal of Medicine and Philosophy 45–78, 74.
[39] ibid.
[40] Young (n 19) 160.
[41] ibid.
[42] Finn, 'The Philosophy of Reproduction' (n 5) 54.
[43] Kingma, 'Were You a Part of Your Mother?' (n 2) 609–10; Elselijn Kingma, 'Lady Parts: The Metaphysics of Pregnancy' (2018) 82 Royal Institute of Philosophy Supplements 165–87.
[44] ibid.
[45] ibid 623.
[46] Kingma, 'Lady Parts' (n 43) 174.
[47] Kingma, 'Were You a Part of Your Mother?' (n 2) 624.
[48] ibid 626.

from the rest of the body (for example, a donated organ).[49] Further, the immunological tolerance of the fetus by the pregnant body, Kingma suggests, signals that the fetus is accepted as one of the pregnant body's parts.[50] The fetus, thus, should be properly understood as part of a person's physiology—as the reason why the person has become a *pregnant* person, as opposed to being understood as a distinct creature that exists within the physical boundaries of the pregnant person.

For some, the fact that a fetus can (and likely will) become separate from the pregnant person and have a life of its own, and thus in future will not be a part of the pregnant person, means that it is not (and never was) a proper part of the pregnant person.[51] However, as Kingma points out, many parts of an organism could and do come to exist separately in future, but 'future separation does not preclude present parthood'.[52] Take, for example, the average household plant (as I write this, I am sat next to a *monstera adansonii* called Wilfred) that exists happily within its planter—one whole plant. I could, however, take a pair of secateurs to Wilfred and make a cutting of only a few inches—lifting away a small part of the plant. Left alone in water in indirect sunlight the cutting that was part of—and is no longer part of—Wilfred will form its own roots and eventually I could plant it into its own new planter to be a new independent whole plant. The potential existence of Wilfred Junior does not make Wilfred any less of one whole plant, nor does the fact that Wilfred Junior exists as one whole plant mean that it was not, at a previous point in time, a part of Wilfred. A fetus is a 'flesh-and-blood bonded' part of a pregnant person[53] during a pregnancy, even if it will cease to be as a matter of course.

Kingma's account has been criticized, much like the container model, for being 'a rather static account of pregnancy' overlooking the fact that gestational conditions change ... the kinds of interactions the blastocyst, embryo and fetus have with the maternal body differ greatly'.[54] This is not a fair criticism. As Finn has stressed, 'the Parthood view alone does not dictate what sort of entity the Foster [meaning fetus] is'.[55] The view describes the *mereological relationship*[56]

[49] ibid 634.
[50] ibid 629.
[51] Heloise Robinson, 'Pregnancy and Superior Moral Status: A Proposal for Two Thresholds of Personhood' (2024) 50 Journal of Medical Ethics 12–19.
[52] Kingma, 'Lady Parts' (n 43) 635.
[53] Patricia Williams, *The Alchemy of Race and Rights* (Harvard University Press 1991) 184–85.
[54] Alejandra Martínez Quintero and Hanne De Jaegher, 'Pregnant Agencies: Movement and Participation in Maternal-Fetal Interactions' (2020) 11 Frontiers in Psychology <doi.org/10.3389/fpsyg.2020.01977> accessed 1 September 2024.
[55] Suki Finn, 'The Mereotopology of Pregnancy' (2023) 48 The Journal of Medicine and Philosophy: A Forum for Bioethics and Philosophy of Medicine 283–98, 289.
[56] Mereology is a branch of metaphysics examining the connection between parts and wholes.

between the entity being gestated and pregnant person in general terms—whether we are discussing the first days after the implantation of an embryo or the maturation of a later-term fetus, the same criteria (homeostasis, metabolic integration, topological continuity, immunological tolerance) describe the state of the embryo/fetus-pregnant person relation. After implantation (a process that takes several days after conception), the decidua (uterine tissue) and the blastocyst are topologically continuous following the blastocyst's burrowing into the decidua, which simultaneously engulfs and encapsulates the blastocyst.[57] This integration is immunologically tolerated, and conditions for successful integration are physiologically regulated by the pregnant person. Thus, while the exact nature of the relation (and of the part—developing entity, and the whole—pregnant person) is different, the *mereological relation* can still be described in similar terms—of 'parthood'.

There are, of course, other metaphysical views of pregnancy beyond the container-parthood binary. There are views that consider the fetus and pregnant person as overlapping or underlapping entities.[58] It is one of these positions that Mattingly was adopting when she suggested that we 'might think of the maternal-fetal dyad as an integrated, two-patient ecosystem whose individual components are not conceptually independent'.[59] In advocating this position, Mattingly suggests that whether the 'maternal-fetal dyad is regarded as one patient or two is less relevant to providing ethical prenatal care than the fact of the dyad's biological unity'.[60] I agree with Mattingly that the physical enmeshment in pregnancy speaks for itself—in pregnancy, there is no easy differentiation between the entity being gestated and pregnant person. While she illustrates the inaccuracy of the container model, however, she fails to provide further defence of the fetus as an overlapping/underlapping entity (either encompasses a conceptualization of two entities which might share parts),[61] as opposed to a part of the pregnant person. While the dyad overlap/underlap view is distinct from the parthood view I do not explore it in much more detail because I take the parthood view as indicative of how we *should* understand pregnancy. The dyad view implies something of a symbiotic relationship, when in reality the fetus does nothing to sustain the pregnant person (the pregnant

57 Michael Power and Jay Schulkin, *The Evolution of the Human Placenta* (Johns Hopkins University Press 2012) 214.

58 See Suki Finn, 'Methodology for the Metaphysics of Pregnancy' (2021) 11 European Journal for Philosophy of Science 69, 1–19, 4.

59 Susan Mattingly, 'The Maternal-Fetal Dyad Exploring the Two-Patient Obstetric Model' (1992) 22 The Hastings Center Report 13–16, 17.

60 ibid 16.

61 Finn, 'Methodology for the Metaphysics of Pregnancy' (n 58).

person facilitates all life functions). A pregnancy is a state of being, of which the entity being gestated is a constituent part. While there can be a pregnant person without there being an entity being gestated as a part, and there could one day be a gestating entity that does not exist in topological continuity with a pregnant person—in a pregnancy where there is an entity being gestated, that entity is a part of the pregnant person.

Making Space for Ontology and Experience

There is a difference between the pregnant body as matter and how that body is *experienced*. While the fetus *is* in physiological terms and arguably metaphysical terms a part of the pregnant person, a pregnant person's subjective experience of that parthood will be unique (and there will be instances where a pregnant person has no awareness of their state/the fetal part of them).[62] I take it as critical that we do not wholly collapse ontological and phenomenological accounts of pregnancy onto each other—how something is experienced is important but does not always tell us what something *is*, and conversely what something *is* is important but does not tell us how it will be experienced. In pregnancy we can distinguish between the state of the body and the experience of the state of the body (while recognizing both). Both the nature of something and the experience of something are critical to ethical and legal analysis of it. Even though law has non-epistemological dimensions, it must reflect in some way what something is, while also leaving space for the fact that there may be substantial variance in how individuals may experience it and feel about it.

While the fetus is a part of the pregnant person (just like a kidney is a part of a pregnant person), we can recognize that they may feel differently about the fetus as a part compared to other parts of them (eg their kidney). People feel differently about all sorts of parts of themselves. Willing organ donors can be reluctant to donate parts that they think of as critical to their sense of self (eyes are a common example).[63] Persons with body dysmorphia or bodily identity integrity disorder experience parts of their body (eg a whole limb) as alien from themselves. Being pregnant can, for some, entail a 'split subjectivity'[64] like 'an *experiential* alienation of the gestating self from herself[/their sense of

[62] eg persons who are unaware that they are pregnant.

[63] Mitchell Lawlor and others, 'Specific Unwillingness to Donate Eyes: The Impact of Disfigurement, Knowledge and Procurement on Corneal Donation' (2010) 10 American Journal of Transplantation 657–63.

[64] Young (n 19) 160–65.

self]'.[65] For some this is because, although the fetus is a part of them, they are invested in the future in which it is no longer a part of them and they become a parent. In other cases, this alienation results from there being a part of the body that is wholly unwanted, dysphoric, and scary—like a tumour. In this section, I briefly outline two features of pregnancy that I take to be critical orientations pertinent to the analysis throughout this book.

First, pregnancy is an embodied state, a corporeal happening—evident in the fact that the pregnant person has a new part of their physicality. Being pregnant is, more often than not,[66] a mode of being that encompasses profound alteration from one's non-pregnant state.[67] Woollard argues that pregnancy is 'the most rapid and dramatic changes to the shape and functioning of one's body experienced in healthy adult bodies' (there is no experience remotely comparable, she explains, in terms of the gravity of bodily change since puberty).[68] The shift in one's sense of their body can vary significantly, but it is not uncommon for people to remark on the 'capaciousness' of pregnancy and the surprise in the ways in which the body 'literally *makes space* where there wasn't space before'.[69] While there are ontological features that we can generalize about pregnancies (eg that it is an embodied state), it is much harder to generalize about experience and what that embodiment comes to mean to different persons. There is no 'one experience explains all'. As Miglio writes, 'every pregnancy is peculiar' and that there are significant qualitative variations in pregnant people's experiences is not an incidental matter but rather a core facet of pregnancy.[70] It remains pertinent though that these experiences are framed through the pregnant person's body and how they feel in that body. Woollard argues that pregnancy is an epistemically transformative experience.[71] Being pregnant can fundamentally alter one's 'somatic experience'.[72] Nelson describes, for example, pregnancy as a 'radical intimacy with—and radical alienation from—one's body'.[73] The split subjectivity that Young and

[65] Miglio (n 6) 149 (emphasis added).

[66] There are some people who are unaware that they are pregnant until they miscarry or deliver a baby—for these people, while their body will be in a profoundly altered state, they will not experience this. While they might experience some sensations that are a result of the pregnancy, they do not experience that 'split subjectivity' described—there is no sense of anything other than their body as it usually is exhibiting sensations that they do or do not recognize from other experiences.

[67] Maggie Nelson, *The Argonauts* (Greywolf Press 2015) 16.

[68] Fiona Woollard, 'Mother Knows Best: Pregnancy, Applied Ethics, and Epistemically Transformative Experiences' (2020) 38 Journal of Applied Philosophy 155–71, 159.

[69] ibid 128.

[70] Miglio (n 6) 72.

[71] Woollard (n 68).

[72] Emily Ross, 'Gestating Bodies: Sensing Foetal Movement in First Time Pregnancy' (2019) 41 Sociology of Health & Illness 95–111, 98.

[73] Nelson (n 67) 16.

others describe is the result of a person feeling a certain way about the body that they inhabit. Pregnant persons feel increasing movement over which they have no control (eg 'kicking') that can be interpreted as 'other' to their self.[74] There are many bodily sensations over which we as embodied entities have no conscious control—pins and needles, hiccups, cramps etc. Fetal movement, however, Miglio explains, is distinct because it is a sensation that is 'primarily enhanced by the [perception of] fetal-other'.[75] Recognition of pregnancy as an embodied state, and of the subjective experience emerging from this embodiment, must be at the forefront of analysis to ensure that the pregnant person is not rendered invisible. While this seems intuitive, where the law pays attention to bodies they are 'framed in a manner which fails to address the complexity of embodiment, and the messy instability of bodies'[76] as will become evident in the next section.

Second, pregnancy is not mothering.[77] Pregnancy is a state of doing generative work in which one's body is facilitating the creation of a human entity. Mothering, while it can result from one's having undertaken pregnancy, is a wholly different enterprise. As Ruddick explains, 'neither pregnancy nor birth is much like mothering'.[78] Although pregnant people may experience pregnancy 'as a moment leading to motherhood . . . no necessity or causality is at work here'.[79] The assumption that pregnancy is the natural source of motherhood (the way in which social bonds are grounded in biology) is critiqued in greater detail in Chapter 6. Here, I highlight the distinction between pregnancy and mothering. To understand pregnancy as mothering is in complete contention with the fetal parthood model of pregnancy because it is rooted in the construction of the fetus as distinct from the pregnant person.[80] Mothering (parenting) is relational work (that has embodied aspects); pregnancy is embodied work. A fetus is 'not a separate *parentable* entity'.[81] Recognizing this materiality does not deny the importance that persons who intend to parent can (and do) invest in a fetus, but rather acknowledges the dangers of conflating a pregnant person's embodiment with a parent–child relationship.[82]

[74] Miglio (n 6) 196.
[75] ibid.
[76] Chris Dietz and others, 'Nobody, Anybody, Somebody, Everybody: A Jurisprudence of the Body' in Chris Dietz and others (eds), *A Jurisprudence of the Body* (Palgrave Macmillan 2020) 2.
[77] Zaina Mahmoud and Elizabeth Chloe Romanis, 'On Gestation and Motherhood' (2023) 31 Medical Law Review 109–40.
[78] Sara Ruddick, *Maternal Thinking: Towards a Politics of Peace* (Beacon Press 1989) 51.
[79] Miglio (n 6) 197.
[80] Mahmoud and Romanis (n 77) 112.
[81] cibid 114.
[82] ibid.

Such conflation can—and does—result in serious social and legal limitations on pregnant people's bodies and decision-making.[83]

The Law and Pregnancy

The metaphysics of pregnancy is under-utilized in legal commentary[84] with little attention afforded to what the law takes a pregnancy to be. Exploring how the law conceptualizes pregnancy makes visible the ontological orientations of law, including the underlying assumptions and premises that come to affect the determinations made about pregnancy. To explore what the law says a pregnancy is, we must look to sources of law concerning pregnant embodiment and the fetal body and interrogate what they reveal about whether the fetus is considered a part of the pregnant person, merely contained by them, or something else. Looking at how the law describes pregnancy to uncover what it takes pregnancy to be should not be seen as uncovering evidence about what pregnancy is (what the law says does not explain which metaphysical theory best describes the state of the world).[85] However, it does tell us something about what socio-cultural conditions pervaded lawmakers' sense of the world at the time the law was written. Moreover, as an instrument with considerable normative force on individuals' lives, how the law describes pregnancy—and the relevant legal, social, ethical, and political questions about pregnancy resulting from this description—shapes the broader context in which individuals live their pregnancies.

The law is an inevitably blunt instrument: it must regulate and make decisions one way or the other where things are (in fact and experience) much more complex. As Kuberska and others acknowledge, 'legal structures tend to require unambiguity as a condition to function'.[86] The boundaries of pregnancy are a clear example. Pregnancy is a binary in the law; a person is either pregnant or they are not.[87] Legislation relating to the prohibition of discrimination on the grounds of pregnancy stipulates that 'the protected period in relation to a woman's pregnancy begins when the pregnancy begins'.[88] This

[83] ibid.

[84] ibid 111.

[85] Finn, 'The Mereotopology of Pregnancy' (n 55).

[86] Karolina Kuberska and others, 'Death Before Birth: Liminal Bodies and Legal Frameworks' in Dietz and others (n 76) 154.

[87] See Sheelagh McGuiness, 'Abortion, Criminal Law and Transgression' in *Women's Studies International Forum* 105 Women's Studies International Forum 102917 <https://doi.org/10.1016/j.wsif.2024.102917> accessed 3 July 2024 for a careful analysis of the complex subjectivities of pregnancy recognition trajectories and how little space is made for this in law.

[88] Equality Act 2010, s 18(6).

protection has not been afforded to people who are attempting to become pregnant but are not yet pregnant, for example, early stages of IVF (hormone treatment, egg harvesting etc).[89] A person is only pregnant—for the purposes of the law—once implantation has happened.[90] In handing down a decision that administration of the morning-after pill is not an abortion, Munby J stated that 'the word miscarriage today means the ending of an established pregnancy, and there is no established pregnancy prior to implantation'.[91] Great emphasis in this judgment was placed on medical indicators that a person is pregnant—that is, identifiability of pregnancy from the presence of human chorionic gonadotrophin hormone in the bloodstream (produced at the/close to the commencement of implantation).[92] In reality, it might be other subjective experiences that direct a person to believe they are pregnant (and indeed believe they are pregnant) for example morning sickness, a missed period, or similar.

It is often observed that the legal status of the fetus is 'ostensibly clear':[93] it has no legal rights because it is not a legal person.[94] That a fetus is *not* a legal person, however, does not tell us what a fetus *is*—is it recognized as a part of the pregnant person or is it something else? As I illustrate in this section, the law in England and Wales adopts an unstable position regarding the metaphysical status of pregnancy because different schemas in the law take different approaches. The inconsistency means that there is instability in how the fetus is ontologically conceptualized in the law. However, the container model seems to be adopted to describe pregnancy more often than not—with a few notable exceptions.

Termination of pregnancy

Section 58 of the Offences Against the Person Act 1861 criminalizes the unlawful procurement of miscarriage, as described earlier in this chapter. Herring postulates that 'the fetus is protected' by this provision.[95] While the

[89] See jurisprudence of the European Union: *C-506/06 Sabine Mayr v Bäckerei und Konditorei Gerhard Flöckner* [2008].

[90] While this can be seen as a clear starting point, implantation is not an instantaneous event, and it can be hard to ascertain exactly when it has happened. This undermines the fact that implantation is discussed as the point that there is a pregnancy (a pregnancy has been established) on the basis of certainty.

[91] *Smeaton* (n 33) [17].

[92] ibid [126].

[93] Sara Fovargue and José Miola, 'The Legal Status of the Fetus' (2010) 5 Clinical Ethics 122–24, 122.

[94] *Paton v British Pregnancy Advisory Service* [1979] QB 276; *R v Tait* [1990] 1 QB 290; *Re MB (Caesarean Section)* [1997] EWCA Civ 1361.

[95] Jonathan Herring, 'The Loneliness of Status: The Legal and Moral Significance of Birth' in Fatemeh Ebtehaj and others (eds), *Birth Rites and Rights* (Hart Publishing 2011) 99.

effect of the offence in practice (limiting terminations to those circumstances prescribed as lawful)[96] means that the fetus is constructed as inviolable (in that the pregnancy of the pregnant person that it is part of cannot be ended in circumstances that are not deemed legally permissible), it is questionable that fetal protection is the objective of the offence.[97] The offence can be committed where a pregnancy is ended but the fetus survives the ending of the pregnancy.[98] Indeed, the offence can be committed where a person attempts to unlawfully procure another person's miscarriage and it transpires that they are not pregnant at all.[99] There is no reference to the fetal body (or its condition) at all in the offence.[100] These particulars of the construction of the offence speak to the conclusion that the crime was introduced for the protection of pregnant people as opposed to the protection of fetuses (another clue being in the offence being contained in the Offences Against the *Person* Act when the fetus is not recognized in law as a person).[101] The protection of pregnant people was thought necessary due to the concerning safety credentials of abortion in 1861.[102] That the object of the offence is the regulation of the embodied state of pregnancy (that can only be ended in prescribed circumstances), rather than the protection of the fetus, is a fact that is often ignored and yet it is material[103] (not least in that it means the offence is incredibly broad).[104] But what does this tell us about what a fetus is taken to be? Since the offence says nothing directly about what the fetus is (or is not), this is open to interpretation.

The inference could be made that the fetus is constructed as a part of the pregnant person. The unlawful ending of a pregnancy is an offence on the *pregnant person's body*. It could be inferred then that the fetus is taken to be a part of the pregnant person's body—it is what makes the person a pregnant person.[105] However, the provision may be read differently. The term 'miscarriage' is used

[96] *R v Bourne* [1939] 1 KB 687; Abortion Act 1967, s 1(1).

[97] Romanis, 'Artificial Womb Technology and the Choice to Gestate Ex Utero' (n 36) 357–59; Emma Milne, 'Putting the Fetus First – Legal Regulation, Motherhood, and Pregnancy' (2020) 27 Michigan Journal of Gender & Law 149–211.

[98] ibid.

[99] Offences Against the Person Act 1861, s 58.

[100] Romanis, 'Artificial Womb Technology and the Choice to Gestate Ex Utero' (n 36) 358.

[101] ibid.

[102] John Keown, *Abortion, Doctors, and the Law: Some Aspects of the Legal Regulation of Abortion in England from 1803 to 1982* (CUP 2002) 35.

[103] Not least in that it bolsters the case for decriminalization of abortion given the safety of contemporary abortion medications (even without medical supervision)/procedures performed by trained professionals.

[104] Elizabeth Chloe Romanis, '*R v Foster*: Exemplifying the Urgency of the Decriminalisation of Abortion' (2023) 31 Medical Law Review 606–14.

[105] That the offence can be committed even where the person is not pregnant is consistent with the view that the offence construes the fetus as a part of the pregnant person—the offence is still committed where action is taken to end a pregnancy because a person believes another person to be pregnant.

to describe how 'the conveyance of the usual good of pregnancy (the baby) has failed or is intentionally prevented'.[106] As Browne argues, 'carriage' 'arguably conjures up the image of the pregnant person as a "carrier" or "vessel"'.[107] In invoking imagery of 'carrying' or 'transporting' something (and with 'miscarriage' this has failed to happen), the language itself imagines the pregnant person as carrying something separate from themselves: it imagines them as a container. The inference from carriage is more clearly seen in provisions that relate not to the termination of pregnancy but to the determination of legal parenthood. The Human Fertilisation and Embryology Act 2008 defines a mother as the 'woman who is carrying or has carried a child'.[108] In this provision, the language of carriage does a lot of heavy lifting; it has the same inferences of 'carrying' and thus it works to individuate the fetus, setting aside its integration as part of the pregnant person. One would not describe a person as 'carrying' another part of themselves (even where that was, for example, a donated part).

Moreover, as Mahmoud and I have argued elsewhere, 'this wording [of this provision] conflates the person's legal status while pregnant with that afforded to them at birth as a description of their relationship'.[109] In describing a person as a mother to the fetus, the fetus is constructed as separate from them, as being cared for by them, as something being held and transported by them. Moreover, to be a mother, or to mother, is relational: it describes care work for another person. The statutory definition of mother, thus, implies a container model of pregnancy because it describes pregnancy as mothering.[110] While the offence of unlawfully procuring miscarriage is not constructed with the same explicit commitment to the container model of pregnancy, there may implicitly be the same commitment.

A second offence relating to the termination of pregnancy is that of 'child destruction', committed where a person intentionally causes the death of a 'child capable of being born alive' unless necessary for the 'preservation of the life of the mother'.[111] The language used here reiterates the imagery of the fetus as atomistically situated—described as a 'child' and the pregnant person as 'mother'—the entities are imagined as related to each other but wholly distinct. Indeed, the language of 'capable of being born alive' reveals a sentiment that

[106] Romanis, 'Artificial Womb Technology and the Choice to Gestate Ex Utero' (n 36) 362.

[107] Victoria Browne, *Pregnancy Without Birth: Feminist Philosophy of Miscarriage* (Bloomsbury 2023) 25.

[108] Human Fertilisation and Embryology Act 2008, s 33(1).

[109] Mahmoud and Romanis (n 77) 126.

[110] For an exploration as to why this is metaphysically inaccurate and has problematic implications, see ibid.

[111] Infant Life (Preservation) Act 1929, s 1(1).

the entity is only temporarily contained within the pregnant person, their current status a matter of geography. Therefore, this offence much more clearly adopts the container model.

Pregnancy remains and registration

All live-births and still-births in England and Wales must be registered (there are distinct registers kept for live-born and still-born babies).[112] A 'still-born child' is defined as a 'child which has issued forth from its mother after the *twenty-fourth week* of pregnancy and which did not at any time after being completely expelled from its mother breathe or show any other signs of life'.[113] After twenty-four weeks, fetal death in utero is considered a still-birth; *before* twenty-four weeks the loss is legally categorized as a miscarriage. A miscarriage is not legally registered or recorded, though a 'baby loss certificate' (an official but not legal document) can be requested.[114] A distinction is clearly drawn in the law between an entity that is ontologically recognized as *having existed*—through a legal registration—and one that is not (even where a loss certificate can be obtained). The introduction of a loss certificate was motivated by the desire to support persons affected by miscarriage in 'acknowledging their pain and ensuring they feel heard'.[115] It does not, however, change the status of a fetus that dies in utero before twenty-four weeks' gestation. While the still-born fetus (that died in utero) is legally recorded in a system that acknowledges that a separate entity did exist, the fetus is not recorded in such a way: which speaks to the fact that before twenty-four weeks the law recognizes the fetus as the pregnant person's tissue. The very distinction between still-birth and miscarriage is significant. Describing the former in terms that make it recognizable as an entity that *did exist* as something distinct from the pregnant person (even if the fetus was never alive and thus never a legal person) is significantly different from the latter being treated as material that is simply a part of pregnant person. Middlemiss suggests that the 'bureaucratic recording of a still-birth, including the name of the baby and the names of its parents, confers official existence alongside a form of legal parenthood and makes these beings and their

[112] Births and Deaths Registration Act 1953, s 1(1).
[113] ibid s 41 as amended by the Still-Birth (Definition) Act 1992, s 1(1) (emphasis added).
[114] Department of Health and Social Care, 'Baby loss certificate launched to recognise parents' grief' (2024) <https://www.gov.uk/government/news/baby-loss-certificate-launchedto-recognise-parents-grief> accessed 22 April 2024.
[115] ibid.

relationships legible to the state'.[116] Those who have experienced miscarriage have described this registration 'as an official, formal acknowledgement of the ontological reality and existence of the baby'.[117] By way of contrast, in not conferring the same recognition to entities that die before birth before twenty-four weeks, those entities, as far as the state is concerned, never existed.

The remains of miscarriage are treated as human 'surplus tissue', defined in the Human Tissue Act 2004 as relevant material which has come from the human body and not stored for designated purposes (eg transplantation or research).[118] The Human Tissue Authority's Code of Practice, confirming that there is—as a matter of law—no distinction between fetal tissue and other tissue from the living person, stipulates that 'fetal tissue of less than 24 weeks gestation is considered to be the mother's tissue, as are non-fetal products of conception (i.e. placenta, membranes, umbilical cord, amniotic fluid)'.[119] The Human Tissue Authority's specific guidance on the disposal of pregnancy remains reiterates that 'pregnancy remains are regarded as the tissue of the woman'.[120] While consent is not technically required for the disposal of fetal tissue[121] (treated as surplus tissue of the pregnant person), the guidance directs that 'the particularly sensitive nature of this tissue means that the wishes of the women, and her understanding of the disposal of the disposal options open to her, are of paramount importance and should be respected and acted upon'.[122] That the guidance highlights the potentially sensitive nature of the tissue (depending on the perspective of the pregnant person) does not undermine the notion that the tissue was a part of the pregnant person. Indeed, as Austin and McGuiness explain, the importance of people having a choice with 'what is done with those remains once they cease to be physically connected to them forms part of their interest in their physical integrity'.[123] That this consent is written about with respect to the pregnant person, rather than the genetic progenitors of the fetus, is indicative of an understanding that the fetus was

[116] Middlemiss (n 30) 85.
[117] ibid 85–86.
[118] s 44.
[119] Human Tissue Authority, 'Code of Practice: Guiding Principles and the Fundamental Principle of Consent' (2020) <https://content.hta.gov.uk/sites/default/files/2020-11/Code%20A.pdf> accessed 22 April 2024, [141].
[120] Human Tissue Authority, 'Guidance on the disposal of pregnancy remains following pregnancy loss or termination' (2015) <https://content.hta.gov.uk/sites/default/files/2021-06/Guidance%20on%20the%20disposal%20of%20pregnacy%20remains.pdf> accessed 22 April 2024, [4].
[121] Though it is legally required for other purposes such as storage or research. However, the Human Tissue Authority, 'Code of Practice' (n 119) advises that 'because of the sensitivity surrounding pregnancy loss, consent should always be sought, even where it might not be lawfully required'.
[122] Human Tissue Authority, 'Guidance' (n 120) [4].
[123] Louise Austin and Sheelagh McGuiness, 'Reproductive Loss and Disposal of Pregnancy Remains' (2019) 70 Northern Ireland Legal Quarterly 131–53, 146.

a part of the pregnant person and thus decisions about what happens to it are theirs to make—in the same way that if my tonsils had been of interest to medical science when they were removed, it would have been my call whether they could be used for research.

Judicial *obiter*

There are few cases in which the courts have made any indications about the ontological nature of pregnancy. Indeed, there is only one case I am aware of in which the question of the metaphysics of pregnancy was considered directly relevant to the matter at hand. In *Attorney General's Reference (No 3 of 1994)* the courts were tasked with determining if a fetus could be a victim of homicide. The House of Lords ultimately determined that it could only be where it is born alive before dying of injuries sustained in utero (on the facts of the case in front of the court there was no murder, but it was unlawful act manslaughter).[124] The opinion of the Court of Appeal[125] describes deliberate infliction of injury to a fetus in the following terms:

> to cause injury to the foetus is just as unlawful as any assault upon *any other part* of the mother.[126]
>
> In the eyes of the law the foetus is to be taken as *a part of* the mother until it has an existence independent of the mother. Thus an intention to cause serious bodily injury to the foetus is an intention to cause serious bodily injury to *a part of* the mother just as an intention to injure her arm or her leg would be so viewed.[127]

As these passages make clear, the Court explicitly adopts a parthood view in which they describe the fetus as an 'integral part' of the pregnant person.[128] At the time the decision was subject to considerable academic disquiet by commentators who described the parthood approach taken as 'illogical . . . and there appears to be no authority for it'.[129] The House of Lords also resoundingly rejected the parthood view, concluding that 'the foetus cannot be

[124] *Attorney General's Reference (No 3 of 1994)* [1998] AC 245.
[125] [1996] QB 581.
[126] ibid 591 per Taylor LCJ.
[127] ibid 593.
[128] ibid 597.
[129] Mary Seneviratne, 'Pre-Natal Injury and Transferred Malice: The Invented Other' (1996) 59 Modern Law Review 884–92, 891.

regarded as an integral part of the mother . . . notwithstanding its dependence upon the mother for its survival until birth';[130] 'the mother's leg [is] a part of the mother; the foetus [is] not'.[131] Lord Mustill rejected the conclusion that the fetus is a part of the pregnant person as 'non sequitur' reasoning—that the fetus does not have legal personality, he posited, does not mean that it shares 'personality with its mother'.[132] He instead suggested that the fetus is a 'unique organism';[133] '[t]he mother and the foetus [are] two distinct organisms living symbiotically, not a single organism with two aspects'.[134] While Lord Mustill's *obiter* conclusions can be read as rejecting the binary between parthood and container models of pregnancy, there is not the same concrete dismissal of the container model as there is of the parthood model. In his judgment, Lord Hope did not stop at dismissing the parthood view—the reasoning adopted in *obiter* actively (though implicitly) endorsed the container view of pregnancy. He provides two reasons (both are flawed—the purpose here is, however, just to describe how the fetus is conceptualized in legal sources). First, he remarks that the fetus cannot be part of the pregnant person because the creation of a fetus 'requires the bringing together of genetic material from the father as well as from the mother'.[135] Second, he opines that the IVF 'serves to remind us that an embryo is in reality a separate organism from the mother from the moment of its conception'.[136] These statements are *obiter* and, though not binding, are indicative of the way that judges conceptualize the fetus when making their decisions.

Legal issues that occur during pregnancy (eg disagreements about treatment decisions) are not uncommon before the courts. How pregnancies and pregnant people themselves are described in these judgments give us an indication of how pregnancy is thought of in ontological terms. Most frequently, the language used by judges *obiter* is indicative of the container view. There is a noticeable tendency for judges in the (en)forced caesarean section cases (in which courts decisions are sought to overrule pregnant person's refusal of medical interventions in/for birth) to describe the fetus as a baby[137] or, sometimes, an 'unborn baby'.[138] In *Norfolk and Norwich (NHS Trust) v W*, Johnson

[130] *Attorney-General's Reference* (n 124) 267 per Lord Hope.
[131] ibid 255 per Lord Mustill.
[132] ibid 255–56.
[133] ibid 256.
[134] ibid 267.
[135] ibid 267. Note that there can be parts of persons with distinct genetic profiles.
[136] ibid. Note that an embryo is a distinct entity from a fetus.
[137] See eg *Guys and St Thomas' NHS Foundation Trust, South London and Maudsley NHS Foundation Trust v R* [2020] EWCOP 4; *United Lincolnshire Hospitals NHS Trust v CD* [2019] EWCOP 24; *Mental Health Trust v DD* [2015] EWCOP 4.
[138] *Re AA* [2012] EWHC 4378 (COP).

J, though noting that a pregnant person's interests are paramount, remarked that 'the reality was that the fetus was a fully formed child, capable of a normal life if only it could be delivered from the mother'.[139] The language is a striking example of how the fetus is constructed as 'merely located within' the pregnant person. The use of language in these cases (revealing how judges are thinking of the pregnant person as a container) reveals something about the court's frame of reference, which impacts the decisions made.[140]

Pregnancy and the ontological orientations of law

Ultimately, what these reflections reveal is a problem with coherence in the law: a dead fetus before twenty-four weeks is considered a part, however, it is not clear that a living fetus at the same point in gestation is conceptualized in the same way. Post-twenty-four weeks, the living fetus (and dead fetus) is consistently described in terms that make it clear that it is 'contained' within the pregnant person. Where the law does treat the fetus differently in different contexts, this always disadvantages pregnant people because their needs are considered less material. The way pre-twenty-four-week fetal remains are recorded (not registered) and treated as waste tissue can be of deep distress to persons who experience pregnancy loss.[141] Simultaneously, someone experiencing early pregnancy, however, is subject to the assumption that their fetus is a distinct entity (which can, of course, come to limit pregnant people's autonomy). The description of the fetus as a 'baby' or 'child', consistent in the case law, has the effect of shifting attitudes inevitably: if something is repeatedly described as a baby, it becomes a baby in the decision-making frame of the decision-maker. Thus, such language is reducing the pregnant person to a baby-container. Ontological premises in law (across different contexts) enable the unstable (and sometimes inaccurate) framing of legal, ethical, social, and political questions. This instability and inconsistently lends itself (consistently) to flexible interpretation—not in ways enabling recognition of the subjectivity involved in pregnancy—but in ways serving only to limit pregnant people's expression of their pregnant subjectivity.

139 [1997] 1 FCR 269, 273 per Johnson J.
140 Mahmoud and Romanis (n 77) 132.
141 Middlemiss (n 30); Austin and McGuiness (n 123).

Birthing and Being Born

According to the fetal container view, birth is simply a change of environment.[142] This perspective is echoed in much philosophical thought. Singer argues that 'the fetus/baby is the same entity whether inside or outside the womb'.[143] Foster, making the same point, rather crassly describes birth as a matter of being 'on one side of the woman's vagina rather than the other'.[144] However, the parthood view makes space for recognition of birth as much more complex than merely a change in environment. As Kingma argues, fetuses 'are not simply "babies in tummy's": there are many differences (internal, structural, functional, relational and topological)' between fetuses and babies.[145] Here, birth is a moment of significant transformation for the fetus in which it shifts from a part to a distinct entity. As Flessas and Jackson point out:

> the fetus does not exist as an independent entity, whose characteristics can be measured and compared with those of a newborn baby. A live fetus is necessarily inside a woman's body and wholly dependent upon her body to sustain its live. This is not 'just' a question of location . . . rather it is what the fetus *is*.[146]

As they quite rightly identify, birth is not merely a change in environment, but a process involving *intrinsic* changes to the entity that is birthed.[147] Greasley explains that 'many significant biological and behavioural changes are triggered at birth', all of which are adaptations in physiology.[148] These adaptations are the result of a fetus no longer being a part but, instead, a *whole* that can survive in the external environment. Once a whole (existing not independently because a neonate is dependent on physical care for survival), a neonate is an entity that enters a particular context constituted of physical relationships with others and develops (quickly) a sense of differentiation of self from other, for example through the exercise of imitation behaviours (long before it develops self-consciousness).[149]

142 Finn, 'The Philosophy of Reproduction' (n 5) 49–62, 55; Kingma, 'Lady Parts' (n 43) 169.
143 Peter Singer, *Practical Ethics* (CUP 1979) 108.
144 Charles Foster, 'Medical Law too often Doffs its Cap to the Doctor's White Coat', *The Times* (London, 21 May 2009) <https://www.thetimes.co.uk/article/medical-law-too-often-doffs-its-cap-to-the-doctors-white-coat-z63b5xtgx93> accessed 14 May 2024.
145 Kingma, 'Lady Parts' (n 43) 176.
146 Tatiana Flessas and Emily Jackson, 'Too Expensive to Treat? Non-Treatment Decisions at the Margins of Viability?' (2019) 27 Medical Law Review 461–81, 475.
147 ibid.
148 Kate Greasley, *Arguments about Abortion: Personhood, Morality, and Law* (OUP 2017) 191.
149 José Luis Bermúdez, 'The Moral Significance of Birth' (1996) 106 Ethics 378–403, 390, 400.

Kingma and Finn elaborate on the different elements of birth—they note two significant occurrences that are conflated under the same heading of 'birth'. First, there is birth-by-location change (denoting the change in the fetus's location from a part of a pregnant person to being in the external environment) and birth-by-physiology change (denoting the structural change from parthood to independent entity).[150] These are two distinct, but in the general course of nature coextensive, occurrences[151]—they are, however, not *necessarily* coextensive, as ectogestation illustrates.[152] Where ectogestation is facilitated by an artificial placenta, Kingma and Finn outline, a human entity is born-by-location change, but not born-by-physiology change, because the entity is still gestating although it is no longer a part of a pregnant person.[153] I agree with Kingma and Finn's conclusions; indeed I made very similar arguments prior to their intervention into the debate, but I used different language—that of birthing (to describe the change of location) and being born (to describe the physiology changes the entity being gestated makes).[154] The difference in language here is material because it is illustrative of the fact that birthing is not only a matter of location change but a state change on the part of the pregnant person. I choose this language now because it is less fetal-centric. Birthing describes the entity being gestated no longer being part of the pregnant person and is simultaneously indicative of the fact that birthing is primarily an experience of the pregnant person. 'Birthing' also centres how there is as much a state change for the pregnant person (in the 'location change') as it is for the fetus. Birthing is the state change for the pregnant person (in that they no longer have a gestating part), while being born describes the state change of the fetus (in the usual course of things from parthood to being an independent entity, though this is more complex in ectogestation as the fetus is no longer a part of a pregnant person but might be considered part of an artificial placenta). The moment of transformation for the pregnant person in their state change needs recognition in its own right. Thinking in this way makes

150 Kingma and Finn (n 3) 360.

151 In earlier work I had observed that these two occurrences appear only as independent processes that merely *happen* to be naturally synchronized, but Elselijn Kingma has since pointed out to me that it is rather an evolutionary necessity that the two occur at the same time as a matter of course (unless something goes wrong).

152 Elizabeth Chloe Romanis, 'Artificial Womb Technology and the Significance of Birth: Why Gestatelings are not Newborns (or Fetuses)' (2019) 45 Journal of Medical Ethics 728–31, 728.

153 ibid.

154 Romanis, 'Artificial Womb Technology and the Significance of Birth' (n 152); Elizabeth Chloe Romanis, 'Challenging the Born Alive Rule: Fetal Surgery, Artificial Wombs, and the English Approach to Legal Personhood' (2019) 28 Medical Law Review 93–123. See also later Elizabeth Chloe Romanis, 'The Ethical and Legal Status of "Fetonates" or "Gestatelings"' (2023) 23 The American Journal of Bioethics 90–92.

visible the 'psychofleshy' work of birth that Chadwick describes as (among other things) 'the challenges of letting go, of opening and releasing the body to become other'.[155] As Katz Rothman puts it:

> We don't as the language of patriarchy would have it, 'enter the world' or 'arrive'. From where? Women who give birth . . . don't feel babies arrive. We feel them leave.[156]

It is rather odd, or rather unsurprising giving the dominance of patriarchy in the West, that 'rituals celebrating women's actual birth-giving are rare'.[157] Using the term 'birthing' (an active verb) to describe birth-by-location change can reorient our thinking about what is significant in birth, and in ensuring we do not erase the significant state changes that occur for pregnant people.

While birthing is significant, especially in terms of the subjective experience of the pregnant person/birth-giver, being born is also significant. The subject of extra uterum gestation—that has been birthed but has not been born—is unique. This entity might no longer be a part of a person, but it is not yet fully 'in the world' in the sense that it is an entity that can be held, smelled, or touched by those around it.[158] While still undergoing gestation, even if no longer part of a pregnancy, a gestating entity (which I have termed the 'gestateling' in earlier work)[159] is meaningfully distinct from both a fetus (in having been birthed) and a neonate (in not having been born)—thus, it has distinct physicality, behaviour, and natality/physical situatedness from these entities.[160] Birthing matters because, without recognition of this, we forget to centre the experience of (formerly pregnant persons). Being born matters because this is what indicates that a new entity has transitioned into the external environment in the way in which we all (to date) have done. Being born is the emergence. The insistence that both aspects of birth are relevant also affords separate significance to pregnancy and to gestation and allows proper separation of both forms of generative work in bringing new life into being from the care work that is undertaken for (newborn) children.

155 Rachelle Chadwick, 'Visceral Acts: Gestationality as Feminist Figuration' (2022) 48 Signs 229–55, 229.

156 Barbara Katz Rothman, 'Daddy Plants a Seed: Personhood under Patriarchy' (1996) 47 Hastings Law Journal 1241–48, 1246.

157 Held (n 26) 371.

158 Romanis, 'Artificial Womb Technology and the Significance of Birth' (n 152).

159 Elizabeth Chloe Romanis, 'Artificial Womb Technology and the Frontiers of Human Reproduction: Conceptual Differences and Potential Implications' (2018) 44 Journal of Medical Ethics 751–55, 753.

160 Elizabeth Chloe Romanis, 'Regulating the "Brave New World": Ethico-Legal Implications of the Quest for Partial Ectogenesis' (PhD thesis, University of Manchester 2020) 203–07.

Legal Conceptualizations of Birth

A great deal of emphasis is placed on birth in the law. Birth is the point at which a human entity obtains legal personality (and all associated rights and protections).[161] Some lawyers point out that the existence of this rule is not necessarily indicative of the fact that the law regards the fetus and newborn baby as wholly different entities.[162] Indeed, we have seen that at times the law adopting a fetal container view of pregnancy can blur the boundaries between the two, even while staunchly reiterating the hard and fast rule that a fetus has no legal personality. While the legal rule is defensible on purely pragmatic grounds (as some claim),[163] legal scholars have also argued that birth as the 'bright line' for legal personality is defensible on metaphysical grounds.[164] It matters then how the law defines birth.

That birth is the focal point of legal personhood is a product of both the civil and criminal law. As I have argued elsewhere, the test for legal personality in English law is nuanced in that it encompasses conditions that mirror that of birthing (birthed) and being born (born alive).[165] Where an entity is birthed but not born alive, the entity is still-born, and while the entity is legally recognized in a way that has ontological significance, that entity is never afforded (neither is it recognized that they at any point had) legal personhood.[166] An entity, thus, must be more than no longer a part of a pregnant person in order to obtain legal personhood. An entity with legal personhood:

1. is birthed (meaning completely detached from the pregnant body)[167]
2. is breathing or exhibiting 'any other sign of life'.[168]

[161] Kristin Savell, 'Is the Born Alive Rule Out-dated and Indefensible?' (2006) 28 Sydney Law Review 625–64, 625.

[162] Amel Alghrani and Margot Brazier, 'What Is It? Whose It? Re-positioning the Fetus in the Context of Research?' (2011) 70 Cambridge Law Journal 51–82. In this article they argue that it is 'physiologically nonsense' to take the position that a late term fetus and newborn baby are distinct. As is evident from the arguments in this chapter, I do not agree.

[163] Elizabeth Wicks, 'Terminating Life and Human Rights: The Fetus and the Neonate' in Charles Erin and Suzanne Ost (eds), *The Criminal Justice System and Health Care* (OUP 2007) 202.

[164] Greasley (n 148); Romanis 'Challenging the Born Alive Rule' (n 154).

[165] Herring (n 95); Romanis 'Challenging the Born Alive Rule' (n 154).

[166] Romanis 'Challenging the Born Alive Rule' (n 154) 100.

[167] *Paton* (n 94); *Rance and Another v Mid-Downs Health Authority and Another* [1991] 1 QB 587. The issue was discussed in further detail in nineteenth-century case law, eg *R v Poulton* (1832) 5 Car & P 328; *R v Crutchely* (1837) 7 Car & P 814; see discussion in Romanis 'Challenging the Born Alive Rule' (n 154) 102.

[168] Births and Deaths Registration Act 1953, s 41 as amended by the Still-Birth Definition Act 1992, s 1(1).

While there is clarity that *both* of these conditions must be satisfied, there remains some debate about each condition.

What is it to be completely birthed? Decisions have clarified (though not offering much clarity) that to be birthed, an entity must not be in the 'process' being birthed, but 'completely separated'.[169] Other cases make clear that being birthed is expulsion from the pregnant person—being attached by the umbilical cord, however, is irrelevant (such an entity is still expelled).[170] While the law does not endorse the parthood view of pregnancy (indeed, the language of expulsion lends itself more naturally to notions of container rather than parthood), the law does adopt a position that the fetus is birthed at the point at which it is no longer a part of the pregnant person—when it is no longer functionally integrated as a part of their person.

There is much more active debate about what it is to be 'born alive'—both in law and in medicine. Breathing and/or the broad 'any other signs of life' are taken as the basis of the legal definition of life at birth in many jurisdictions. The statutory term 'signs of life', and what might be considered sufficient evidence of 'signs of life', is in need of interpretation. In my existing work, I have argued that 'signs of life' is clearly intended to mean activity that is indicative of exertive activity that exhibits interaction with the external environment[171]—for example, that evidences that gestation has ended; the entity has transitioned from 'the process of being biologically created' to the 'process of developing'. This is both a normative claim and a descriptive one. I do believe strongly that this is what the law *should* be (in order for the 'born alive' criterion to effectively discriminate between entities that have made some physiological adaptations for an independent existence versus entities that have not—whether biologically alive or not). However, precedent on the matter does also seem to support this conclusion. In *C v S*, the Court of Appeal precluded the possibility of recognizing aspects of fetal physiology that are indicative of biological life (those like a primitive heartbeat that some who dispute my position have sought to rely on).[172] In this way, the law does distinguish between signs of biological life (eg that illustrate fetal physiology—primitive circulation, movement of cardiac muscle) and signs of life in a legal sense (eg that evidence life after birth, which fetal physiological functions never would). For this reason, I argue that it is

[169] *Rance* (n 167) 620 per Brooke J.
[170] *R v Reeves* (1839) 9 Car & P 25, 26 per Vaughan J.
[171] Romanis, 'Artificial Womb Technology and the Significance of Birth' (n 152).
[172] *C v S* (Foetus: Unmarried Father) [1988] QB 135, 155 per Donaldson MR.

at least plausible that a gestateling—with only fetal physiology—extra uterum may not satisfy the legal definition of 'born alive'.[173] This is not to deny that it is biologically alive but to highlight that the signs of life it exhibits are fetal in nature because it has not been 'born-by-physiology change' to borrow Kingma and Finn's terms. A gestateling has not made its emergence.

Colgrove has disputed my conclusion, arguing that an entity gestating extra uterum 'just is' a newborn (the same as a baby in neonatal intensive care). He argues that I have read 'evidence of self-sufficiency' into 'signs of life' when this is not its plain meaning.[174] He uses as an example the World Health Organization (WHO) definition of 'born alive', which lists the beating of the heart as a sufficient sign of life to determine that a human entity is born alive.[175] Thus, Colgrove argues, a gestateling with a heartbeat must meet this definition (and thus my case for exertive activity is irrelevant).[176] However, the WHO definition was developed for a particular purpose—statistical purposes. What Colgrove has failed to appreciate, however, is that 'signs of life' are not a matter of biological fact or statistical reporting, but a legal term of art. English law has been specific that signs of life (sufficient to demonstrate that an entity is 'born alive') are inclusive of (only) those that are actively exertive and seemingly involve some interaction with the external environment in some sense.[177]

The phenomena unpicked in this chapter—pregnancy, gestation, and birth—for what they are metaphysically and what the law takes as its ontological premises surrounding these phenomena—are critical to the analysis in this book. This chapter is not just scene-setting: undertaking a metaphysical examination of these phenomena, and importantly doing something original in examining the metaphysical assumptions that the law makes about them, is important work in itself. Making visible the complexities and richness of the embodied experience of pregnancy and birthing and the nuances and transformations in the condition of human entities at the beginning of life are instructive exercises. We must be interested in them because of what they tell us about the becoming of life and the processes from which we all come.

[173] Nick Colgrove, 'Artificial Wombs, Birth and "Birth": A Response to Romanis' (2020) 46 Journal of Medical Ethics 554–56.
[174] ibid 555.
[175] ibid.
[176] eg *C v S* (n 172).
[177] Romanis, 'Challenging the Born Alive Rule' (n 154) 112.

3

CLASSIFICATION OF TECHNOLOGIES ENABLING GESTATION

Having presented my conceptual approach to identifying what gestation is (and how it is distinct from pregnancy),[1] this chapter considers how biotechnologies, both that are already in use and that are on the horizon, have the potential to fundamentally alter the nature of gestation with implications across a number of legal contexts. This analysis adds another dimension to the metaphysical approach adopted in Chapter 2 in carefully considering the nature of technologies and what they change about gestation. This critical conceptual foregrounding, which provides more understanding about what these technologies are, what they do, and how they relate to each other, enables better appreciation and exploration of the practical ethico-legal issues that will be explored in the following chapters.

In this chapter, I defend two claims. First, that it is useful to think about assisted gestation or technologies enabling gestation as a genus of technologies. I explore why thinking collectively about technologies enabling gestation allows us to better consider the implications of these technologies. A taxonomic approach allowing for the classification of these technologies is useful in illustrating the degrees of similarity and difference between them. In earlier work I defined assistive gestation as technologies that support persons who want to reproduce (potentially using their own gametes) but are unable, or even unwilling, to engage for a variety of reasons (biological, social, psychological) in the undertaking of gestational work.[2] This support might involve interventions that enable the individual (unable to become pregnant and physiologically support a gestation) to sustain a pregnancy, or supporting individuals preferring not to sustain a pregnancy, with interventions that mean gestational work is undertaken by another person or a machine.[3] In this chapter,

[1] See Chapter 2.
[2] Elizabeth Chloe Romanis, 'Regulating the "Brave New World": Ethico-Legal Implications of the Quest for Partial Ectogenesis' (PhD thesis, University of Manchester 2020) 228.
[3] Elizabeth Chloe Romanis, 'Assisted Gestative Technologies' (2022) 48 Journal of Medical Ethics 439–446.

Biotechnology, Gestation, and the Law. Elizabeth Chloe Romanis, Oxford University Press.
 DOI: 10.1093/9780191986574.003.0003

I delve further into this definition by exploring the boundaries of 'technologies enabling gestation' as a genus, what it encompasses and what it does not. I present a taxonomy of gestation on the basis of an inductive classificatory analysis of surrogacies, uterus transplantation (UTx), ectogestation, and *reciprocal effortless* in vitro fertilization.[4]

Second, I argue that technologies within the genus 'technologies enabling gestation' have the potential to fundamentally alter the nature of gestation in different ways. In particular, I consider how the procreative experience of intended parent(s) is markedly different where different technologies are used. For this reason, each of these technologies (surrogacies, UTx, and ectogestation) serve different procreative needs.

The Utility of Classification

There is a need to think collectively about procreative technologies—what do they *collectively* change about the state of the world, and what are their *collective* implications?[5] Thinking collectively is not to deny the importance of specificity where necessary or appropriate, but to acknowledge that technologies do not exist in isolation. Thinking collectively about technologies/practices surrounding gestation can help improve our conceptual understanding of both gestation itself (the process) and of assisted/assistive gestation as a practice,[6] the different technologies that might (not) be recognized as technologies enabling gestation, and the relationships between them. The exercise of classifying procreative technologies and practices on the basis of their relationships to each other can help us think through the essence of gestation and what is taken to be valuable about gestation. Thinking collectively is also important because the relationships between the technologies impacts on how they are each understood (since some of their conceptualization is sometimes understood in opposition to technologies with different features). It is hard to fully appreciate where these technologies are best suited (or not) to individuals' procreative preferences where they are not considered alongside other

[4] Reciprocal effortless IVF (ReIVF) is a process in which two people are supported to carry a conceptus in their bodies (often described as a form of assisted gestation; I explain later in this chapter why this is a mischaracterization).

[5] There is utility in an approach beyond mine here which thinks at the family level about assisted procreation (encompassing assisted gestation and assisted conception) about the similarities and differences between these practices and how their nature may change with novel technologies (I hope this will be my next project!).

[6] Romanis, 'Assisted Gestative Technologies' (n 3) 439.

possibilities. Questions about the permissibility of these technologies, where they are often framed as alternatives or as having alternatives (like adoption), are a clear example of how failing to think collectively as we consider regulatory questions like access to these technologies will have inevitable ramifications.[7] Appreciating the differences between these technologies, both in terms of what they offer those seeking assistance with gestation and those who wish to do the assisting, is as critical an element of their nature.

As a means of thinking collectively about technologies with sufficient space for appreciating the ways in which closely related technologies can have both subtle and substantial differences, I am drawing inspiration from the terminology and methods adopted in taxonomy (also known as theoretical systematics). This is the theory and practice of classification (developed for plants and animals); effectively a system for classifying objects of interest into conceptually distinct and helpful categories.[8] Classification (that can be thought of as a 'filing system'[9]) is '*the grouping of objects into classes owing to their shared possession of attributes*'.[10] Classification can help us to think collectively because it allows us to see the ways in which technologies are similar and the ways in which they are not—we can elucidate what makes them similar and what does not. Of course, how things are classified depends on what are taken to be the organizing principles; what these are must be dependent on context in order to ensure that the groupings have utility for the intended purpose.[11]

Classification is not simply a descriptive exercise (that would merely be identifying what things are); rather it is the usage of inductive reasoning to order and organize[12] (and organizing things into new categories that have specific utility). As such, there is considerable judgement embedded in the premises of the exercise, for example, in deciding what yardstick to use to measure or compare things by.[13] It is *gestation* that is the central concept I am using to guide my classification, given the focus on the process in this book. In circumstances in which people are seeking to become parents, gestation is a process that *must* occur in order for an entity that they can parent to come into being. As such, that gestation is undertaken is the primary goal for many seeking to become a parent. Though for others, *how* that gestation is undertaken will also matter.

[7] ibid.
[8] Ernst Mayr and Peter Ashlock, *Principles of Systemic Zoology* (2nd edn, Donnelley & Sons Company 1991) 2.
[9] ibid 116.
[10] ibid 113 (emphasis original).
[11] ibid 115
[12] ibid 4.
[13] Donald Rogers, 'The Philosophy of Taxonomy' (1958) 50 Mycologia 326–32, 327

Pregnancy can (and, for some, will be) a critical goal. For example, cases where a person decides that surrogacies are not an option for them because they care about pregnancy and not just that there is a successful gestation. Overall, however, the pregnancy remains a second order desire; the person wants the pregnancy because they want a certain kind of procreative experience—something that results in an entity they can parent. Consequently, in cases where persons need technological assistance to procreate, the birth of the child remains the first order desire, and the pregnancy may be the second order desire where it is the person's preferred means of achieving that parenthood.[14] Thus, as the first order desire, I focus on gestation as the central organizing concept. There can be considerable preferences about the nature of gestation where there are options—would a person who wants to become a parent prefer a so-called 'natural' or 'artificial' gestation, or to be or not to be pregnant themselves? These are encompassed within a classification system when we take gestation as the central concept.

Koplin has argued that my proposal of thinking collectively (in describing assistive gestative technologies as a 'genus' of technologies) 'should provide neither the only nor the main level of ethical analysis' of surrogacies, UTx, and ectogestation.[15] While these technologies share parallels with each other, he argues, they have greater similarities with other technologies. By way of example, he points out that surrogacies are not only a form of technology enabling gestation but a 'contested commodity'[16] similar to sexual services and organ donation.[17] He concludes that 'it is not only—or even primarily—the connections between AGTs [assisted gestative technologies] that matter' and that these ethical issues might be better appreciated by thinking about the other genera that these technologies might belong within.[18] His argument is effectively that I am adopting the wrong concept as the organizing principle: perhaps he is suggesting that it is better to focus on what technologies demand of others than the specific function they are intended to provide to a

[14] In cases where persons seek to conceive and become pregnant, the way that pregnancy is thought of as a desire may be very similar (a person wants to become a biological parent and pregnancy is 'the way it is done' within their means so that is how they will do it) and thus they think of pregnancy as something they want to be because of the result. There is no doubt that there are some people who may enjoy a pregnancy so much they would endeavour to do this again (and maybe not even to procreate themselves, maybe they do it to act as a surrogate). For others, the desire for pregnancy may never come into it because of their socialized expectations of their physiology, eg a person assigned male at birth.

[15] Julian Koplin, 'How Useful is the Category of "Assisted Gestative Technologies?"' (2023) 49 Journal of Medical Ethics 350–51, 350.

[16] Koplin draws this term/categorization from Radin's work see Margaret Jane Radin, *Contested Commodities* (Harvard University Press 2001).

[17] Koplin (n 15) 350.

[18] ibid 351.

person seeking the technology. The classification of these technologies in the way advocated does not preclude the possibility of undertaking a different classification exercise if we want to think about challenges related to issues raised by a different central organizing concept. This does not mean that there is no utility in thinking about technologies enabling gestation as a genus (a genus is a higher order category of a number of species which all have *some* common features/a 'correlated character complex'[19])—this will have significant utility in many contexts, which I demonstrate over the context of this book. It allows us to interrogate the essence of gestation itself across contexts. Moreover, it is particularly useful to use as an organizing concept that is the first order desire of potential service-users of technologies, as this is what is guiding use of the technologies in the first place (and centrally describes the function they are intended for). Moreover, Koplin's objection (and the critique, raised by Cavaliere, that considering assisted gestation as a unified category means failing to appreciate political and moral aspects of different technologies)[20] neglects consideration of the fact that although technologies enabling gestation is the genus, differences like that which he highlights can be appreciated within a classification system—these are precisely the things that speak to the fact that UTx, surrogacies, and ectogestation are not the same *species* of technologies enabling gestation (a more specific classification) even though they are all a technology enabling gestation (a less specific classification).[21] This is illustrated in the next section.

A Taxonomy of Technologies Enabling Gestation

Taking a phenetic approach (examining the degree of overall similarity between things),[22] the general principles of classification dictate that:

1) objects are assembled into classes that are as homogenous as possible;
2) objects are included in the class with others that they share the greatest number of attributes with;

[19] Mayr and Ashlock (n 8) 136.

[20] Giulia Cavaliere, 'Assisted Gestative Technologies, or on Treating Unlike Cases Alike' (2022) 48 Journal of Medical Ethics 452–53.

[21] Some commentators saw clearly what I was trying to do (in that a genus is not the smallest taxon, there would be species within the genus assisted gestation) and agreed see JY Lee, 'Framing Gestation: Assistance, Delegation, and beyond' (2022) 48 Journal of Medical Ethics 448–49.

[22] Mayr and Ashlock (n 8) 120.

3) a new class is established where there is an object/(s) that is too distinct to be included in an already established class; and
4) the degree of differences between classes is expressed by a hierarchy;[23] in this hierarchy each categorical level 'expresses a certain level of distinctness'.[24]

As an illustrative example, *calathea* (also known as prayer plants) are a grouping of plants native to tropical environments (but fare well as houseplants) known for their colourful striped patterns and the dramatic way their leaves curl up at night and open for the morning sun. While united in these features, my Makoyana (called Malice) and Ornata pinstripe (called Jane) are distinguishable. Malice has large oval medium-green leaves with decorative darker green patterns on each leaf. Whereas Jane has broad dark-green leaves with thin pink stripes. Malice has dark purple undersides that are also patterned, while the undersides of Jane's leaves are a flushed purple. As a consequence, although these two plants must be of one class in some senses (that they have similar care needs eg high humidity, medium indirect light etc)—their distinctions (appearance) lead us to recognize that as we add in more specificity they are of different classes. Thus, they are of the same genus, but not the same species. In what follows, I illustrate the application of these principles to technologies enabling gestation. I argue that technologies enabling gestation should be considered a *genus*,[25] of which different technologies encompass different *species* (and their different uses, potentially *subspecies*). The dendrogram[26] in Figure 3.1 depicts the result of my reasoning.

Surrogacies, UTx, and ectogestation as species of technology

Species, when adopting a phenic approach, refers to a 'set of discrete entities all of which possess the unchanging defining property or properties'.[27] A species will often be defined in a relational way—eg a dog is not a cat, and a cat is not a dog (because these animals have a distinct set of defining properties from each other which mean that they cannot reproduce with one another). This concept is translatable into the current context by thinking about a species as

[23] ibid 114.
[24] ibid.
[25] Romanis, 'Assisted Gestative Technologies' (n 3).
[26] The term used to describe a taxonomic 'map'—Mayr and Ashlock (n 8) 123.
[27] Mayr and Ashlock (n 8).

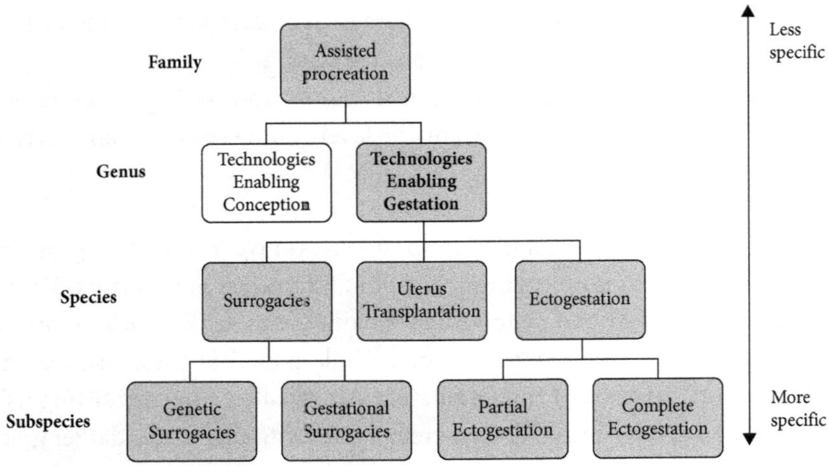

Figure 3.1 Taxonomy of technologies enabling gestation: family to subspecies

a collective of technologies that perform the same function in the same way. The defining feature or property being the *mode of gestation*. Ectogestation is distinguishable from surrogacies and UTx because gestation is facilitated by machine rather than a human person. While surrogacies and UTx both involve gestation sustained by a human person, one involves the person who was born with a functional uterus undertaking the work on behalf of others, the other involves the gestation being facilitated within a transplanted uterus and the work undertaken by the person who intends to parent. Although both human gestations, UTx and surrogacies are not the same species. The environment of the gestation is different in these cases because of things like immunosuppressive drugs altering the pregnant persons' physiological chemistry.[28] More significantly, *who is undertaking the gestational work* is distinct between each of these technologies. UTx is not a surrogacy because it involves an even greater physical change to the body of the pregnant person (in addition to the body transforming from the non-pregnant state, the body is becoming a body with a uterus), and the pregnant person intends to parent the resulting entity after birth. Because the converse is true on each count, surrogacies are not UTx.

Within a species, there can emerge different subspecies. In the animal/plant kingdom, these are subdivisions within the range of a species that are meaningfully different from other populations of the same species.[29] Natural diversity

[28] Kavita Shah Arora and Valarie Blake, 'Uterus Transplantation: Ethical and Regulatory Challenges' (2013) 40 Journal of Medical Ethics 396–400, 398.

[29] Mayr and Ashlock (n 8) 43.

exists within a species, but sometimes a difference is significant enough to warrant classification as a subspecies. Usually this will be accounted for in evolutionary terms. While complete ectogestation and partial ectogestation are both forms of artificial gestation, one technology is designed to 'take over' a gestation where it becomes necessary, or potentially one day to offer people the freedom to choose how long they would want to be pregnant for, and the other is designed to 'grow babies' from scratch. Thus, the technologies could be used in different environments for different purposes—one as a form of 'rescue' (and incidentally as a procreative technology), and the other as a procreative technology. Similarly, surrogacies might be thought of as having two subspecies—gestational surrogacies and genetic surrogacies, while both still being options available today, evolved as products of their time. Gestational surrogacies allow intended parents to procreate with their own genetic material (the ovum), whereas in genetic surrogacies the surrogate donates both genetic material and their gestational work. These differences between the forms of surrogacies and of ectogestation do not take away from their fundamental nature (in the case of surrogacies, gestation sustained by pregnancy where the pregnant person does not intend to parent, and in the case of ectogestation, artificial gestation of whatever length).

That these technologies are distinct and would be thought of as different species from each other is rather self-evident, and unlikely to be much contested. That these species make up a genus, however, might need greater explanation.

Technologies enabling gestation as a genus

Species within a genus all have *some* common features/a 'correlated character complex'.[30] Whatever character complex is the commonality between the species that makes up the genus will be clearly delineated from another/other groups at the same rank (that have their own distinct character complex).[31] Surrogacies, UTx, and ectogestation all have in common that they are a form of assisted procreation—the technological process of medical interventions that are intended to address involuntary childlessness. They are all technologies that enable people to procreate who otherwise may not be able to or would not be able to do so in a way that met their specific needs or desires in procreating. There are, of course, many other technologies that would belong to this

[30] ibid 136.
[31] ibid 134.

category 'assisted procreation'—artificial insemination, in vitro fertilization (IVF), and intracytoplasmic sperm injection (and all of these processes can be undertaken with donated gametes). In addition to these technologies all being some form of assisted procreation, some will inevitably have properties similar to that of UTx, surrogacies, and ectogestation. For example, where undertaken with donated gametes, practices like IVF are similar to UTx because they both encompass the use of donated material. However, despite these similarities, I argue that these technologies are of a fundamentally different character complex as a result of their (intended) function. While there may be parallels between technologies like artificial insemination and IVF and surrogacies, UTx, and ectogestation, their fundamental property—that defines what function they perform for a service-user—is wholly distinct.

Both conception and gestation are necessary stages in the process of assisted procreation, but they are wholly distinct processes.[32] There can be no gestation without conception, and without gestation a conceptus fails to become. This does not, however, make the processes the same. I have been struck by the extent of the conceptual conflation that often occurs between conception and gestation in the philosophical literature. In his essay, 'The Philosophy of Gestation', Feibleman describes what he takes to be the interesting ontological facts of procreation, and yet, despite its title his focus is on 'the commitment to being' which he attributes primarily to events that are, in reality, of conception, rather than gestation:

> With the fertilized ovum, something now will be produced, an organism. The genes are committed to sorting themselves out, to a selection which has not yet taken place beyond the elimination of other sperm and other ova. But what a decision has been made! To develop into a human individual! But by whom? For what? The chance operation of a determinative mechanism?[33]

Conception and gestation are distinct events in the grand scheme of procreation. Conception is the process in which a human zygote is formed from an ovum and a sperm:[34] this fusion (or 'fertilization') often takes around twenty-four hours. Conception can occur in the oviduct of a person with the physiology to become pregnant following the deposit of sperm either through sexual intercourse or a technological mechanism of insemination. It can also,

[32] See Romanis, 'Assisted Gestative Technologies' (n 3) 440–41.
[33] James Feibleman, 'The Philosophy of Gestation' (1967) 16 Journal of Theoretical Biology 355–65, 357.
[34] Richard E Jones and Kristin Lopez, *Human Reproductive Biology* (4th edn, Elsevier 2014) 163.

following the development of IVF, take place outside of the body in laboratory conditions in which there is greater control over which egg and which sperm form the zygote. Ethical and legal questions about conception are, as the quote from Feibleman above illustrates, about *what unique genetic entity* comes into being. As established, gestation, by way of contrast, is the process of becoming: the generative process between conception and birth.[35] When we are talking about the ethical and legal issues in gestation, we are reflecting on *how* an entity is facilitated to come into being (not what genetically unique entity is brought into being). Thus, technologies assisting with gestation and technologies assisting with conception we can say are of a wholly different nature. The distinction becomes material in the ethical and legal assessment of these technologies.[36] Given the fundamental difference between technologies enabling conception and technologies enabling gestation that delineates them so clearly, we should recognize them as two distinct genera that both belong to the family 'assisted procreation'.

In arguing that surrogacies, UTx, and ectogestation, are encompassed within the genus technologies enabling gestation, I am not (despite what others have suggested) arguing that these technologies must be treated the same, or that there must be consistency in how they are regulated.[37] Because they are technologies sharing the fundamental character complex explained earlier—enabling gestation where a person is unable or unwilling to do so—there are some unique ethico-legal issues that are raised in the context of *all* of these technologies. These are all issues that speak directly to the nature of the technologies as enabling gestation for persons unable/unwilling to do so—for example, access to technologies and the attribution of parentage where technologies are utilized.[38] This is not the same as saying that these technologies will not raise their own unique ethico-legal issues (though some have misinterpreted my claim as meaning this[39]).

I have been criticized for labelling the genus I have described as 'assisted gestative technologies' in earlier work[40] because, critics argue, doing so inappropriately conceptualizes procreative practices as procreative technologies. Kendal argues that UTx and surrogacies do not involve technologies—they are practices of 'people rather than technologies'.[41] However, Kendal's

[35] Romanis, 'Assisted Gestative Technologies' (n 3) 441.
[36] ibid 440.
[37] See Cavaliere (n 20).
[38] Romanis, 'Assisted Gestative Technologies' (n 3) 441–44.
[39] Cavaliere (n 20); Koplin (n 15).
[40] Romanis, 'Assisted Gestative Technologies' (n 3).
[41] Evie Kendal, 'Commentary on Romanis' Assisted Gestative Technologies' (2022) 48 Journal of Medical Ethics 450–51.

conceptualization, conflates 'technology' with the 'technological'.[42] Technology is not merely machinery. Rather, in an instrumental and anthropological sense, it can be broadly described as 'a means' and 'human activity',[43] which is encompassing of more than machines. Firestone conceptualized technologies as methods of generating and deploying knowledge and skills to manipulate the physical environment.[44] UTx is the (technologically assisted)[45] enterprise of surgically altering the body to create gestational capacity where there was none before (and simultaneously in another person, potentially, to remove this capacity where it may have existed). Gestational surrogacies obviously involve technological intervention in conception and implantation but do not in the gestation. It might be argued, therefore, that since a surrogate pregnancy progresses just as a 'natural' pregnancy does, that describing the pregnancy as a technology is inaccurate. Rather, we might label gestational surrogacies a 'practice'.[46] However, when thinking about technology in the instrumental, anthropological sense, surrogacies can be understood as a human intervention into the physical environment (and the embodied physicality of persons) creating new possibilities—namely, gestation that does not follow from coitus,[47] and in which the fetus and pregnant person have a more limited genetic relationship.[48] For this reason, surrogacies and UTx ought properly to be understood as technologies.

On reflection, however, I have concluded that 'assisted gestative technologies' was not the appropriate descriptor for what the genus encompasses. These technologies all make the process of gestation possible in instances where the person(s) who want to procreate are unable (or unwilling) to facilitate it. The term that best describes how they function then is that they 'enable' the gestation. Labelling the technologies as 'assisted' denotes only technologies that do a share of the work (and an alternative 'assistive'[49] only those technologies that enable a person to perform a function). Technologies enabling gestation

[42] Martin Heidegger, 'The Question Concerning Technology' in David Kaplan (ed), *Readings in the Philosophy of Technology* (Rowman & Littlefield Publishers 2009) 9.
[43] ibid.
[44] Shulamith Firestone, *The Dialectic of Sex: The Case for Feminist Revolution* (William Morrow and Company 1970) 154. See also discussion in Victoria Margree, *Neglected or Misunderstood: The Radical Feminism of Shulamith Firestone* (Zero Books 2017) 75.
[45] Surgery is a technological enterprise in all of the various machines that make it possible eg the anaesthetic machine, suction apparatus, patient monitoring equipment etc.
[46] I am grateful to Dr Laura O'Donovan and Dr Nicola Williams for raising this with me in various discussions over the last few years.
[47] This also occurs where a person utilizes a method of assisted conception.
[48] I say more limited because a pregnant person and the fetus they sustain will always have a genetic relationship because of phenomena like microchimerism. What is significant, however, is that the fetus, when conceived as a zygote, was not formed with the pregnant person's genetic material.
[49] I am grateful to Dr Katharine Jenkins for discussions on this point.

is thus a better descriptor of what it is that delineates these technologies from technologies enabling conception. A subgenus of 'assisted gestative technologies' could be used to describe surrogacies and ectogestation (in some forms), and a subgenus of 'assistive gestative technologies' could be used to describe UTx and ectogestation (in some forms). These categories, however, are very much subgenera, subordinate to the genus 'technologies enabling gestation' because they are unified in their characteristic function of performing gestational work on the part of a person who cannot or is unwilling.

Classifying carefully

Undertaking classification forces us to closely examine the nature of technologies—their purpose, functions, and features—and it is how we can isolate those that are related from those that are not. There is increasing interest in the bioethics literature in Reciprocal effortless IVF (ReIVF)[50] that some have implied constitutes a technology enabling gestation.[51] Reciprocal IVF describes a form of assisted procreation in which a same-sex assigned female at birth couple both play a vital role in the birth of a child (one by donating the genetic material, and the other by undertaking the gestational work).[52] Thus, both parties can describe themselves (in a factual sense, though not in a legal one) as biological parents of the child.[53] This process, in terms of how it is assisted, encompasses only an element of assisted conception—IVF is used in order to allow a couple who both produce eggs to procreate together: a 'joint' effort—but there is no technology enabling the gestation (this is facilitated by a pregnancy without any technical intervention). Reciprocal *effortless* IVF, describes a more novel practice adopted as a part of reciprocal IVF, which utilizes intravaginal culture supporting two people assigned female at birth to 'carry' a conceptus in their bodies.[54] This process combines what is known as 'effortless'

[50] Sara Babcock Gilbert and Alex Polotsky, 'Vaginal Culture for IVF Allows Two Mothers to Carry the Same Pregnancy: Is More Always Better?' (2019) 21 Case Reports in Women's Health <doi.org/10.1016/j.crwh.2019.e00099> accessed 1 September 2024; Emanuele Mangione, '"Recombining" Biological Motherhoods: Towards Two "Complete" Biological Mothers' (2024) Journal of Medical Ethics <doi:10.1136/jme-2023-109610> accessed 1 September 2024; Emanuele Mangione, 'Carrying the Same Pregnancy: A Bioethical Overview on Reciprocal effortless IVF and Similar Techniques' (2023) 18 Clinical Ethics 271–79.

[51] See Mangione ibid.

[52] S Marina and others, 'Sharing Motherhood: Biological Lesbian Co-mothers, A New IVF Indication' (2010) 25 Human Reproduction 938–41.

[53] ibid. For more discussion on legal parentage see Chapter 6.

[54] Mangione, 'Recombining' (n 50).

IVF (intravaginal culture of embryos) with reciprocal IVF.[55] In this process, as Mangione describes it:[56]

1) Sperm and eggs are mixed in a special device that is then placed in the vagina (or womb)[57] of individual A
2) The device supports fertilisation and incubation (including early zygote development)
3) After a period of time, which can be days or hours, the device is extracted from the body of A
4) Embryos are retrieved from the device
5) Embryos are then implanted in the womb of person B with the intention that they become pregnant

As Mangione notes, since the first reporting of this technique in 2018, in the literature and the press this has been referred to as 'carrying the (same) pregnancy' or equivalent phraseology that implies that both person A and B in the steps above have been pregnant with the same entity.[58] While noting that there is a need for 'more accurate linguistic revision in describing ReIVF',[59] Mangione nonetheless continues to perpetuate a category mistake regarding the nature of the process. He argues that 'ReIVF and the other similar techniques' allow two people to 'share' a gestational bond with the same entity'.[60] He reaches this conclusion by conflating gestation and pregnancy[61] and, relying on the dubious claims of Watt and McCarthy,[62] he stipulates that pregnancy begins at the point of conception, not the point of implantation and as such a person who has the incubation device in their vagina or uterus is pregnant.[63] Since the same entity is 'carried' within both A and B, Mangione stipulates, both can be considered to have gestated the entity (and thus be considered 'gestational mothers').[64] This

[55] Mangione, 'Carrying the Same Pregnancy' (n 50) 273.
[56] Mangione, 'Recombining' (n 50) 2–3.
[57] Some devices are designed to be placed in the vagina, others have been designed to be placed in the uterus: see Mangione, 'Carrying the Same Pregnancy' (n 50) 271–74; Joanna Delange, 'World's First Baby Carried as an Embryo in Two Wombs has been Born' <https://www.progress.org.uk/worlds-first-baby-carried-as-an-embryo-in-two-wombs-has-been-born/> accessed 8 June 2024.
[58] Mangione, 'Carrying the Same Pregnancy' (n 50) 271–72.
[59] ibid 272.
[60] ibid 275.
[61] ibid 272.
[62] Helen Watt and Anthony McCarthy, 'Targeting the Fetal Body and/or the Mother-Child Connection: Vital Conflicts and Abortion' (2019) 87 The Linacre Quarterly 147–60.
[63] Mangione, 'Recombining' (n 50) 3; Mangione, 'Carrying the Same Pregnancy' (n 50) 272.
[64] Mangione, 'Recombining' (n 50) 3.

conceptualization would lead to this technology being classified as a species with the genus of technologies enabling gestation.

However, the conceptualization of ReIVF as facilitating a 'double gestation' (gestation within two bodies) is flawed. First, as explored in depth in Chapter 2, pregnancy and gestation are *not* the same. Even if the insertion of a device containing an embryo could be considered as establishing pregnancy (we will come back to this in a moment), this does not necessarily mean that the device supports gestation. A person can be pregnant but not be sustaining a gestation (see the examples in Chapter 2 of molar pregnancies and fetal death in utero). The device inserted in the vagina/womb of person A supports the fertilization and incubation (including early zygote development) of the embryo. Fertilization and incubation, however, are not constituent elements of gestation, but wholly different processes.[65] The bridge between fertilization/conception and gestation is implantation[66] (which proceeds the development of the placenta—the organ that facilitates gestation). Since the device in ReIVF contains the embryo in a distinct cavity from the body of person A, it cannot implant into the uterine wall of person A. The process in ReIVF that takes place in the period of time in which the device is located in the vagina/womb being of incubation, while meaningful to individuals, and potentially akin to how animals other than mammals incubate fertilized eggs, is not a gestational experience. This is because—in order for there to be gestation—there must be a form of implantation to initiate the process of becoming between conception and birth (in pregnancy, this is necessary to enable the body to facilitate the process, the same would be the case where gestation is facilitated by a device).

Furthermore, I argue that it is inaccurate to describe the device being inserted into the vagina/uterus as establishing a pregnancy. Chapter 2 argued that pregnancy is a state of being.[67] One cannot be in the state of pregnancy where one's physiology is not altered (this occurs where there is implantation and remodelling of uterine tissue).[68] In what might be termed 'natural' procreation, following coitus, sperm fertilize ovum in the oviduct of persons with the capacity to become pregnant. Approximately forty to sixty per cent of concepti, however, pass from the body without ever being implanted.[69] In such

[65] Romanis, 'Assisted Gestative Technologies' (n 3) 440.

[66] In which the blastocyst in invades and settles in the decidua of the uterine wall—Michael Power and Jay Shulkin, *The Evolution of the Human Placenta* (Johns Hopkins University Press 2012) 102.

[67] Elizabeth Chloe Romanis and Victoria Adkins, 'Artificial Placentas, Pregnancy Loss, and Loss-sensitive Care' (2024) 50 Journal of Medical Ethics 299–307.

[68] Power and Shulkin (n 66) 46.

[69] Gavin Jarvis, 'Early Embryo Mortality in Natural Human Reproduction: What the Data Say [version 2; peer review: 2 approved, 1 approved with reservations]' (2017) 5 FI000Research 2765 <doi.org/10.12688/f1000research.8937.2> accessed 1 September 2024.

cases, the person with the physiology to become pregnant would not experience that a conception had happened (though it is important to note that some people may experience considerable anxiety about whether they *are* pregnant following coitus).[70] While the process of conception occurred, without implantation (taking place two to three days later), there is no state change in the person's body; they are not pregnant. Where a conceptus is passed from the body before implantation, this is not a lost pregnancy, rather it is a case of unrealized pregnancy (it is not a case of a pregnancy being established and then ending, rather it is one of the potential for a pregnancy never coming to fruition). The case of ReIVF is even further removed from a pregnancy than the case of a passed conceptus because where a conceptus is in the device (rather than directly in the oviduct of person A) there is never any potential for it to implant. I mentioned that Mangione sought to show that ReIVF is a pregnancy. While he asserts that pregnancy begins at conception, he provides no justification for this claim, rather he provides justification for the claim that a pregnancy is established even if it is not a viable pregnancy that could go to term.[71] Mangione explains that a person is still pregnant even if the embryo implanted in some other part of their body rather than their reproductive tract.[72] One can agree[73] and would still have to reach the conclusion that ReIVF is not pregnancy—the difference between the embryo implanted in the abdomen and the embryo in the ReIVF device inserted into a part of a person's body is that the latter is never implanted into the person: it never alters their physiological state of being. That implantation is a process and not an instantaneous event does not undermine the point here—that there must be some implantation of some nature for a pregnancy to have begun. Moreover, if the insertion of the device into the vagina/uterus during the incubation phase of ReIVF was pregnancy, then the removal of the device in the vagina/uterus would constitute a termination of pregnancy (in English law, defined as an intentional ending of a pregnancy)[74] —a characterization that I think most people would find counterintuitive.

The conclusion of this analysis is that ReIVF is better categorized within the genus of technologies enabling conception. I do not deny that this technique

[70] Romanis, 'Assisted Gestative Technologies' (n 3) 441.

[71] Watt and McCarthy (n 62) 155.

[72] ibid.

[73] It should be clear from my analysis in Chapter 2 that I do not believe pregnancy begins at conception. Pregnancy is a state of being in which the body usually has a gestating part.

[74] Offences Against the Person Act 1861, s 58—see analysis on this point: Elizabeth Chloe Romanis, 'Artificial Womb Technology and the Choice to Gestate Ex Utero: Is Partial Ectogenesis the Business of the Criminal Law?' (2020) 28 Medical Law Review 342–74.

may embody important procreative preferences for some people. Mangione makes the compelling case for same-sex people assigned female at birth wanting to procreate as a joint enterprise[75]—I imagine it could also be a preference that many people with vaginas but without the capacity to become pregnant might hold in high regard. However, that this is a meaningful ritual for many undergoing assisted procreation and that can involve body parts that are conducive to gestation (in the case of the device that incubates in the womb) does not mean that it is a technology that enables gestation. It does not, it enables conception. Misclassifications could have problematic implications, especially in the context of regulation.

Existing regulatory structures and technologies enabling gestation

When the delineation between technologies enabling conception and those enabling gestation is placed at the foreground of thinking about assisted procreation, it becomes evident that technologies enabling gestation cannot simply be subsumed into a framework of regulation that was designed with assisted conception in mind. The Human Fertilisation and Embryology Acts (HFE Acts) 1990 and 2008, that apply across all the jurisdictions of the UK, speak directly (as the name suggests) to assisted conception. The HFE Act 1990 was introduced to address developments in the 1980s (specifically IVF) that constituted fertility treatment and embryo research. Since its inception the framework has only been subject to piecemeal reform. Most notably with the passage of the HFE Act 2008.

Alghrani described the HFE Act 2008 as a 'missed opportunity' to consider how to better regulate for technologies encompassing a 'third era' of reproduction[76] (she was describing UTx and artificial placentas).[77] While I agree with Alghrani that it is disappointing that horizon-scanning did not take a greater role in reform efforts, I think it is wholly unsurprising that reform efforts did not take account of future technologies enabling gestation (and it might be thought unfair to criticize them for a failure to consider what Alghrani considers the 'third era'). In the process of reform there was little scope for

[75] Mangione, 'Carrying the Same Pregnancy' (n 50) 275.

[76] Amel Alghrani, 'The Human Fertilisation and Embryology Act 2008: A Missed Opportunity?' (2009) 25 Journal of Medical Ethics 718–19; Amel Alghrani, *Regulating Assisted Reproductive Technologies: New Horizons* (CUP 2018) 5.

[77] Though, as Williams points out, there is no clear definition or explanation of the concept of 'third era of reproduction' in Alghrani's work—see Nicola Williams, 'Amel Alghrani, *Regulating Assisted Reproductive Technologies – New Horizons*' (2020) 38 Medical Law Review 431–36, 431.

fundamental change, as McCandless and Sheldon explain, '[n]owhere was a blank piece of paper offered for reform in a way that allowed for a thorough and fundamental rethinking of the kind of regulation which might best suit this area'.[78] As a consequence the ethico-legal issues surrounding technologies assisting conception, as the focus the regulatory regime, were thus the focus of reform efforts in 2008.

Fox explains that the key reforms in 2008 can be grouped into four broad categories: (1) 'the impact of fertility treatment on the family', (2) data collection and management, (3) 'choices made by parents about the characteristics of children', and (4) embryo research.[79] At their root, all of these major reforms spoke directly to those issues concerning the fundamental nature of technologies enabling assisted conception—*who* comes into existence, in what familial circumstances, and what are the consequences. There is no reflection on those matters that relate to the nature of technologies enabling gestation (*how* entities come into being). While surrogacies were considered in the reforms, section 54 of the HFE Act 2008 did make expansive changes to the parental order process in uncontested surrogacy arrangements,[80] these reforms continued to neglect the nature of surrogacies as a technology enabling gestation. This is because parental orders did not disrupt the function of the law holding that gestation is determination of legal motherhood. They merely established a mechanism by which other people could parent the resulting child.[81] This approach did not engage with the essence of the arrangement of surrogacies in their truest sense (that the surrogate does not consider themselves the mother and the gestation is performed to assist others to become parents).

In both 1990 and 2008 UTx had not yet resulted in a live birth, and ectogestation was wholly science fiction, and the use of technologies enabling conception were (and remain) far more common than surrogacies. As a consequence, it is hardly surprising that there was not consideration of technologies enabling gestation. The legal framework that has developed in the UK, therefore, not only does not address the ethico-legal issues unique to technologies enabling gestation (as distinguished from technologies enabling conception), but it does also not have the capacity to deal with them without comprehensive overhaul. There may be merit in considering the utility of a distinct (but

[78] Julie McCandless and Sally Sheldon, 'The Human Fertilisation and Embryology Act (2008) and the Tenacity of the Sexual Family Form' (2010) 73 Modern Law Review 175–207, 180.

[79] Marie Fox, 'The Human Fertilisation and Embryology Act 2008: Tinkering at the Margins' (2009) 17 Feminist Legal Studies 333–44, 337–40.

[80] ibid 338.

[81] Zaina Mahmoud and Elizabeth Chloe Romanis, 'On Gestation and Motherhood' (2023) 31 Medical Law Review 109–40, 118.

complementary) regulatory framework for technologies enabling gestation.[82] O'Donovan agrees that the suggestion of a novel regulatory structure focused on gestation, rather than conception, 'has obvious merit and warrants further exploration given the similar ends and outcomes [that these] ... technologies attempt to achieve'.[83] Such an approach would recognize that technologies enabling conception and technologies enabling gestation are genera of the same family and that where people utilize assisted conception they may also utilize technology enabling gestation. However, the distinctness of the framework would also create the space for the kinds of ethico-legal issues that are particular to the nature of what is enabled when we are discussing technologies enabling conception rather than those enabling gestation (and vice versa). As Cavaliere agrees, 'Romanis successfully shows that there are relevant distinctions between the process of gestation and that of conception and the process of gestation entails a unique form of labour [which might be better described as work] due to the biological, political, and cultural dimensions associated with it'.[84] The precise formulation of questions about access to technologies and their impact in the context of choice about what work one undertakes in becoming a parent, abortion, sexed and gendered impacts, and how we attribute parenthood are wholly different—as is explored in the following chapters of this book.

The Spectrum of Enablements

Critics of my proposal to recognize technologies enabling gestation as a genus kept referring to the salient biological, political, cultural, differences between surrogacies, UTx, and ectogestation.[85] As noted, I agree there are meaningful differences between these technologies—which is what makes them *different species within the genus*, rather than all members of the same species. The fundamental character property of surrogacies, UTx, and ectogestation is that they enable gestation, though they do so in different ways. As Lee agrees, 'there is descriptive and normative heterogeneity between the individual species of

[82] Romanis, 'Assisted Gestative Technologies' (n 3); Elizabeth Chloe Romanis, '"The Law is Very, Very Outdated and not Keeping Up with the technology': Novel Forms of Assisted Gestation, Legal Challenges, and Perspectives of Reproductive Rights Advocates in England and Wales' (2023) 10 Journal of Law and the Biosciences lsad027 <doi.org/10.1093/jlb/lsad027> accessed 1 September 2024.

[83] Laura O'Donovan, 'Gifting the Womb: A Legal and Ethical Analysis of Uterine Transplantation' (PhD thesis, University of Manchester 2021) 222.

[84] Cavaliere (n 20).

[85] ibid; Koplin (n 15).

AGTs [assisted gestative technologies], which are worth further ethical analysis'.[86] These technologies, thus, appeal to different people who need or want (for whatever reason) gestational support to procreate for different reasons because of the unique support they each can offer. Some persons without the capacity to become pregnant will seek out technologies that enable them to become pregnant (and thus facilitate gestation); others may not value pregnancy to the same degree, or even actively seek to avoid it, and seek alternative means of gestation in their procreative project (where a surrogate undertakes the pregnancy, or a machine facilitates the gestation).

While I maintain that pregnancy is a unique form of bodily work, and that we must pay proper regard to the social, political, and cultural ramifications of undertaking this work, I remain neutral on the issue of whether pregnancy is an inherent good or not, and I believe this to be a critical commitment. For as many people who describe their pregnancy as a joyful, powerful, and identity-forming mode of being, an equal number will proclaim it to be miserable, energy-consuming, and identity-rupturing, and then there are those who would not use such visceral language in either direction to describe it. Making space for contradictory experience, and the diversity of value that different individuals place in experiences, and that the reasons for individuals valuing (or not) valuing experiences can be contextual, is a central feminist commitment.[87] Pregnancy can be both dangerous and worth celebrating; worth avoiding and empowering; invigorating and terrifying. Surprisingly, or maybe unsurprisingly, this is a rather uncommon stance amongst those writing about technologies enabling gestation. Usually, scholars will generally defend technological intervention, or generally oppose it, based on some value-laden understanding of pregnancy (that exclusively celebrates it[88] or denounces it[89]).

[86] Lee (n 21) 449.

[87] Katharine Bartlett, 'Feminist Legal Methods' (1990) 103 Harvard Law Review 829–88, 880.

[88] eg some scholars are anti-surrogacies because it defies the 'natural' 'caretaking' that takes place in a pregnancy (that they argue makes one a mother). See Jennifer Hendricks, *Essentially a Mother: A Feminist Approach to the Law of Pregnancy and Motherhood* (University of California Press 2023). Others argue against ectogestation on the basis that it 'would directly result in kidnapping and extinction of biological motherhood': Jordi Vallerdu and Sarah Boix, 'Ectogenesis as the Dilution of Sex or the End of Females?' in Janina Loh and Mark Coeckelbergh (eds), *Feminist Philosophy of Technology* (Springer 2009) 118.

[89] eg some scholars universally problematize pregnancy in order to make the case for ectogestation, eg Bidoli and Di Nucci argue that 'gestation and childbirth should be recognized as unsafe, painful processes and to convey the idea that the proper way to deal with such harm is to offer an alternative to pregnancy': Andrea Bidoli and Ezio Di Nucci, 'Beyond Pregnancy: A Public Health Case for a Technological Alternative' (2023) 16 International Journal of Feminist Approaches to Bioethics 103–30, 103. This paper reiterates the central argument made earlier by Kendal: Evie Kendal, *Equal Opportunity and the Case for State Sponsored Ectogenesis* (Palgrave 2015) 3–5; 12 though Kendal adopts a much more nuanced and moderate position in stressing that ectogestation does not necessarily mean that pregnancy and birth are 'denigrated or undermined' at 8.

Instead, I take the position that, where there are a range of technologies enabling gestation available, what technological intervention might be best for an individual needing some enablement with gestation for their procreative project will depend on their values and preferences surrounding pregnancy. Cavaliere suggests that parental projects are a critical part of persons' individual and social identities 'and are closely connected to their well-being and sense of self'.[90] Gestation, and the mode that it takes, is an important part of the way a person/persons together imagine their parental project. As I have argued with Kendal elsewhere, '[d]ecisions about gestation are highly significant to individuals many of whom may feel that fundamental aspects of their identities as a "parent", "gestator" or "woman" are at stake'.[91]

The principal objective of many people who seek technologies enabling gestation is to pursue a particular conception of parenthood—that of a genetic tie between them and a child.[92] Though this will not universally be the case, an aspiration of a genetic relationship is often what makes seeking becoming a parent through accessing surrogacies or UTx, rather than pursuing adoption, more appealing to them.[93] In much of the literature on UTx, the procedure is defended as important to allow people to 'shape their families according to their values and preferences',[94] however the values and preferences explored are usually related to a genetic tie or a legally recognized parental relationship at birth.[95] In a future where a person may have other technologies enabling gestation at their disposal in ways that enable them to become a genetic parent and legally recognized as such at birth,[96] UTx may come to be valued

[90] Giulia Cavaliere, 'The Public Provision of Uterus Transplantation: What Should Feminists Do if They win?' in Natasha Hammond-Browning and Nicola Williams (eds), *International Legal and Ethical Perspectives on Uterus Transplantation* (Edward Elgar 2024) 24.

[91] Elizabeth Chloe Romanis and Evie Kendal, 'Subjective Experience, Gestational Preferences and Justice: Valuing Both Uterus Transplantation and Ectogestation' in Natasha Hammond-Browning and Nicola Williams (eds), *International Legal and Ethical Perspectives on Uterus Transplantation* (Edward Elgar 2024) 106.

[92] Ruby Catsanos, Wendy Rogers, and Mianna Lotz, 'The Ethics of Uterus Transplantation' (2013) 27 Bioethics 65–73, 72. I remain neutral on the desire to have genetically related children. The desire is something that people do feel and pursue, and this does come to impact on their choice of how to procreate currently. It will likely, in the future, impact which novel technologies enabling gestation are available.

[93] Benjamin Jones and others, 'Options for Acquiring Motherhood in Absolute Uterine Factor Infertility; Adoption, Surrogacy and Uterine Transplantation' (2021) 21 The Obstetrician & Gynaecologist 138–47, 142.

[94] David Orentlicher, 'Toward Acceptance of Uterus Transplants' (2012) 42 Hastings Center Report 12–13, 13.

[95] See eg Jones and others (n 93) 142.

[96] This is because the law affords parental status to the person who births—see explanation and critique in Chapter 7.

for something more specific: for enabling people to experience pregnancy—to 'become visibly pregnant, emotionally pregnant, and socially recognized as pregnant'.[97]

O'Donovan has observed that 'part of the experiential value of UTx is the experience of gestation and abdominal birth'.[98] The experience of 'gestation' that O'Donovan refers to here, should be read as meaning the experience of pregnancy in which the body facilitates gestation. As others have noted, the experience of pregnancy that is offered by UTx is not that of a pregnancy where there was no need for uterus transplant.[99] First, in the sense that when the uterus is transplanted a number of nerves are not transplanted with it, which means that fetal movement and other sensations will not be felt in the same way.[100] Second, in that the pregnancy will necessarily be highly medicalized because of the complexities of managing the body's immune response to the transplanted organ meaning that more monitoring (treating the pregnancy as innately 'high-risk') is recommended.[101] These distinguishing features, however, may hardly signify for those who value *undertaking pregnancy*. For individuals without the capacity to undertake pregnancy—UTx offers the choice of experiencing pregnancy, even if that choice is between experiencing a pregnancy that necessitates medical intervention and where a lack of nervous innervation means they will experience less 'pregnant' sensation and experiencing no pregnancy at all. However, for those who value a particular experience of *vaginal birthing* as their reason for wanting to be pregnant, what UTx can deliver may be less promising. Catsanos and others note that the lack of sensation and of, what they term, 'normal' delivery, may mean that UTx does not deliver what an individual means by the value in pregnancy (where they attach this to *vaginal birthing* rather than *being pregnant*).[102] That said, this assumes that persons who value being pregnant may mean actually that they value being a birther, and that valuing being a birther means that they *only* value vaginal birth, which I think to be a narrow conception of what being a birther can mean to people. These authors also note that some people who seek UTx may find that it does not meet their expectations.[103] This is, however,

[97] Julian Koplin and Evie Kendal, 'Ethical Issues in Uterine Transplantation' (2020) 34 Korean Journal of Transplantation 78–83, 80.

[98] O'Donovan (n 83) 37.

[99] Arora and Blake (n 28) 398.

[100] ibid; Mats Brännström and others, 'Uterus Transplantation – Substantial Progress in Research but Not Yet Ready for the Clinic' (2007) 12 Middle East Fertility Society Journal 86–95, 91; Ruby Catsanos, Wendy Rogers, and Mianna Lotz, 'The Ethics of Uterus Transplantation' (2013) 27 Bioethics 65–73, 69.

[101] Jones and others (n 93) 142.

[102] Catsanos and others (n 100) 69.

[103] ibid 70.

the case of any pregnancy and not just those facilitated by UTx. The experience of pregnancy offered by UTx is not something that should be considered sexed—people assigned male at birth may also wish to experience pregnancy where their partner assigned female at birth is unwilling/unable, or where they are single or in a relationship with someone of the same sex, or just because they value the experience.[104]

Pregnancy can have value in different ways. As Brännström and others note the value that is or is not placed on pregnancy are varied because 'viewpoints on reproduction and family building are culturally embedded concepts'.[105] Being pregnant and giving birth may speak to a person's preference for a physical, biological link between them and a resulting child.[106] O'Donovan describes how some people may perceive this linkage as making their parenthood 'more authentic'.[107] The desire for a link is not wholly about the consequences of that link (procreation being visible to others and parenthood being legally recognized)—but about the emergence of a child into the world being an event of one's own making—a meaningful series of events mediated as part of their own psychofleshy mode of being. Pregnancy, in using one's body to make another person, can be an empowering experience; to experience a new part of the self, and to both constitute and create using one's physicality, and to feel that the change in the future one is creating for themselves (or, in some cases, for others). Pregnancy is an intimacy within the self that can be transcendent. A person using their body to create life can feel like an artist and all the satisfaction that comes from making (and not just the enjoyment of the finished product). In a group of people who underwent UTx, a number described the procedure as important because it led to a change in their self-perception: that their body could (even if it did not) become a pregnant body.[108] Being pregnant is not just a matter of the work that the body is doing, or the value one feels in the state of being in themselves, it is also about pregnancy being a state of being that is visible to others. In some contexts and cultures, pregnancy commands considerable respect,[109] which also speaks to why pregnancy is highly

[104] Timothy Murphy, 'Assisted Gestation and Transgender Women' (2014) 20 Bioethics 389–97, 390–91.

[105] Mats Brännström and others, 'Uterus Transplantation: From Research, through Human Trials and Into the Future' (2023) 29 Human Reproduction Update 521–44, 536

[106] Laura O'Donovan, 'Pushing the Boundaries: Uterine Transplantation and the Limits of Reproductive Autonomy' (2018) 32 Bioethics 489–98, 490.

[107] ibid 490.

[108] Stina Järvholm and others, 'Uterus Transplantation: Joys and Frustrations of Becoming a "Complete" Woman – A Qualitative Study Regarding Self-image in the 5-year Period after Transplantation' (2020) 35 Human Reproduction 1855–63, 1861.

[109] Reyes Lázaro, 'Feminism and Motherhood: O'Brien vs Beauvoir' (1986) 1 Hypatia 87–102, 95.

valued by some individuals.[110] Some of this may relate to how pregnancy can be, to some extent, a performance in the social practices and customs that surround it (like baby showers).[111] The desire to experience pregnancy should not be narrowly reiterated as a sexed or gendered desire, as Mavuso and Chadwick stress, people of many genders and sexes desire to be pregnant.[112]

Where people perceive pregnancy as important, but they are born without the capacity to become pregnant (or no longer have the capacity to become pregnant), technologies like UTx speak to their needs (help to gestate) in ways that match their individual values (that pregnancy is a meaningful experience). For other individuals who can become pregnant but are worried about being able to be pregnant for the full duration of pregnancy, for example, because of concerns about their health,[113] partial ectogestation may meet their needs by helping them *complete* a gestation in a way that speaks to what they value (pregnancy as a meaningful experience). Such individuals would still get to experience pregnancy but know that they do not have to risk unplanned premature delivery of their fetus.

Pregnancy is not universally empowering, however. For some, the creative power in pregnancy is not felt (even where the person wants to become a parent), rather, it is drowned out by dysmorphic relationship with one's body and confusion about shifting bodily boundaries, and where one begins and ends. Pregnancy can also be characterized, for many, by discomfort, pain, stress, and fear. Some scholars emphasize that pregnancy and birth always encompass serious physical risks—including risk to life.[114] Pregnancy, for people who feel or anticipate it as unpleasant or scary, may see it only a means to an end—a necessary evil in the pursuit of genetic parenthood. Technologies enabling gestation without pregnancy have an important place in thinking about procreative preferences in thinking about the needs of persons who would wish to never be pregnant. Complete ectogestation could enable people to procreate—potentially using their own genetic material—without having to experience the burdens of pregnancy.[115]

[110] Romanis and Kendal (n 91) 111–12.

[111] Angel Petropanagos, 'Pronatalism, Geneticism, and ART' (2017) 10 International Journal of Feminist Approaches to Bioethics 119–47, 124.

[112] Jabulile Mavuso and Rachelle Chadwick, 'Cisgender Men's Narratives about their Desires to be Pregnant: Re/constructing Reproduction, Gender, and their Entanglement' (2024) Journal of Family Studies 1–21 <doi:10.1080/13229400.2023.2301586> accessed 1 September 2024.

[113] Romanis, 'Artificial Womb Technology' (n 74) 350–51.

[114] Anna Smajdor, 'The Moral Imperative for Ectogenesis' (2007) 16 Cambridge Quarterly for Healthcare Ethics 336–45, 336; Kendal (n 89) 3; Bidoli and Di Nucci (n 89).

[115] Kendal (n 89) 5.

It is also important to acknowledge the preferences of people who wish to assist others with procreative work as these will also be relevant in determining the right option for individuals.[116] In the UK, surrogacies must be motivated by altruism (since commercial surrogacies are prohibited)[117] in helping people to build their families through gestational work. However, how they may want to help enable gestation may vary based on their subjective experiences—for example, some may prefer to donate their uterus so the intended parent can sustain a pregnancy themselves, others may prefer to undertake the pregnancy themselves—all for a variety of reasons.[118] Thus, the preferences of those who intend to assist with gestation should also be considered important.

Murphy argues that '[p]eople turn to all these technologies to become parents, yes, but their choices also involve becoming parents according to their own self understandings of what it is to be a parent' and what is meaningful in the journey of becoming a parent.[119] Technologies enabling gestation work in different ways: some enable pregnancy, some eliminate the need for pregnancy. These technologies, thus, serve distinct functions that will be important to different individuals. In addition to enabling the realization of different preferences, it is important to note that these technologies provide completely different procreative experiences. The below table summarizes some of these differences—not only are there differences between them in terms of pregnancy, but there are also distinctions between them in who is pregnant, in how a pregnant person (where there is one) can give birth, and in how giving birth and the being born of a child is experienced. These intricate details will each speak to people's more specific preferences about procreation—this might be a matter of what becoming a parent means to them, or about what experiences they value more generally. The details will also be material from the perspective of another person (if there is one) intending to assist with gestation. These species of technologies enabling gestation can be compared in how their fundamental character that makes them part of the genus is undertaken in distinct ways.

[116] Alexandra Mullock, Elizabeth Chloe Romanis, and Dunja Begović, 'Surrogacy and Uterus Transplantation using Live Donors: Examining the Options from the Perspective of "Womb-Givers"' (2021) 35 Bioethics 820–28.

[117] Strictly speaking, it is not unlawful to pay a surrogate, but it is unlawful for arrangements to be commercial in nature eg third parties profiting, per the Surrogacy Arrangements Act 1985, s 2. Though it is important to note that the distinction between altruism and commercial surrogacies is not so clear nor a distinction that should be steadfastly maintained. See JY Lee, 'Surrogacy: Beyond the Commercial/Altruistic Distinction' (2023) 49 Journal of Medical Ethics 196–99.

[118] Mullock and others (n 116).

[119] Murphy (n 104) 393.

	Gestational surrogacies	**Uterus transplantation**	**Partial ectogestation**	**Complete ectogestation**
Is there a pregnancy?	Yes, complete duration of gestation	Yes, complete duration of gestation	Yes, partial duration of pregnancy	No pregnancy
Who is the pregnant person?	Commissioned individual (who does not intend to parent)	Person who intends to parent	Usually, person who intends to parent (but could also be a surrogate, or a person who plants to pursue adoption)	/
By what means does the pregnant person give birth?	Vaginal or surgical delivery at full term (if there are no complications)	Surgical delivery at full term (if there are no complications)	Vaginal/ surgical delivery pre-term	/
When is the new human entity born?	When the entity is delivered from the pregnant person	When the entity is delivered from the pregnant person	When the entity is delivered from the artificial placenta	When the entity is delivered from the artificial placenta

As Lee and others anticipate, in the event that there are multiple technologies available that facilitate gestation, 'competing values over the "proper" or "good" way to gestate will add to the contentious hierarchy of gestation methods, and divide groups of aspiring parents'.[120] The reality is that choices about gestation are not just individual choices; they are situated in social and legal context and have broader social and political ramifications. Koplin and Kendal raised the point that what value we should afford to gestation (and to what extent) remains an open philosophical question.[121] Such a question is not only philosophical in nature, but socio-political, because social and cultural factors are embedded in the ways values in procreative experiences are described. In societies that value pronatalism (a social bias towards 'childbearing . . . toward creating a child in a particular kind of way'[122]) people are 'bombarded with messages that normalize, praise, and mandate pregnancy'.[123] Thus, some have raised

[120] JY Lee, Andrea Bidoli, and Ezio Di Nucci, 'Does Ectogestation have Oppressive Potential?' (2023) Journal of Social Philosophy <doi.org/10.1111/josp.12512> accessed 1 September 2024.
[121] Koplin and Kendal (n 97) 80.
[122] Angel Petropanagos, 'Pronatalism, Geneticism, and ART' (2017) 10 International Journal of Feminist Approaches to Bioethics 119–47, 120.
[123] ibid 123.

concerns about the authenticity of the desire for UTx, and/or raised concerns about the promotion of UTx because of the pronatalist signalling this can embody.[124] Similarly, some scholars have raised concerns that ectogestation could also propagate signalling harms—for example, in enabling greater medicalization of pregnancy and birth,[125] or pathologizing pregnancy in such a way that excludes the experiences of those who describe pregnancy as joyful.[126] Social messaging around procreative technologies, especially those concerning *how* procreative work is undertaken and influence the bodily boundaries of so many in different ways, is important to examine, remain attentive to, and address. That said, the solution to harmful social pressures is not to deny the procreative needs of individuals in the ways that they describe them. Pronatalism exists whether or not UTx is permitted. The pathologization and medicalization of pregnancy exists whether or not ectogestation is permitted. Thus, we need to think about how to address societal expectations in procreation more directly, and we must do so in a manner that does not deny the significance of the wishes, feelings, and experiences of individuals that frame their procreative preferences.

These technologies, because of their sharing the character complex of providing a person A who needs assistance with gestation with some assistance (whether to have it performed for them, or to perform it themselves), are inevitably consistently compared to each other. Making visible that they are *related* technologies—all enabling gestation in their own species-specific ways—by classifying these technologies is useful. It makes the conceptual similarities and distinctions between these technologies clearer, and thus makes it easier to appreciate where each technology is (or is not) facilitating individuals' procreative preferences. These preferences all have social and political ramifications related to their central character complex in how they shift the nature of gestation and our understanding of it. In this chapter, with the conceptual clarity of a taxonomic approach, I have described the various different modalities of gestation that technologies enabling gestation can offer, and why they might be valuable to different individuals. In Chapter 4 I consider when and where we should facilitate access to technologies enabling gestation.

[124] Kathryn MacKay, 'The "Tyranny of Reproduction": Could Ectogenesis further Women's Liberation?' (2020) 34 Bioethics 346–53.

[125] Victoria Adkins, 'Impact of Ectogenesis on the Medicalisation of Pregnancy and Childbirth' (2021) 47 Journal of Medical Ethics 239–43; Elizabeth Chloe Romanis and others, 'Reviewing the Womb' (2021) 47 Journal of Medical Ethics 820–29.

[126] Suki Finn and Sasha Isaac, 'Evaluating Ectogenesis via the Metaphysics of Pregnancy' in Robbie Davis-Floyd (ed), *Birthing Techno-Sapiens: Human Evolution and the Future of Reproduction* (Routledge 2021); Romanis and others (n 125).

4
ACCESS

Technologies enabling gestation offer different experiences for persons wanting to become parents (and potentially third parties). Were all to be readily available, different individuals may seek to make different choices about gestation—about *how* they bring a new human entity into being. This inevitably raises the question of who would or should have access to technologies enabling gestation, and in what circumstances. In this chapter, I explore a pivotal issue that undergirds access to these technologies. Social, legal, and clinical regulation of procreative technologies has been centred around notions of the 'biological' and the 'natural' and as such, they are structured by and re-embed these notions reinforcing conservative values in procreative regulation. This is likely to have structural impacts on the choices individuals seek to make about gestation—both in terms of the choices they *want* to make and that they *can* make.

Even before we get to thinking of legal, social, and clinical regulation, in the very development of this technology conceptions of the 'natural' are built into how they are envisaged. Technologies do not speak for themselves; they are defined by who designs them and what they designed them for. Science and scientists do not operate in a social and political vacuum. Science as an institution is not value-neutral,[1] nor does it exist in a different realm from social context: thus 'social views are always embedded or sedimented' in technologies.[2] How researchers discuss the primary motivations for their development of technologies enabling gestation are revealing of their conceptions of medical need. The technologies are brought into being as solutions to what researchers have identified as a problem in need of a medico-technological solution. In the case of uterus transplantation (UTx) most describe the importance of the procedure in relation to people born assigned female at birth

[1] Elisabeth Lloyd, *The Case of the Female Orgasm: Bias in the Science of Evolution* (Harvard University Press 2005) 242.

[2] Marilyn Strathern, 'Still Giving Nature a Helping Hand? Surrogacy: A Debate about Technology and Society' in Rachel Cook, Shelley Day Sclater, and Felicity Kaganas, *Surrogate Motherhood: International Perspectives* (Bloomsbury 2003) 281–82.

Biotechnology, Gestation, and the Law. Elizabeth Chloe Romanis, Oxford University Press.
 DOI: 10.1093/9780191986574.003.0004

(AFAB) who cannot experience pregnancy. Those working on UTx have positioned it the 'only treatment' for absolute uterine infertility affecting people AFAB who want to reproduce.[3] Those working on the development of artificial amnion and placenta technologies (AAPT) have stressed that they envisage the technology not as a procreative technology, but an alternative to neonatal intensive care.[4] As Kendal and I have observed elsewhere, the framing of the technology as serving *these* purposes may come to limit other uses.[5] For example, the motivations behind the development of these technologies could come to prevent transformative future uses, such as, the use of UTx to enable people who are not AFAB undertaking pregnancy. That said, some surgeons have begun turning their attention to whether uterus transplantation could be of clinical benefit to trans women,[6] which does illustrate that envisaged uses of technologies can shift over time. At the time of writing, in reading the work of those developing AAPT, it is hard to envisage the use partial ectogestation as a procreative choice (potentially in the future).[7] This is because of just how much it is insisted and reiterated that AAPT is a solution to prematurity.

In this chapter I first consider the claims made by some scholars that the right to procreate (in both a moral and legal sense) should encompass the liberty to make decisions about gestation. I argue that neither such a moral nor legal right exists, but more importantly, even if it did, it would not be absolute. The better way to approach questions of access, therefore, is not to dwell on the matter of a 'right to gestation' but instead consider how we should afford access to technologies enabling gestation appropriately bearing in mind the importance of equality of opportunity and the harms of stratified procreation. I critique the legal framework regulating assisted procreation (conception) that is contained in the Human Fertilisation and Embryology Acts 1990 and 2008 (HFE Acts 1990 and 2008) (applying across the UK) for its focus on 'biological' needs in procreation, rather than procreative needs. I argue that such an approach results in biological essentialism that has limited access to assisted procreation in ways that impact marginalized groups, and without reform, a

[3] Elliott Richards and others, 'Uterus Transplant: State of the Art in 2021' (2021) 38 Journal of Assisted Reproduction and Genetics 2251–59, 2251.

[4] Alan Flake, 'A Supportive Physiologic Environment for the Extreme Premature Infant: Improving Life Outside the Womb' (2022) 57 Journal of Pediatric Surgery 167–71, 169.

[5] Elizabeth Chloe Romanis and Evie Kendal, 'Subjective Experience, Gestational Preferences and Justice: Valuing Both Uterus Transplantation and Ectogestation' in Natasha Hammond-Browning and Nicola Williams (eds), *International Legal and Ethical Perspectives on Uterus Transplantation* (Edward Elgar 2024) 118.

[6] Benjamin Jones and others 'Uterine Transplantation in Transgender Women' (2019) 126 British Journal of Obstetrics & Gynaecology 152.

[7] ibid.

legal framework for technologies enabling gestation that builds on the premises of that which exists would come to limit access to uterus transplantation and ectogestation in concerning ways. Finally, I consider the problems of stratified access to novel technologies enabling gestation. How we facilitate access to technologies, including thinking about who they are accessible to—and who they are not—is a critical step in thinking through the implications of shifting modalities of gestation. These technologies bring new possibilities, but only where there are means for accessing technologies in ways that facilitate the realization of these possibilities.

A Right to Opt In or Out of Gestational Work?

In the ethico-legal literature on UTx, there has emerged debate about whether there is a right to gestate.[8] Amongst those debating the issue, the 'right to gestate' is seen as an extension of procreative liberty/the right to procreate.[9] In the ordinary sense of the word, however, a right to gestate seems intuitive in most cases. Where a person has become pregnant, forced termination of pregnancy (and thus the ceasing of that person undertaking gestation) would be a violation of a person's right to non-interference with their bodily integrity as well as the negative right to procreate that is recognized as a part of the right to respect for family life in the European Convention of Human Rights.[10] For clarity, the question might better be asked in this way—is there a moral or a legal right to gestation? Can a person demand access to assistive technology (like UTx) that can enable them to sustain a pregnancy? Or can a person demand access to a replacement technology (like surrogacies or ectogestation) that can undertake gestational work for them? This framing makes it clearer that the question that is being asked is one of *positive* rather than *negative* rights and that we might reach different answers when considering moral and legal rights[11] (though I do not in this case). Moreover, asking the question in this way broadens the conversation from one just related to UTx, but the full spectrum of technologies enabling gestation.

[8] John Robertson, 'Is There a Right to Gestate?' (2017) 4 Journal of Law and the Biosciences 630–36; Amel Alghrani 'Uterus Transplantation In and Beyond Cisgender Women: Revisiting Procreative Liberty in Light of Emerging Reproductive Technologies' (2018) 5 Journal of Law and the Biosciences 301–28.

[9] ibid.

[10] European Convention on Human Rights, Article 8.

[11] Gulzaar Barn, 'A Right to Gestate? Uterus Transplants and the Language of Rights' in Natasha Hammond-Browning and Nicola Williams (eds), *International Legal and Ethical Perspectives on Uterus Transplantation* (Edward Elgar 2024) 60.

Robertson argues that procreative liberty (freedom of procreative choice)[12] encompasses 'a right to gestate when gestation is essential to or a part of a person's way to have genetic offspring for rearing, just as use of IVF [in vitro fertilization] embryo freezing, sperm and egg freezing, and related activities are'.[13] He explains that these important technologies all enable individuals to procreate and thus must be encompassed under the liberty of procreative liberty. This limits the use of UTx, and within his logic also surrogacies and ectogestation, to persons who *need* such technologies to procreate. He stipulates that, '[b]ecause gestational surrogacy is essential for genetic reproduction when a woman is unfit or unable to gestate, a robust conception of procreative liberty should extent to gestational surrogacy as well'.[14] The inference is that it would not be a matter of procreative liberty for a person with a functioning uterus to be granted access to ectogestation—Robertson would presumably not have thought that this preference was encompassed within the right to procreative liberty. Moreover, if a person without a uterus or any gametes wanted UTx to procreate by sustaining a pregnancy using donor material, that would not be a matter of procreative liberty by Robertson's reasoning. Alghrani disagrees with Robertson's conception of gestation in relation to procreative liberty.[15] The inference is that if we are recognizing the value of choice in procreative activities, then *how* that procreation is facilitated will be just as critical to the concept than what entity is created. What is tricky, however, and is not addressed within her argument is what statements are made about the obligations of others where we recognize a moral right to gestation. This is pertinent in the case of all technologies enabling gestation, but most especially surrogacies and UTx.

Hall argues that there can be no such thing as a moral right to procreate as an instrument an individual can assert 'because an individual cannot reproduce on their own. Reproductive projects are necessarily collaborative, and all collaborators have the right to agree or to refuse to join the project. The hopeful parent can, at best, assert the right to *try* to reproduce'.[16] This is not to say there is not a moral right of non-interference with procreation (for example, forced sterilization is wrong) but this is wholly consistent with recognizing that there

[12] See John Robertson, *Children of Choice: Freedom and the New Reproductive Technologies* (Princeton University Press 1994) 22.

[13] Robertson, 'Is There a Right to Gestate?' (n 8) 631.

[14] ibid 632.

[15] Alghrani (n 8) 307–08.

[16] Georgina Antonia Hall, 'Reproduction Misconceived: Why There is No Right to Reproduce and the Implications for ART Access' (2022) Journal of Medical Ethics <doi:10.1136/jme-2022-108512> accessed 1 September 2024 (emphasis added).

is straightforwardly no *right* to use the body of (or materials resulting from) another for one's procreative purposes. A person assigned male at birth (AMAB) cannot demand that their partner assigned female at birth (AFAB) facilitate a pregnancy as much as a person AFAB morally cannot demand that their partner AMAB inseminate them. There can be no moral *positive right* to UTx and surrogacies because of what this means that individuals can demand of the bodies of others.[17] Just as there is no right to gestation in cases where individuals seek to interfere with the abortion choices of others (eg to prevent individuals having an abortion and thus continue facilitating gestation and birth so that they can parent the resulting entity),[18] there is no right to demand another individual act as a surrogate (which would be very similar co-opting to the prevention of abortion) or to donate their uterus. As Barn argues:

> A positive right to UTx that involved forcible redistribution of reproductive materials or coerced access to reproductive means would of course be straightforwardly in conflict with other people's negative rights and therefore unsustainable.[19]

These are rights to bodily integrity—but there is no positive right to become pregnant, nor to have gestation facilitated by another person. Ectogestation, however, is distinguishable from surrogacies and UTx in the sense that a right to (ecto)gestation would not be demanding work of other bodies (parts from them or the performance or pregnancy), but this is not to say that it would not be demanding work of others at all (eg professionals managing machines). This distinction might still be material in that a right to make a choice about gestation in the sense of whether to facilitate it oneself or to opt for a machine does not transgress the bodily boundaries of another person. The question of resources and implications becomes more material where the potential interference with the negative rights of other individuals is less pertinent. If one accepts that there is a positive right to other forms of procreative assistance (like IVF), one should accept that there should be a positive right to ectogestation. Essentially if one accepts a moral right to procreate, then one *must* accept a moral right to ectogestation. However, I agree with Hall that there can be no moral right to procreate because it requires bodily resources of others, in the case of ectogestation this is *still* the case because I cannot demand the use of

[17] Barn (n 11) 71.
[18] See Chapter 7.
[19] Barn (n 11) 71.

another person's genetic material for the purposes of my procreation (whether that is facilitated by my body or by a machine)—I need their agreement, which they might provide to me directly or to a clinic if they are donating their material. It might be fair to say that I have a right to try, however, since this would encompass situations where I have the agreement (or active collaboration) of another person to use their genetic material. This argument is limited to procreative possibilities in the present of course, we might need to ask different questions about whether there is a right to procreate in instances where procreative possibilities as we know them are no longer in anyway limited to biosex. For example, where persons can generate their own gametes (through in vitro gametogenesis (IVG)) and facilitate pregnancy (because they were born with a uterus or a bioengineered uterus) or using a machine.[20] In these instances no bodily resources are being demanded of another person at all, only potentially state assistance (in a publicly funded health system).

Hall explains that clinicians and the state are collaborators in the procreative project when an individual needs procreative technological assistance to reproduce. She then argues that since they are collaborators they are free (morally) to 'refuse or restrict access to treatment, when asked to join the project' though the grounds for appropriate refusal are debateable.[21] By this logic, the state would be free to restrict or refuse access to ectogestation on the basis of whatever criteria it deems appropriate (Hall concedes that we can debate what the right criteria might be, but the argument is that they are entitled to introduce access criteria because there is no moral right to procreate). While Hall's framing of procreation as collaborative is generally appropriate within the confines of reproductive biology as we know it,[22] the framing of the state or clinicians as collaborators affords them too much power and legitimates intrusion into decisions that we ought to shield from external interference and public–political interference.[23] Furthermore, it ignores the socio-political realities of the ways that states design and weaponize procreative policies to the detriment of marginalized groups.[24] In legal terms, state involvement is

[20] See Elizabeth Chloe Romanis and Alan Brown, 'Legal Parenthood, Novel Reproductive Practices, and the Disruption of Reproductive Biosex' Modern Law Review <doi.org/10.1111/1468-2230.12914> accessed 1 September 2024.

[21] Hall (n 16).

[22] Romanis and Brown (n 20).

[23] This point is not that we must or need to fund every instance of procreative assistance, but that decisional privacy about procreation without state interference must be respected. This is analogous to the argument that Jackson makes about why we should not interrogate the fitness to parent of people seeking fertility treatment: see Emily Jackson, 'Conception and the Irrelevance of the Welfare Principle' (2002) 65 Modern Law Review 176–203, 178.

[24] See Dorothy Roberts, *Killing the Black Body: Race, Reproduction, and the Meaning of Liberty 20th Anniversary Edition* (Vintage Books 2017).

relevant because—where assistance is publicly funded—there might be claims that the state ought to support it. We can acknowledge this dimension of procreative decision-making without actively encouraging the framing of the state as a 'collaborator' in procreative projects.

Alghrani's argument is not only that there is a moral right to gestation, but also a *legal* right. In making this claim she subsumes a 'right to gestate' under a 'right to procreate' within 'the right to respect for family life' in the European Convention for Human Rights.[25] There are, however, two errors in Alghrani's construction of the legal right to gestate.

First, in Strasbourg jurisprudence there is no right to procreate—only a right *to respect for decisions about procreation.* Because the right to respect for private life protects decisions related to identity, procreation does readily come under its scope.[26] In *Dickson v United Kingdom,*[27] the case on which Alghrani relies to establish a right to procreate, the European Court of Human Rights (ECtHR) reiterates, on the basis of established precedent, that article 8 encompasses 'a right to respect for *their decision to become genetic parents*'.[28] Eijkholt, however, warns against the dangers of equating the right to respect for private life to a *positive right* to procreate, since in its substance is requires nothing more than an individual right to 'respect' *for decision-making about procreation.* Claiming there is a right to procreate 'obscures the degree of protection that can be expected'.[29] Individuals can make private choices about procreation; they cannot demand that the state subsidize or facilitate their access. Although there are circumstances where the ECtHR has interpreted the right to respect for private life as encompassing positive obligations, they have yet to do so in the context of a 'right to decisional privacy about procreation'.[30] The ECtHR considered it unnecessary in *Dickson* to make a determination about whether there is a positive or a negative right to procreate as the decision was actually one about whether there was excess public interference into a private matter: decision-making about procreation in the particular context (which concerned a married couple seeking artificial insemination because the husband was incarcerated).[31] Even where the ECtHR does recognize that there are positive obligations in relation to the right to respect for private life, they will

[25] Alghrani (n 8) 310.

[26] Pieter Dijk and others, *Theory and Practice of the European Convention on Human Rights* (4th edn, Intersentia 2006) 66.

[27] *Dickson v United Kingdom*, Application No 44362/04 (2007).

[28] ibid [66] (emphasis added).

[29] Marleen Eijkholt, 'The Right to Found a Family as a Stillborn Right to Procreate?' (2010) 18 Medical Law Review 127–51, 142.

[30] ibid.

[31] *Dickson* (n 27) [71].

never be absolute. Positive obligations mean that states must create a framework that contains the appropriate safeguards for such practices to go ahead. They would be permitted under such a framework to derogate from the right to respect for private life in contexts where interference is in accordance with the law, and:

> necessary in a democratic society in the interests of national security, public safety or the economic well-being of the country, for the prevention of disorder or crime, for the protection of health or morals, or for the protection of the rights and freedoms of others.[32]

As such, states are permitted where they have such a justification to put in place legal frameworks that enable access to assisted procreation, but restrict its use to some circumstances, or specifically prohibit it in others, where such provisions are related to the conditions for permissible derogation in the convention. The decision in *Dickson* means that where assisted procreation is made available to some individuals, it should be made readily available to all unless a refusal is justified by way of the permissible derogations afforded to member states. Consequently, a right to privacy around decisions about assisted procreation will always be a *qualified* right.

Second, ECtHR jurisprudence when it refers to a right to respect for procreative decisions is referring specifically to the right to decisions about whether to become a genetic parent,[33] not about gestation. Convention jurisprudence, therefore, exemplifies reasoning on the point of the nature of procreation that resembles more what Robertson (rather than Alghrani) constructed as encompassed within a right to procreate (decisions only about genetic parenthood). Though unlike Robertson, the ECtHR has never encompassed means of gestation as falling within the realms of procreative decision-making that must be respected as a matter of private life. Prohibitions on surrogacies across members of the Council of Europe are not considered, in themselves, violations of the right to private life. In cases where individuals have sought to claim that their home state refusing to recognize them as the parent of their child is a violation of their right to respect for private life have consistently failed.[34] It is notable that in the same cases it is often found that non-recognition of parenthood is a violation of the right to respect for private life of resulting children.[35] This is

[32] Art 8(2).
[33] *Evans v United Kingdom*, Application No 6339/05 (2007) [72].
[34] *Labassee v France*, Application No 65941/11 (2014); *Mennesson v France*, Application No 65192/11 (2014); *DB and others v Switzerland*, Application Nos 58817/15 and 58252/15 (2022).
[35] ibid.

likely because decisions about technologies enabling gestation are not wholly a private matter. As Eijkholt explains—the involvement of a third person like a surrogate or a uterus donor could transform procreative arrangements into 'not quite private ones'.[36] We cannot simply collapse the matter of gestation into the existing jurisprudence on procreation, which is explicitly referring to matters of assisted conception where it references a right to respect for decisions about procreation. This is crystal clear in that there has never been a decision that stipulates that decisions to access surrogacy must be respected.

Despite the above, I am not arguing that we should not facilitate access to technologies enabling gestation. Rather I am illustrating, in agreement with Barn, that rights-based justifications to their access encompass complications.[37] Even if we were to determine that there is a moral or legal right to procreate, we are still left with questions about what obligations this imposes on, for example, the state (in moral and legal terms) to facilitate the realization of that right. As a consequence, determinations about rights hardly move the debate about access to technologies enabling gestation along that much. Moreover, that there may be no moral or legal right to certain experiences over others in assisted procreation does not mean that we should not respect the choices people make in valuing some experiences over others. Even if there is no legal right to procreation, there would be a violation of a person's right to respect for private life (or right to non-discrimination) if the *conditions* that are placed on access to procreative technologies systemically exclude some groups and not others.[38] Involuntary childlessness 'can provoke a life crises at a deeply existential level, threatening one's sense of identity, purpose and role functioning, and may require a complete revision of life goals'.[39] It is also the case that how one becomes a parent can matter to individuals and can be a part of the procreation, and their identity in relation to that, that they imagine for themselves. We do not have to recognize a right to procreate (and as a constituent part of this the right to gestate or the right to gestation) in order to recognize that facilitating access to technologies enabling gestation can be a moral and social good that can meaningfully help people to lead the lives that they envisage for themselves. The issue at hand is, therefore, not about whether there is a right to gestation, rather about how we afford access to technologies

36 Eijkholt (n 29) 143.

37 Barn (n 11) 72.

38 See Kirsty Horsey and Emily Jackson, 'The Human Fertilisation and Embryology Act 1990 and Non-Traditional Families' (2023) 86 Modern Law Review 1472–88.

39 Bernadette Bartlam and Susan Birch, 'Review: A Right to Parenthood' (1998) 2 Journal of Child Health Care 36–40, 36.

enabling gestation appropriately bearing in mind the importance of equality of opportunity and the harms of stratified procreation.

Access, Procreative Need, and Biological Need

Procreative needs are broader than 'biological' needs in procreation. An individual's (or couple's) biological needs in procreation encompass what has been traditionally understood as 'infertility', which the World Health Organization defined as 'a disease of the male or female reproductive system defined by a failure to achieve a pregnancy after 12 months or more of regular unprotected sexual intercourse'.[40] This might result, for example, from a person AMAB not producing (good-quality) sperm, a person AFAB not producing (good-quality) eggs, or 'abnormalities' in the uterus or endocrine system that make a pregnancy difficult to establish or sustain.[41] A person's (or couple's) biological needs in procreation, thus, encompass interventions that enable procreation to occur (eg hormone therapy, or donor material). Procreative needs do not relate *only* to individuals' biological needs because what are framed as matters of fertility reflect only the cis-heteronormative nuclear model of procreation (family-building). They also encompass broader social and psychosocial factors—for example, sexuality, identity, economic circumstances. These factors can mean that not everyone can or wants to reproduce sexually. Attending to biological needs and *not* to broader procreative needs is a matter of propagating biological essentialism: that procreation is the result of biological factors only, rather than a range of socio-cultural factors. Assisted procreation makes transcending the 'biological' possible. Where we use technology only as a mirror to the 'biological', this is perpetuating the notion of the 'biological' as inviolable.

Assisted procreation is highly regulated activity in England and Wales and many jurisdictions, though there are some notable exceptions (the United States, for example, is referred to as 'the wild west' of assisted reproduction).[42] The framework in England and Wales, while not directly imposing specific rules on who can and cannot procreate, does impose conditions that could

[40] World Health Organization, 'Fact Sheet: Infertility' (nd) <https://www.who.int/news-room/fact-sheets/detail/infertility> accessed 21 June 2024.

[41] ibid.

[42] I Glenn Cohen, 'The Right(s) to Procreate and Assisted Reproductive Technologies in the United States' in David Orentlicher and Tamara K Hervey, *The Oxford Handbook of Comparative Health Law* (OUP 2021) 1009.

indirectly limit some people from procreating. For example, there are provisions that enable clinics to make decisions about who should be able to access procreative services.[43] Moreover, where there are new procreative developments, those developing technology will develop criteria for access based on what 'problem' they envisage their technology to be addressing. In this section, I argue that what is deemed permissible in assisted procreation (in both social and legal terms) is constructed around notions of the 'biological' and thus a matter of medical need. This narrow lens of constructed need limits recognition of the *procreative* needs of individuals. It is likely, I argue, that without significant reform, and a change in the approach to law-making, that technologies enabling gestation will be subject to significant restrictions—tying their use to medically constructed notions of need (that reflect the 'biological') in ways that exclude marginalized persons.

'Biological need' and legal limitations

That access to procreative technologies should be underpinned by *need* is in the fabric of the legal framework. In a publicly funded health system, a notion of 'need' might not be thought so problematic in determining or prioritizing access to resources. However, the lens through which 'need' is interpreted and constructed should always be subject to careful, critical interrogation (for who it includes and who it excludes). Since its inception, the legal framework, with its origins in the HFE Act 1990), had the cis-heteronormative nuclear family in mind. As Horsey and Jackson note, since assisted conception was stigmatized and highly controversial at the time it was assumed necessary to subject access to strict controls.[44] In the 1990 Act, there were no provisions allowing for same-sex family recognition in the attribution of parenthood and included provisions that expressly required clinics consider the need for a child to have a father and mother when considering whether to provide procreative services (effectively signalling that single people and same-sex female couples should not be assisted to procreate).[45] Essentially, assisted procreation was envisaged as a means of enabling traditional families to procreate where there were biological limitations preventing sexual procreation. Speaking to the social stigma surrounding assisted procreation, the provisions of the Act assumed

[43] Michael Thomson, 'Legislating for the Monstrous: Access to Reproductive Services and the Monstrous Feminine' (1997) 6 Social & Legal Studies 401–24, 410.
[44] Horsey and Jackson (n 38) 1472.
[45] ibid 1473.

and enabled the 'invisibility' of the assistance (eg with donor anonymity).[46] This was mirrored in the discussions of surrogacies. The Warnock Committee, an inquiry set up in 1982 to investigate the regulate human reproduction in the UK, made recommendations[47] which (though only some were accepted)[48] resulted in the Surrogacy Arrangements Act 1985. While they made recommendations about regulation, most of Warnock's members hoped that surrogacies would just go away by constructing a regulatory regime that did not make surrogacies appealing.[49] In making surrogacies more legally complex, surrogacies might be thought to be limited to people who *need* (have a 'compelling medical need' for) assisted gestation, rather than those who might want to outsource gestation.

Reforms introduced in the HFE Act 2008 did make some space for families outside of the heteronormative nuclear model of the family in introducing the recognition of female same-sex parents[50] and in changing provisions referring to the need for a 'father' to requiring clinics to consider whether a child resulting from fertility treatment would have a supportive parenting environment.[51] To some extent, these provisions move on from the concept of 'medical need' in the construction of assisted procreation because they are accounting for circumstances in which people wanting to build their families together may not be biologically limited in their ability to procreate, but their specific needs are not served by biological possibilities (eg two people AFAB may both be capable of becoming pregnant, but would not be able to procreate together). However, there remain aspects of the legal framework that maintain assumptions of the 'biological' that could or can limit access to persons wanting to reproduce outside of the cis-heteronormative nuclear family model. Furthermore, that the 2008 Act has changed the letter of the law does

[46] Per the Human Fertilisation and Embryology Authority (Disclosure of Donor Information) Regulations 2004 persons conceived from donated material after 1 April 2005 are entitled to request identifying information about their donors from the Human Fertilisation Authority when they turn 18. However, it is notable that children must know they are donor conceived to know they can apply for information about the donor. There is inevitably some difference between the children of heterosexual and same-sex couples: see Andrew Bainham, 'Arguments about Parentage' (2008) 67 Cambridge Law Journal 322–51.

[47] Department of Health and Social Security, *Report of the Committee of Inquiry into Human Fertilisation and Embryology* (Cmnd 9314, 1984).

[48] Margaret Brazier, 'Regulating the Reproduction Business?' (1999) 7 Medical Law Review 166–93, 169.

[49] ibid 179.

[50] Notably, however, this recognition is simply extending the nuclear family to the inclusion of female same-sex parents, rather than any kind of radical reform—see Julie McCandless and Sally Sheldon, 'The Human Fertilisation and Embryology Act (2008) and the Tenacity of the Sexual Family Form' (2010) 73 Modern Law Review 175–207.

[51] For commentary see Marie Fox, 'The Human Fertilisation and Embryology Act 2008: Tinkering at the Margins' (2009) 17 Feminist Legal Studies 333–44, 337.

not necessarily mean that notions of 'biological need' have not been baked into assisted procreation in other ways. Guidelines, for example, build notions of the 'biological' into access criteria—for example, in relation to age and assisted conception.[52] Moreover, decisions about what is and is not funded across the jurisdiction, or at a local level, in the health service can reflect notions of 'biological need'. It was only in 2022 that funding for same-sex couples for fertility treatment was introduced[53]—before this, in order to establish a 'fertility issue', lesbian couples had to go through several rounds of intrauterine insemination before they could be considered for NHS-funded treatment.[54] Finally, where new technologies become available, it is often the case that they are restricted to their clinically envisaged use—for example, mitochondrial replacement techniques, legally regulated in the UK since 2015—have been restricted to cases of 'medical necessity'.[55]

There remain several barriers to access to procreation embedded within the legal framework that limit access to assisted procreation generally for marginalized groups. It is hardly surprising that this is the case given the endemic marginalization of 'non-traditional' procreative arrangements in the evolution of the law (including that pre-dating the HFE Acts).[56] These barriers, still embedding the concept of 'biological need' for assistance to some extent, may come to limit who can access technologies enabling gestation.

First, who is envisaged as a person that can become pregnant in the legal framework may come to limit access to UTx for procreative purposes. The limitations of current transplantation techniques mean that the organ is not connected to a person's fallopian tubes (if they have them).[57] A pregnancy can thus only be established by IVF. Even if the science were to change here, it is likely that for people AMAB, a pregnancy from UTx could only be achieved by IVF. As a consequence, provisions relating to who can become pregnant in assisted conception are relevant. Hammond-Browning observes that the HFE

[52] National Institute for Health and Care Excellence, 'Fertility Problems: Assessment and Treatment [CG156]' (2017) <https://www.nice.org.uk/guidance/cg156/chapter/Recommendations#access-criteria-for-ivf> accessed 20 May 2024 [1.11.1.4]

[53] Lowenna Waters, 'Discriminatory NHS Rules on IVF for Lesbian Women to be Scrapped' (2022) *The Standard* <https://www.standard.co.uk/news/uk/nhs-discriminatory-rules-ivf-lesbian-women-to-be-scrapped-b1013565.html> accessed 20 May 2024.

[54] ibid.

[55] Human Fertilisation and Embryology (Mitochondrial Donation) Regulations 2015, Reg 5 (a). For critique see Romanis and Brown (n 20).

[56] Sarah Cooper, *Analysis Gender in Healthcare: The Politics of Sex and Reproduction* (Palgrave Macmillan 2022) 171–74.

[57] Dominique de Ziegler and others, 'Assisted Reproductive Technology Strategies in Uterus Transplantation (2019) 112 Fertility and Sterility 19–23, 20.

Acts prohibit the transfer of human embryos into a person who is not AFAB.[58] There is no express prohibition in either Act (1990 or 2008) stipulating that it is an offence to implant embryos in the uterus of a male person (whether that is a uterus they were born with or that has been transplanted into them). Rather, the legislation directs that 'no person shall place in a woman— (a) an embryo other than a permitted embryo . . . or (b) any gametes other than permitted eggs or permitted sperm'.[59] In the next sub-section (that defines permitted eggs as from a woman's ovaries, and permitted sperm as from a man's testes), it is specified that '"woman" and "man" include respectively a girl and a boy (from birth)'.[60] This can be interpreted either as saying that it is only permitted embryos/gametes can then *only* be implanted into women AFAB (explicitly prohibiting the practice of using such material in men AMAB and, potentially, people AFAB who have changed their legal gender to male). Hammond-Browning stresses that anything other than this interpretation is difficult to foresee.[61] If this first interpretation is adopted, a person AMAB could have a uterus transplant, but they could not lawfully become pregnant. However, the provision can be interpreted as merely omitting to acknowledge the realities of male pregnancies (it does not explicitly say *only* women).[62] Per this interpretation, persons AMAB could be supported to become pregnant after uterus transplantation because it is not strictly prohibited. Horsey and Jackson note that this provision is not a direct prohibition on trans women and cis men undertaking pregnancy, it was simply that it was taken for granted that only people AFAB could become pregnant.[63] In any event, the law as written is clearly not friendly to procreation outside of the cis-heteronormative because it exists in a regulatory gap. This creates considerable uncertainty[64] that could come to affect access to UTx for people AMAB if it is not altered. The overall construction of the provision still is revealing—it seems deliberate in its intention maintain some preservation of 'biological procreation' even where procreation is technologically assisted. Such normative judgments underpinning regulatory structures could come to

[58] Natasha Hammond-Browning, 'UK Criteria for Uterus Transplantation: A Review' (2019) 126 British Journal of Obstetrics and Gynaecology 1320–26, 1322.

[59] Human Fertilisation and Embryology Act 2008, s 3(2).

[60] ibid s 3ZA(6).

[61] Natasha Hammond-Browning, 'Author's Reply Re: Uterine Transplantation in Transgender Women: Medical, Legal and Ethical Considerations' (2018) 126 British Journal of Obstetrics & Gynaecology 546, 546.

[62] Elizabeth Chloe Romanis, 'Male and Nonbinary Pregnancy in the Law: Ontic Injustice and/or Invisbilization' (forthcoming).

[63] Horsey and Jackson (n 38) 1475.

[64] Alan Brown, 'Trans Parenthood'; Horsey and Jackson (n 38).

impact on ideas about where and when people can access technologies that defy the 'biological'—such as ectogestation.

Second, there are indirect barriers to access to assisted procreation that may come to impact access to technologies enabling gestation. Many jurisdictions have 'child welfare' requirements within their domestic law surrounding assisted procreation that could become a barrier to subversive uses of assisted gestation even if there were no longer direct prohibitions. Legislation in England and Wales dictates that:

> [a] woman shall not be provided with treatment services unless account has been taken of the welfare of any child who may be born as a result of the treatment (including the need of that child for supportive parenting), and of any other child who may be affected by the birth.[65]

Thomson argues that this section 'embodies dominant contemporary gender definitions. The doctor defines which women exist within these definitions, therefore also defining those—the monstrous—who fall outwith'.[66] In this way, the provision could be understood as directly reinforcing 'biologically' constructed biosexed roles. Moreover, the provision, O'Donovan notes, is a 'threshold requirement' for access to embryo implantation,[67] and thus it can easily be used to discriminate against individuals. In UTx, since it will involve IVF to establish a pregnancy, clinics are mandated to consider the welfare of a potential future child that might be delivered from a UTx pregnancy. Similarly, the provision is not explicit that it applies only where gestation takes place inside a person's body, and so it is foreseeable that this could also be used to determine whether persons should be assisted with procreation by ectogestation (by way of an analysis of the potential future welfare of a child born from these person/s having treatment).[68]

McGuiness and Alghrani have questioned whether this 'welfare clause' could be and is 'being used as a smoke screen to hide prejudices regarding the parental fitness of prospective patients', and stipulated that this might particularly impact on gender/sex minorities seeking to become parents through

[65] Human Fertilisation and Embryology Act 1990, s 13(5), as amended by HFEA 2008, s 14(2).

[66] Thomson (n 43), 410–11.

[67] Laura O'Donovan, 'Why Uterine Transplantation Requires Us to Rethink the Role of the Preconception Welfare Principle (2022) Journal of Law and the Biosciences <doi.org/10.1093/jlb/lsac028> accessed 1 September 2024 1–32, 16.

[68] Natasha Hammond-Browning, 'A New Dawn? Ectogenesis, Future Children and Reproductive Choice' (2018) 14 Contemporary Issues in Law 349–73, 357.

assisted procreation.[69] Historically, this provision has been used to discriminate against single women and same-sex female couples (the need of a child for supportive parenting read, before amendment in 2008, the need of a child for a father).[70] Dunne has explained that one of the principal aims of the sterilization of trans and nonbinary people across Europe was to 'protect any future child from the potential dangers of having a trans parent, in particular a parent who has played a non-normative role (eg woman producing sperm in the child's conception)'.[71] It is easy to imagine similar notions can be projected into the 'welfare clause' when applied to novel technologies enabling gestation—especially when used outside of the reproductive binary eg trans women or, more so, cis men gestating.

In addition, O'Donovan has raised concerns about the child welfare principle being used to determine priority-setting for UTx,[72] suggesting that this could lead to an indirect discrimination policy that prioritizes some people over others. Some have noted that there might come a point where demand for a uterus to gestate outstrips supply, and difficult decisions must be made about how to prioritize need for uteri.[73] It is not hard to imagine the need to determine priority being used to reinforce 'the traditional "goal-standard" model of the nuclear family'[74] in determining that women AFAB without uteruses are in greater need. In a recent focus group study with reproductive rights advocates in England, this was raised by several participants who had concerns that people deemed '*deserving recipients*' would be the exclusive recipients of any donor organs. For example, people with Mayer-Rokitansky-Küster-Hauser Syndrome (born AFAB with a deformed or absent uterus and/or vagina) may be afforded priority over trans women because '*it starts to go down this really bizarre deserving/non-deserving, moral/immoral path*'.[75] The concern would be that if biosexed roles in procreation continue to be reinforced,

[69] Sheelagh McGuiness and Amel Alghrani, 'Gender and Parenthood: The Case for Realignment' (2008) 16 Medical Law Review 261–83, 268.

[70] For discussion of this reform, see McCandless and Sheldon (n 50); Rachel Anne Fenton, D Jane Rees, and Sue Heenan, '"Shall I Be Mother?' Reproductive Autonomy, Feminism and the Human Fertilisation and Embryology Act 2008' in Jackie Jones and others (eds), *Gender, Sexualities and Law* (Routledge 2011) 241–54, 250.

[71] Peter Dunne, 'Transgender Sterilisation Requirements in Europe' (2017) 25 Medical Law Review 554–81, 569.

[72] O'Donovan (n 67) 28–30.

[73] Elizabeth Chloe Romanis and Jordan Parsons, 'Directed and Conditional Uterus Donation' (2022) 48 Journal of Medical Ethics 810–15, 812.

[74] Susie Bower-Brown, 'Beyond Mum and Dad: Gendered Assumptions about Parenting and the Experiences of Trans and/or Non-Binary Parents in the UK' (2022) 18 LGBTQ+ Family: An Interdisciplinary Journal 233–40, 233.

[75] Elizabeth Chloe Romanis, 'The Equality-Enhancing Potential of Novel Forms of Assisted Gestation: Perspectives of Reproductive Rights Advocates' (2023) 37 Bioethics 637–46, 644.

it can be reasoned that people AFAB without a uterus are in greater need than trans women or cis men. The Canadian Assisted Human Reproduction Act 2004 contains some key principles that underpin the scheme of regulation. These principles include a similar declaration to that of the English 'Welfare Clause',[76] however, this is qualified by another principle that declares that 'persons who seek to undergo assisted reproduction procedures must not be discriminated against, including on the basis of their sexual orientation'.[77] While this may go some way to preventing some of the problems described, in not making explicit that discrimination on the basis of gender/sex, it still leaves open the possibility of people seeking to subvert the biosex binary in procreation being denied treatment depending on the social context.

While complete ectogestation is unlawful,[78] were it to become possible and lawful in itself, some of the barriers discussed above determining who can use it and in what circumstances raise normative questions. The welfare provisions will still apply because assisted conception is inevitably a prerequisite to the beginning of gestation facilitated by machine. Since the regulation of assisted procreation has long been premised on constructed notions of need that reflect the 'biological' and on 'welfare reflections' that can easily reflect conservative values, would use of ectogestation be limited to people or couples where one is unable to sustain a pregnancy?

Clinical gatekeeping

Partial ectogestation has been identified as a technology enabling gestation that is important in facilitating procreative choices. For example, those who cannot sustain a complete pregnancy for health reasons,[79] and some scholars have advocated for partial ectogestation as a procreative choice beyond health needs.[80] Access to partial ectogestation (where there is no assisted conception) would

[76] Assisted Human Reproduction Act 2004, s 2(a) stipulates that 'the health and well-being of children born through the application of assisted human reproductive technologies must be given priority in all decisions respecting their use'.

[77] ibid s 2(e).

[78] See discussion in Chapter 1.

[79] Jennifer Hendricks, 'Not of Woman Born: A Scientific Fantasy' (2012) 62 Case Western Law Review 399–445, 408; Amel Alghrani, *Regulating Assisted Reproductive Technologies: New Horizons* (CUP 2018), 131; Hammond-Browning (n 68) 351; Elizabeth Chloe Romanis, 'Artificial Womb Technology and the Choice to Gestate Ex Utero: Is Partial Ectogenesis the Business of the Criminal Law?' (2020) 28 Medical Law Review 342–74, 351–53.

[80] Anna Nelson, 'Should Delivery by Partial Ectogenesis Be Available on Request of the Pregnant Person?' (2022) 15 International Journal of Feminist Approaches to Bioethics 1–26; Romanis, 'Artificial Womb Technology' (n 79) 354.

not be regulated by the existing legal framework in the HFE Acts. Procreation, however, is subject to considerable regulation beyond this framework. Partial ectogestation involves ending a pregnancy,[81] and as such the provisions that regulate termination of pregnancy in the Offences Against the Person Act 1861 and Abortion Act 1967 are applicable. Any 'unlawful procurement of miscarriage' is a crime: miscarriage is defined as ending of an 'established pregnancy'[82] and thus, *any* unlawful ending of an established pregnancy (and not just those that result in fetal death) is a crime.[83] Pregnancies can lawfully be ended in circumstances deemed lawful codified in the Abortion Act 1967 (AA 1967)—on 'socio-medical grounds' before twenty-four weeks,[84] where continuing the pregnancy poses greater risk to the pregnant woman's life than termination,[85] where termination is necessary to prevent grave permanent injury to the pregnant woman, or where there is a substantial risk that the fetus has 'such physical or mental abnormalities so as to be seriously handicapped' if born.[86] As I have argued elsewhere, for a pregnant person wanting to opt out of gestation, the law here poses a barrier and potentially places on pregnant people not facing an immediate serious risk to health or any risk to life an obligation to undertake gestational work (remaining pregnant) in place of ectogestation where it is available.[87] The construction of the AA 1967 is such that pregnant people must 'convince a doctor that they require intervention into their pregnancy' to end it—and this is the case whether the question is one of abortion or ectogestation.[88] This aligns with the approach in medicine more broadly in that although people are entitled to be informed about reasonable options,[89] doctors must only inform patients of those interventions that they believe are clinically appropriate:[90] and even then patients cannot *demand* one course of action over another.[91] Until there is a change in the law, therefore, partial ectogestation is permissible only when undertaken for clinical reasons. This aligns with the envisaged uses of the technology of those developing the technology.

[81] Romanis, 'Artificial Womb Technology' (n 79) 335.
[82] *R (On the Application of Smeaton) v Secretary of State for Health* [2002] EWHC 610 (admin).
[83] Romanis, 'Artificial Womb Technology' (n 79) 358–59.
[84] Abortion Act 1967, s 1(1)(a).
[85] ibid s 1(1)(b).
[86] ibid s 1(1)(c).
[87] Romanis, 'Artificial Womb Technology' (n 79) 363.
[88] Abortion is discussed in Chapter 7.
[89] *Montgomery v Lanarkshire Health Board* [2015] UKSC 11.
[90] *McCulloch v Forth Valley Health Board* [2023] UKSC 26.
[91] *R (Burke) v General Medical Council* [2005] EWCA Civ 1003.

It remains to be seen whether partial ectogestation is a procreative choice that would appeal to people—it does, after all, involve major surgery and encompasses risk, therefore, to the pregnant person and to their wanted fetus. There are imaginable circumstances, however, where for some the risk profile of partial ectogestation compared to a complete pregnancy might be such that intervention is desirable to some. That this decision, essentially one of *how* a procreation is facilitated, is confined to the medical profession might be thought problematic for the extent that it disregards the inevitable socio-political elements of such a decision in subsuming it only as a clinical question. It is easy to see how some reasons might readily become more palatable to health professionals than others. We can look to technological interventions in birth as an example, while caesarean rates generally are rising, it has been a long journey for, and there is still much resistance to, recognition of the importance of 'maternal-request caesarean section'[92] even though, in many cases, from the birth-givers perspective their request is often motivated by clinical need.[93]

In the case of other technologies enabling gestation, clinical gatekeeping may also limit access, limiting who can experience pregnancy. Surrogacy UK, a not-for-profit professional organization supporting surrogacies in the UK, have long-endorsed surrogacies in instances where it is necessary for intended parents, and they have encouraged a broad socially attentive definition of necessity to encompass that need for assistance with gestation cannot be defined in purely 'biological' terms.[94] There are some people who are not biologically infertile but do not have the ability to gestate, such as male same-sex couples, or people who may be capable of becoming and sustaining a pregnancy, but they have crippling tokophobia. Access criteria have been developed for UTx, though they vary by provider. It is notable that, as UTx remains, at most centres performing the procedure, an experimental surgery, that drawn up access criteria reflect notions of risk specific to the risk profile of the technology as experimental. As Koplin and Kendal have acknowledged there are ethical

[92] Updated guidance in 2023 in the UK is more supportive of request caesarean that it previously had been: National Institute of Health and Care Excellence, 'Caesarean birth - NG192' (2021) <https://www.nice.org.uk/guidance/ng192> accessed 28 November 2023, [1.2.25] and [1.2.29].

[93] Elizabeth Chloe Romanis, 'Appropriately Framing Maternal Request Caesarean Section' (2022) 48 Journal of Medical Ethics 554–56; Rebecca Brown and Andrea Mulligan, '"Maternal Request": Caesarean Sections and Medical Necessity' (2023) 18 Clinical Ethics 312–20.

[94] Law Commission of England and Wales and Scottish Law Commission, 'Building Families Through Surrogacy: A New Law: Volume II: Final Report' (Law Com No 411, Scot Law Com No 262, March 2023) <https://s3-eu-west-2.amazonaws.com/cloud-platform-e218f50a4812967ba1215eaecede923f/uploads/sites/30/2023/03/2.-Surrogacy-full-report.pdf> accessed 12 June 2024 [6.101].

complexities baked into determinations of who is eligible for UTx.[95] In the UK, criteria have been based on a 'variety of psychosocial and medical factors',[96] which has sparked considerable debate.[97] For example, it has been indicated that UTx recipients should be AFAB, have their own ovum, have a supportive partner, and must not yet be a parent (among other things).[98] Hammond-Browning critically reflects on these criteria,[99] most of which the team have defended in some way as clinically necessary or a matter of fairness.[100] I do not have the space to delve into the assessment of each of these criteria (though I will note, agreeing with Hammond-Browning, that a person already being a parent, especially if they were unable to gestate that child, undermines the goal of the procedure in helping people have a *pregnancy experience* not just to have a child).[101] The point I wish to make is that these are not wholly clinical criteria. Many are, in fact, socio-political judgments on whether someone's self-described need for the experience of gestation is sufficient to be classified as a clinical need. It is easy to see how such normative questions, which are obviously socio-political, might feature in clinical decisions about access to complete ectogestation.

The gatekeeping I have described is exacerbated by the point of scarcity of resources and how need is, often within publicly funded healthcare, constructed as a hierarchy.[102] How those needs constructed as clinical necessity are weighed against those considered more personal preference is a complex matter fraught with ethical judgement. In UTx, where demand is likely to outstrip supply of donor material,[103] how do we determine whose need for

[95] Julian Koplin and Evie Kendal, 'Ethical Issues in Uterine Transplantation' (2020) 34 Korean Journal of Transplantation 78–83, 82.

[96] Laura O'Donovan and others, 'Ethical and Policy Issues Raised by Uterus Transplants' (2019) 131 British Medical Bulletin 19–28, 24.

[97] Natasha Hammond-Browning, 'UK Criteria for Uterus Transplantation: A Review' (2017) 126 British Journal of Obstetrics & Gynaecology 1320–26; Benjamin Jones and others, 'Re: UK Criteria for Uterus Transplantation: A Review' (2019) 126 British Journal of Obstetrics & Gynaecology 1507–08; see also Ryan Tonkens, 'Gatekeeping Uterus Transplants: A Proposal for Eligibility Criteria and the Fair Allocation of Wombs' in Natasha Hammond-Browning and Nicola Williams (eds), *International Legal and Ethical Perspectives on Uterus Transplantation* (Edward Elgar 2024).

[98] Benjamin Jones and others, 'Uterine Transplantation: Past, Present and Future' (2016) 123 British Journal of Obstetrics and Gynaecology 1434–38.

[99] Hammond-Browning (n 97).

[100] Jones and others (n 97).

[101] Hammond-Browning (n 97) 1323.

[102] See Evie Kendal, 'Commentary on Romanis' Assisted Gestative Technologies' (2022) 48 Journal of Medical Ethics 450–51, 450.

[103] There is system of opt-out for organ donation in England and Wales (also referred to as 'deemed consent') per the Organ Donation (Deemed) Consent Act 2019 and the Human Transplantation (Wales) Act 2013. However, the uterus is on the list of organs excluded from the deemed consent model

a uterus to experience is greatest? What normative judgments about who should be undertaking pregnancy (and who should not) might filter into these assessments? Mitra argues that 'if reproductive justice is to be achieved one has to think of ways for uterus allocation that would neither selectively target gendered bodies nor selectively deprive access for some on the basis of their sexuality and gender'.[104] Similarly, in the case of partial ectogestation or ectogestation, where presumably the technology is expensive and there is limited availability, what needs will be considered most significant when assessing whether to support individuals to avoid or opt-out of gestational work? How will these relate to gendered stereotypes?

It has consistently been the case that procreative technologies are limited to 'certain groups that have specific needs that *are* recognized, whereas other groups of people with other different needs may be excluded'.[105] Who is perceived as the appropriate user of novel technologies is co-constructed between notions of the 'biological' and of social judgement influencing whether a 'medical need' is recognized. It remains the case that in assisted procreation, 'individuals must explain their reproductive choices (or choices around reproduction) in clinical terms to ascertain social acceptance'.[106] People who opt for technological assistance, for example, are often ridiculed—for example birthing people who opt for a maternal request caesarean section are labelled 'too posh to push'.[107] Equally, people who refuse to birth in a hospital (they want to birth at home with or without medical support) are also criticized for being 'bad mothers'.[108] While this critique comes from different directions, the essence is always that pregnant people are expected to conform to the recommendations (and often control of) medical professionals.

per The Human Tissue (Permitted Materials: exceptions) (England) regulations 2020. See Nicola Williams, Laura O'Donovan, and Stephen Wilkinson, 'Presumed Dissent? Opt-out Organ Donation and the Exclusion of Organs and Tissues' (2022) 30 Medical Law Review 268–98; Romanis and Parsons (n 73) 810–15.

[104] Sayani Mitra, 'Transplanting the Uterus: A Reproductive Justice Perspective' in Solveig Lena Hansen and Silke Schicktanz (eds), *Ethical Challenges of Organ Transplantation* (Transcript Publishing 2021) 293.

[105] Romanis, 'The Equality-Enhancing Potential' (n 75) 644.

[106] ibid.

[107] For critique see Elizabeth Chloe Romanis, 'Addressing Rising Cesarean Rates: Maternal Request Cesareans, Defensive Practice, and the Power of Choice in Childbirth' (2020) 13 International Journal of Feminist Approaches to Bioethics 1–26, 17.

[108] For critique see Anna Nelson and Elizabeth Chloe Romanis, 'The Medicalisation of Childbirth and Access to Homebirth in the UK: COVID-19 and Beyond' (2021) 29 Medical Law Review 661–87.

Stratified Access

Roberts has argued that procreative 'technologies rarely achieve their subversive potential' because of a constellation of barriers erected to their use.[109] In this section, I argue, that without due attention to the *extra-legal* barriers surrounding procreative technologies, technologies enabling gestation are likely to exacerbate existing disparities in procreative decision-making and pregnancy care. I am not taking the position that because of potential disparities technologies enabling gestation should never be permitted. Räsänen claims that it is not immediately apparent that disparities are always and necessarily unjust (he suggests further thought must be directed to the issue)—'if pregnancy outcomes are "good enough" for everyone, then the fact that some people have access to even better outcomes might not be a problem for justice'.[110] I am not taking this approach either, as the access issues I highlight are absolutely justice concerns given that they disproportionately impact some marginalized groups more than others. My position is that we need to centre the reality of disparities in procreative and pregnancy care in reflections about how to facilitate access to technologies enabling gestation so that such disparities can be addressed. One element of this has been explored thus far in this chapter—in that we must not understand procreative needs as wholly 'biological' needs—as to do so limits use to cis-heteronormative nuclear families. In this section, I note that the access issues related to socio-economic status, class, and race where procreative technologies are not publicly funded.

Notably, most scholars who have written strongly in defence of a technology enabling gestation, have also written strongly in favour of public funding. Kendal advocates for 'state-sponsored' ectogestation,[111] and Wilkinson and Williams advocate for state funding of UTx.[112] The matter of state funding in principle does not go far enough. As Cooper notes, 'the purchase and supply of [assisted reproductive technologies] on the NHS *at a regional level* houses a myriad of considerations that are inextricably linked to the subsequent determination of access'.[113] Decisions about what procreative assistance to fund and for whom is the subject of a lottery across much of the UK. In a recent study, Jones and others found that the accessibility of various forms of assisted

[109] Roberts (n 24) 248.

[110] Joona Räsänen, 'Who Should Have Access to Assisted Gestative Technologies?' (2022) 48 Journal of Medical Ethics 447, 447.

[111] Evie Kendal, *Equal Opportunity and the Case for State Sponsored Ectogenesis* (Palgrave 2015).

[112] Stephen Wilkinson and Nicola Williams, 'Should Uterus Transplants be Publicly Funded?' (2016) 42 Journal of Medical Ethics 559–65.

[113] Cooper (n 56) 170 (emphasis added).

procreation was much greater in areas in England with the 'most advantaged local authorities in terms of average household income and level of deprivation'.[114] There are lesser opportunities, therefore for individuals living in more deprived areas and experiencing involuntary childlessness to pursue assisted procreation.[115] That funding for procreative assistance is better in areas where people are more likely to be able to afford to pay for it themselves exemplifies that procreative technologies, more often than not, benefit more socio-economically privileged individuals. Moreover, it is not just the direct financial costs of procreative technologies that must be considered when we consider who can afford to access them—for example, travel costs, the necessary time off work etc.[116] Disparities are concerning in the context of assisted conception because it affects who is enabled to reproduce at all, but also in the context of technologies enabling gestation, because it affects decisions about the bodily work involved in procreating. Cavaliere warns that even in publicly funded health systems that appropriately recognize the importance of funding procreative technologies, 'it is unlikely that all biologically and socially infertile women would be granted free access to ectogenesis' because resource allocation decisions are inevitable.[117] The same must be true of UTx.

While the conceptualization of legal rights adopts a neoliberal stance—people can procreate how they want but they cannot demand that the state help them—this ignores the socio-political dimensions of procreation—who is routinely excluded from procreating and doing so in a way that enables them to have the meaningful experiences they seek, or without the burdens they seek to avoid. Where ectogestation is reserved for the privileged[118] (because they pay for the service directly or live in areas where it is more likely to be funded), there risks a widening of the gap that exists in pregnancy outcomes. In the UK, and many other western high-income economies, entrenched obstetric negligence, violence, and racism is evident in maternal morbidity such that Black women are five times more likely to die as a result of poor care during

[114] Bobbie Jones, Nitzan Peri-Toten, and Anna Mountford-Zimdars, 'Geographic Opportunities for Assisted Reproduction: A Study of Regional Variations in Access to Fertility Treatment in England' (2023) 26 Human Fertility 494–503.

[115] ibid.

[116] Romanis, 'The Equality-Enhancing Potential' (n 75) 645.

[117] Giulia Cavaliere, 'Gestation, Equality and Freedom: Ectogenesis as a Political Perspective' (2020) 46 Journal of Medical Ethics 76–82, 78.

[118] Suki Finn and Sasha Isaac, 'Evaluating Ectogenesis via the Metaphysics of Pregnancy' in Robbie Davis-Floyd (ed), *Birthing Techno-Sapiens: Human Evolution and the Future of Reproduction* (Routledge 2021).

pregnancy and birth.[119] It is not hard to imagine technologies enabling gestation creating a world in which richer, privileged people, more likely to be educated and white, are able to access ectogestation, and UTx where pregnancy is important to them (and will likely receive good care). All while people with lesser resources who are structurally marginalized by socio-economic status, class, and race (often directly and indirectly as a result of state policies) do not have access to these choices. Technologies enabling gestation make even starker the realities of the procreative disparities that already exist in contemporary conditions.

An analysis attentive to stratification can help make visible how 'state policy, cultural norms directly or indirectly privilege and valorize the reproductive work of certain groups while vilifying the capabilities of others'.[120] UTx could result in the reinforcement of the bioromanticism of *some* pregnancies, while ectogestation is seen as a mechanism to control (and, in extreme cases, replace) others. Horn argues for the importance of looking to contemporary and historical instances of procreative coercion to ensure due attention is paid to 'the harms that might accompany the pursuit of an intended project of . . . technology to improve decision-making in reproductive care'.[121] There may be 'concerns about women from lower socio-economic backgrounds losing even greater degrees of privacy and bodily control as the process of gestation is seen as more publicly owned' (irrespective of location because there is the possibility of it being facilitated by machine).[122] Pregnancy is a fleshy, embodied business. A clear conceptual distinction between *pregnancy* and gestation, I would argue, must be maintained, in law and beyond, in order to reinforce the point that pregnancy as a bodily state cannot be subject to the same interference as gestation facilitated by machine. This speaks to the importance of proper regulation of surrogacies to ensure that intended parents recognize and respect the bodily boundaries of the surrogate: while the surrogate is pregnant, the fetus is a part of them. Some decisions, therefore, must always be the surrogates: decisions about termination, for example, or about birthing.[123]

119 Birthrights, 'Systemic Racism, Not Broken Bodies: An Inquiry into Racial Injustice and Human Rights in UK Maternity Care' (2022) <https://www.birthrights.org.uk/wp-content/uploads/2022/05/Birthrights-inquiry-systemic-racism_exec-summary_May-22-web.pdf> accessed 28 November 2023.

120 Stephanie Paterson, Francesca Scala, and Marlene Sokolon, 'Introduction' in Stephanie Paterson, Francesca Scala, and Marlene Sokolon (eds), *Fertile Ground: Exploring Reproduction in Canada* (McGill-Queen's University Press 2014) 8.

121 Claire Horn, 'Ectogenesis, Inequality, and Coercion: A Reproductive Justice-informed Analysis of the Impact of Artificial Wombs' (2023) 18 BioSocieties 523–44, 532.

122 Claire Horn and Elizabeth Chloe Romanis, 'Establishing Boundaries for Speculation about Artificial Wombs, Ectogenesis, Gender, and the Gestating Body' in Chris Dietz, Mitchell Travis, and Michael Thomson (eds), *A Jurisprudence of the Body* (Palgrave 2020) 249.

123 This is not the same as saying the surrogate is the parent—see Chapter 6.

An important element of stratified access is not just a case of affording access to technologies, but who potentially is pressured or encouraged to utilize technologies that do not speak to their preferences.[124] A number of commentators have raised concerns about the use of ectogestation to facilitate the 'policing of pregnancy' and specifically the coercive power of law.[125] Pregnancy, and pregnancy experiences, as Howard explains, are 'an issue of class, race, religion, relationship status, ethnicity, and ability, among other intersections of identity and oppression'.[126] Cavaliere warned of the dangers of ectogestation coming to label some individuals as 'substandard gestators' where their behaviours do not align with societal expectations.[127] The effect could be exacerbated by UTx in the construction of pregnancy as a meaningful experience that people struggle to these lengths to achieve. Some scholars have suggested that ectogestation could be an important mechanism for fetal protection,[128] for example, for enabling 'fetuses that could have become the victims of maternal alcohol or drug use during pregnancy to have a safe and healthy place for fetal development'.[129] Such an approach, however, is likely—Horn argues—to result in coercive uses of ectogestation[130] (made possible by fetal extraction). Though Horn argues this would be more the result of social pressure and result in some legal change to facilitate (she notes that 'it is improbable' that fetal extraction for gestation ex utero would be lawful).[131] However, the case law relating to disputes about how to proceed where a pregnant person is refusing medical intervention in their pregnancy tells a different story. I have argued elsewhere that it is not wholly implausible that compelled fetal extraction and partial ectogestation could come before the courts.[132] Pregnant people are consistently found to be lacking capacity to refuse surgical intervention in birth where it is considered necessary by medical professionals[133] and decisions seemingly indicate that

[124] Horn (n 121) 531.

[125] ibid; Cavaliere (n 117); Elizabeth Chloe Romanis, '"The Law is Very, Very Outdated and Not Keeping Up with the Technology": Novel Forms of Assisted Gestation, Legal Challenges, and Perspectives of Reproductive Rights Advocates in England and Wales' (2023) 10 Journal of Law and the Biosciences <doi.org/10.1093/jlb/lsad027> accessed 1 September 2024.

[126] Grace Howard, *The Pregnancy Police: Conceiving Crime, Arresting Personhood* (University of California Press 2024) 4.

[127] Cavaliere (n 117) 79.

[128] Räsänen (n 110); Gregory Pence, 'What's so Good about Natural Motherhood? (In Praise of Unnatural Gestation)' in Scott Gelfand and John Shook (eds), *Ectogenesis: Artificial Womb Technology and the Future of Human Reproduction* (Rodopi 2006) 82.

[129] Räsänen (n 110) 447.

[130] Horn (n 121) 531–39.

[131] ibid 536.

[132] Romanis, '"The Law is Very, Very Outdated . . .' (n 125).

[133] *Re S (Adult: Refusal of Medical Treatment)* [1992] 3 WLR 8; *Re MB (Caesarean Section)* [1997] EWCA Civ 1361; *Re AA* [2012] EWHC 4378 (COP); *Guys and St Thomas NHS Foundation Trust v R* [2020] EWCOP 4; *NHS Trust v JP* [2019] EWCOP 23.

the threshold of capacity for decision-making in this context *may* be lower than in others.[134] Where a person is found to be incapacitated, medical interventions can be lawfully performed where they are in the best interests of the individual. The hyper-medicalization of pregnancy and birth, that is legally supported, should be cause for concern—could there be a case where a pregnant person is found to be incapacitated and that it is in their best interests to have their pregnancy ended (and gestation continued ex utero)?

As I have argued in this chapter, without social and legal reform there is the danger that technologies enabling gestation are inaccessible to marginalized groups who *want* to use them, especially those considered to be seeking procreation beyond the cis-heteronormative 'biological' family. A related issue is the transformative gender-rupturing potential of the technologies that these technologies may possess; this is discussed in Chapter 5.

[134] Samantha Halliday, 'Court-authorized Obstetric Intervention: Insight and Capacity, A Tale of Loss' in Camilla Pickles and Jonathan Herring (eds), *Childbirth, Vulnerability and Law: Exploring Issues of Violence and Control* (Routledge 2019) 179.

5

SEX AND GENDER

Pervasive in the ectogestation literature is the claim that artificial amnion and placenta technologies (AAPT) has the capacity to 'free women of the tyranny of gestation'.[1] Takala suggests that ectogestation 'will finally make true equality between humans possible'.[2] Kendal claims that women's equality will always be limited until pregnancy becomes a reproductive choice, rather than a fact of reproducing.[3] Gestation outside of the body, and by similar logic presumably also practices that allow pregnancies to be facilitated by bodies assigned male at birth (AMAB), would or could, according to some scholars, help secure gender equality by 'de-gendering gestation'[4] or, at least, go some way towards securing this. This argument is based on several premises. Here I put them in their strongest forms:

(P1) Gestation sustained by pregnancy is undertaken almost exclusively by women[5]/and exclusively by people AFAB;

(P2) '[G]ender-based oppression is connected to female biological functioning', specifically, the role of female physiology in procreation;[6]

(P3) Technologies enabling gestation have the capacity to challenge the seemingly 'immutable fact of reproduction from the beginning of time: that a fetus must gestate in a woman's body';[7]

[1] Gregory Pence, 'What's so Good about Natural Motherhood? (In Praise of Unnatural Gestation)' in Scott Gelfand and John Shook (eds), *Ectogenesis: Artificial Womb Technology and the Future of Human Reproduction* (Rodopi 2006) 77–88, 83.

[2] Tuija Takala, 'Human Before Sex? Ectogenesis as a Way to Equality?' in Frida Simonstein (ed), *Reprogen-Ethics and the Future of Gender* (Springer 2009) 187–95, 188.

[3] Evie Kendal, *Equal Opportunity and the Case for State Sponsored Ectogenesis* (Palgrave 2015) 8.

[4] Frida Simonstein, 'Artificial Reproductive Technologies and the Advent of the Artificial Womb' in Frida Simonstein (ed), *Reprogen-Ethics and the Future of Gender* (Springer 2009) 177–86; Anna Smajdor, 'The Moral Imperative for Ectogenesis' (2007) 16 Cambridge Quarterly for Healthcare Ethics 336–45; Kathryn MacKay, 'The "Tyranny of Reproduction": Could Ectogenesis Further Women's Liberation?' (2020) 34 Bioethics 346–53.

[5] Smajdor, 'The Moral Imperative for Ectogenesis' (n 4) 337.

[6] MacKay (n 4) 347; Peter Singer and Deane Wells, 'Ectogenesis' in Scott Gelfand and John Shook (eds), *Ectogenesis: Artificial Womb Technology and the Future of Human Reproduction* (Rodopi 2006) 9–26, 14.

[7] Jennifer Bard, 'Immaculate Gestation? How Will Ectogenesis Change Current Paradigms of Social Relationships and Values?' in Scott Gelfand and John Shook (eds), *Ectogenesis: Artificial Womb Technology and the Future of Human Reproduction* (Rodopi 2006) 149–58, 149.

Biotechnology, Gestation, and the Law. Elizabeth Chloe Romanis, Oxford University Press.
 DOI: 10.1093/9780191986574.003.0005

(P4) Where pregnancy can be facilitated by gestation sustained in all bodies or outside of bodies altogether, a fundamental source of gender-based inequality can be eliminated. This is a *necessary (though not sufficient)* condition for gender emancipation.

The argument concludes that where gestation is no longer exclusively 'a woman's job',[8] gender equality becomes possible.[9] In this chapter, I illustrate that this argument of gender equality resulting from novel technologies enabling gestation, or even of being necessary if not sufficient for emancipation, is misguided and reductive.

I place emphasis on the fact that it is not *women* who exclusively bear the burdens of pregnancy but *people with physiology assigned female at birth* (AFAB). Consequently, the argument ought to be reframed as the '*unsexing*' of—rather than the 'de-gendering' of—gestation as a means for emancipation. Indeed, many commentators who make this argument would accept this suggestion (eg it is people AFAB—not exclusively women, but usually women—who gestate). I still take the time to show how the current account of 'de-gendering' gestation as it is consistently reiterated is harmful because this renders invisible trans and nonbinary procreation. Second, citing female biological functioning as the root cause of inequality in (P2) inappropriately locates inequality in certain bodies and their capacities, rather than in the social response to those bodies/capacities.[10] Third, both (P3) and (P4) are unhelpfully acontextual and overstate the capacities of AAPT and uterus transplantation (UTx), which are much narrower than often described when considered in social and legal context. No defender of this argument has yet been able to provide a persuasive account of how changing the locus of gestation challenges normative pronatalist pressures on women and people AFAB. Consequently, removing gestation from the body/exclusively bodies AFAB does not directly result in equality for people AFAB and/or sex and gender minorities. Moreover, to claim that these technologies are necessary for equality is also problematic.

Despite my contention that arguments about novel technologies enabling gestation resulting in gender and sex equality overstate the possibilities, I do believe that AAPT and UTx are potentially equality-*enhancing*, morally

[8] Julien Murphy, 'Is Pregnancy Necessary: Feminist Concerns about Ectogenesis' in Scott Gelfand and John Shook (eds), *Ectogenesis: Artificial Womb Technology and the Future of Human Reproduction* (Rodopi 2006) 27–46, 31.

[9] Takala (n 2); Singer and Wells (n 6) 14.

[10] Claire Horn and Elizabeth Chloe Romanis, 'Establishing Boundaries for Speculation about Artificial Wombs, Ectogenesis, Gender, and the Gestating Body' in Chris Dietz and others (eds), *A Jurisprudence of the Body* (Palgrave 2020) 227–54.

desirable, and will be of value to people AFAB and to sex and gender minorities.[11] There are important mechanisms in which these technologies and practices can contribute to the liberation of marginalized groups, particularly LGBTQ+ people[12] and people AFAB. My object here is to show, however, that sex or gender equality cannot and does not result directly from the availability of these technologies nor should we take it that introduction of these technologies is *necessary* for emancipation. To enable the realization of any equality-enhancing potential from UTx and AAPT, significant social and legal reform is necessary.

Gender, Sex, and Pregnancy

In her case for ectogestation as a 'moral imperative', Smajdor describes the physical necessity that '[b]abies must be gestated in women's bodies' means that 'it is *women* who take on the risks, whereas society in general profits from these sacrifices'.[13] Sander-Staudt notes the relevance of gender in understanding the impact of ectogestation 'because it mimics the biological practice of gestating a child, an ability that currently *only women* possess'.[14] Ferreira argues that ectogenesis is a 'part of the solution' to gender inequality 'as an impetus for driving change and raising awareness of the fact that since *only women can get pregnant it can represent a source of profound inequality*'.[15] Some bioethicists specifically ascribe the benefit of ectogestation to its capacity to 'de-gender' gestation by removing the physical demands of women's bodies that the process of human procreation has naturally required: pregnancy and birth.[16] The same logic could apply to UTx. The development of reproductive practices that enable men to undertake the generative work of pregnancy and birthing means that UTx would surely be recognized as important by those who defend ectogestation for its capacities to 'de-gender' gestation.

[11] Elizabeth Chloe Romanis, 'The Equality-Enhancing Potential of Novel Forms of Assisted Gestation: Perspectives of Reproductive Rights Advocates' (2023) 37 Bioethics 637–46.

[12] Laura Kimberley, Megan Sutter, and Gwendolyn Quinn, 'Equitable Access to Ectogenesis for Sexual and Gender Minorities' (2020) 34 Bioethics 338–45.

[13] Smajdor, 'The Moral Imperative for Ectogenesis' (n 4) 336.

[14] Maureen Sander-Staudt, 'Of Machine Born? A Feminist Assessment of Ectogenesis and Artificial Wombs' in Scott Gelfand and John Shook, *Ectogenesis: Artificial Womb Technology and the Future of Human Reproduction* (Rodopi, New York 2006) 109–28, 111 (emphasis added).

[15] Aline Ferreira, 'The (Un)Ethical Womb: The Promises and Perils of Artificial Gestation' (2022) 19 Journal of Bioethical Inquiry 381–94, 386 (emphasis added).

[16] MacKay (n 4); Smajdor, 'The Moral Imperative for Ectogenesis' (n 4).

Because of the focus on equality for women, the project is clearly described as one of 'de-gendering' throughout the literature. Sander-Staudt explains how ectogestation is 'likely to render gender *less relevant* to reproduction or parenting'.[17] MacKay writes that gestation *extra uterum* is powerfully 'disruptive to the biological foundation of women's oppression because it challenges the "normal view" of gender categories'.[18] Such accounts, however, are implicitly based on an oversimplified, binary understanding of both sex and gender. They assume that there are exclusively two, clearly delineated, classifications of person: 'women' (who have the physiological capacity for gestation) and 'men' (who lack the physical capacity for gestation).[19] There is an assumption that there is a binary conception of gender (one can be either a man or a woman) and a binary concept of sex (one can biologically be either male or female, and this is directly related to reproductive capacities), and that these categories neatly map onto each other (women are female, men are male), but are also readily distinguishable (women/females are not men/males and vice versa).

Biology and anthropology, informed by human experience, show us both that male/female and man/woman are not exclusive gender or sex categories, and that these two categories (male/female, man/woman) are not clearly distinguishable from each other nor are they immutable.[20] There has been much exploration of the ways in which gender is socially constructed,[21] and increasingly there is recognition that the same is true of sex.[22] There is no clear way to delineate what physiological or biological features make a body female or male: '[a] body's sex is simply too complex. There is no either/or. Rather, there are shades of difference'.[23] Looking at any or all of the chromosomes, genitalia, or hormone production within a body cannot clearly delineate that it is either male or female. There are some traits, that for social reasons, we have identified as being indicative of femaleness or maleness but how these biological traits or features came to be grouped and to be labelled as 'male' or 'female' is a social interpretation. Moreover, what features were understood as being 'male' or being 'female' are not wholly stable constructions—they can shift depending on context.

[17] Sander-Staudt (n 14) 111 (emphasis added).
[18] MacKay (n 4) 347.
[19] Horn and Romanis (n 10) 242.
[20] Judith Butler, *Gender Trouble* (Routledge 1990); Anne Fausto-Sterling, *Myths of Gender: Biological Theories about Women and Men* (Basic Books 1993); Anne Fausto-Sterling, *Sexing the Body: Gender Politics and the Construction of Sexuality* (Basic Books 2000).
[21] Kate Millett, *Sexual Politics* (Granada Publishing Ltd 1971); Sally Haslanger, 'Gender and Race: (What) Are They? (What) Do We Want Them to Be?' (2002) 34 Noûs 31–55.
[22] Butler (n 20); Fausto-Sterling (n 20).
[23] Fausto-Sterling (n 20).

Around two per cent of the population are born intersex (having some variation from the biotypically male or female—whether chromosomally, ambiguous or absent genitalia, or a hormone difference).[24] Blackless and others conclude that this, in conjunction with an understanding with the deviation in characteristics assumed male and female in different cultures, leads to the conclusion that 'developmental biology suggests that a belief in absolute sexual dimorphism is wrong. Instead, two overlapping bellshaped curves can be used to conceptualize sexual variation across the population.'[25] That a binary conception of sex is excessively simplistic is a conclusion equally supported by a body of scientific literature,[26] as by the work of gender theorists on the relationship between biological features and culture. Some theorists have argued that 'sex' is as culturally constructed as gender, because how biological features of difference (whichever are reified as determinative) are interpreted is a matter of cultural value.[27]

Despite the clear complications in separating 'female' from 'male' based on biological features (or the claim that some features clearly are only male *or* female), one feature that a biological essentialist approach might insist can differentiate is the capacity to become pregnant. This is a claim that appears in much early feminist jurisprudence that attempts to explain how the androcentrism of law fails women. West describes women being fundamentally different because of their innate connectedness to others (in contrast to the atomistic understanding of existence propagated by law), using, in part, the example of pregnancy.[28] The understanding of the capacity to become pregnant as the defining feature of being female is not as intuitive as it might appear, however, given the many people born with physiology AFAB who struggle with infertility, or who are born without a uterus. As Baer explains, an account like that of West is 'simplistic, exclusionary and illogical'. While the experiences West mentions are unique to people AFAB, they are not common to all people AFAB.[29] It is thus clear that a capacity to become pregnant is not a feature that can be used to identify a person as having female physiology. However, this is a capacity that, given the current confines of human reproductive biology, is almost exclusively limited to people with biotypical physiology AFAB. Thus,

[24] Melanie Blackless and others, 'How Sexually Dimorphic Are We? Review and Synthesis' (2000) 12 American Journal of Human Biology 151–66.

[25] ibid 163.

[26] ibid; Claire Ainsworth, 'Sex Redefined' (2015) 518 Nature 288–91.

[27] Butler (n 20) 9.

[28] See Robin West, 'Jurisprudence and Gender' (1988) 55 The University of Chicago Law Review 1–72.

[29] Judith Baer, 'Feminist Theory and Law' in Robert Goodin (ed) *The Oxford Handbook of Political Science* (OUP 2011) 305–16, 309.

while sex may not be fixed (persons can have hormone treatment and/or genital reassignment), until uterus transplantation becomes more widely available,[30] the capacity to sustain a gestation remains largely limited by biological constraints—that is the having of a working uterus. Pregnancy sustaining gestation is thus an impossibility for people born without a functioning uterus—whether AMAB, AFAB, or intersex. The capacity to become pregnant is not a feature that can be used to identify a person as female.[31] However, this is a capacity that, given the current confines of human procreative biology, is almost exclusively limited to people with biotypical physiology AFAB. Thus, while sex may not be fixed (persons can have hormone treatment and/or genital reassignment), until UTx becomes more widely available, the capacity to facilitate gestation with bodily work remains limited as described above. The salient point here is that proposals of ending or mitigating gender-based oppression with technologies redistributing gestational work to persons of all sexes, or to machines, rely on binary accounts of sex and gender that are overly simplistic. These accounts neglect the existence of men and nonbinary people who undertake gestation and birthing. It is people AFAB who *can* have the physiology to become pregnant, and this encompasses a wide diversity of people in terms of both gender and sex. Neglecting this diversity in speculative literature about novel technologies is symptomatic of a broader problem. Generally, in the public consciousness there is a conceptual integration of gender and gestation (facilitated by pregnancy). Historically, it has been exclusively people AFAB, who either were identified as women or were treated as such, that undertook gestational work (whether to reproduce themselves or acting as surrogates). It remains the case that it is primarily people AFAB that also identify as women who sustain gestation via pregnancy. Pervasive cis-heteronormative understandings and ideals surrounding procreation that 'inextricably link femininity with pregnancy' have thus come to dominate the social perception of pregnancy to the degree that the experiences and needs of LGBTQ+ people, particularly gender queer people, are simply rendered invisible.[32] Trans men and nonbinary people describe difficulties in accessing pregnancy and birthing care because of (a fear of) transphobia,[33] and even report feeling pressure to present as women to conform to the expectations of healthcare providers.[34]

[30] See limitations on this possibility in Chapter 3.
[31] See Chapter 2.
[32] Olivia Fischer, 'Non-binary Reproduction: Stories of Conception, Pregnancy, and Birth' (2021) 22 International Journal of Transgender Health 77–88, 81.
[33] ibid 81.
[34] ibid.

Social scripts that have come to shape, direct, and even dictate how pregnant people are thought of and interacted with are so fixated on gender that space is not made for alternative realities.

The law adds authoritative and expressive force to these understandings of pregnancy. In many jurisdictions, the language used to describe pregnancy and parenthood resulting from gestation remains both gendered and sexed.[35] In England and Wales, gender-neutral drafting in law-making has been in place as standard practice since 2007.[36] Despite this, procreation and pregnancy are areas where gendered terms remain commonplace and are used to perpetuate conceptions of pregnancy as a gendered activity. Significantly, the Human Fertilisation and Embryology Acts 1990 and 2008 make no space for male or nonbinary pregnancy when it defines a mother as '[t]he *woman* who is carrying or has carried a child as a result of the placing in her of an embryo or of sperm and eggs'.[37] Furthermore, equality laws in multiple jurisdictions, for example, the EU[38] frame discrimination against pregnant persons as discrimination on the basis of sex, rather than as a form of discrimination in its own right, which legally entrenches the notion that pregnancy is a sexed activity.

It is, therefore, unsurprising that there is a conceptual failure in much ethico-legal scholarship to properly recognize the 'gender-rupturing potentialities of gestational labour'[39] as it is currently performed. When considered seriously, 'pregnant men engender a critical re(conceive)ing of the idea that sex is biologically determined, that pregnancy is necessarily sexed as female, and that one's sex, gender identity and identification as mother/father neatly align'.[40] However, in practice, male and nonbinary pregnancy is othered, and systematically 'made invisible, pathologized and rendered unrecognized'.[41] Imagining how novel technologies enabling gestation can radically change the oppressive structures surrounding pregnancy and procreation more broadly will be more

[35] Elizabeth Chloe Romanis, 'Male and Nonbinary Pregnancy in the Law: Ontic Injustice and/or Invisbilisation' (forthcoming).

[36] Drafting Techniques Group of the Office of the Parliamentary Counsel, 'Office of the Parliamentary Counsel: Drafting Guidance' (2020) <https://assets.publishing.service.gov.uk/media/660407d091a320001a82b06b/2024.03.19.Drafting-guidance.pdf> accessed 2 November 2022 [2.1].

[37] s 33(1).

[38] The Charter of Fundamental Rights of the European Union prohibits any discrimination on grounds of sex. This Recast Directive 2006/54/EC, s 23 stipulates 'It is clear from the case-law of the Court of Justice that unfavourable treatment of a woman related to pregnancy or maternity constitutes direct discrimination on grounds of sex. Such treatment should therefore be expressly covered by this Directive'.

[39] Rachelle Chadwick, 'Visceral Acts: Gestationality as Feminist Figuration' 48 (2022) Signs 229–55, 237.

[40] Lara Karaian, 'Pregnant Men: Repronormativity, Critical Trans Theory, and the Re(conceive)ing of Sex and Pregnancy in Law' (2013) 22 Social & Legal Studies 211–30, 212–13.

[41] Chadwick (n 39) 247.

constructive, Horn advocates, if we begin 'by rejecting binary understandings of human reproductive roles.'[42]

To return to the main premises of the argument outlined earlier, P1 ('Gestation sustained by pregnancy is undertaken exclusively by women') is clearly untrue, since there are people other than women who sustain pregnancies and birth, and there are important reasons to recognize this. This does not, however, mean that the argument fails here. If we adjust the premise to recognize that only people AFAB (who predominantly identify as women) can sustain pregnancies and birth, and if P2, P3, and P4 are also true, then we can still reach the conclusion that gender equality can be facilitated by novel technologies enabling gestation. There are some clear radical implications from the possibility of gestation outside of the constraints of biology; where it can take place as part of people born without a uterus (whether male, female, intersex or other), or outside of the confines of any body. Before exploring some of these implications, it is necessary to interrogate the premise that gender-based oppression is caused by, or connected to, female biological function.

Bodies and Social Oppression

Proponents of the 'gender equality from removing gestation from bodies AFAB and/or bodies entirely' argument place the focus of the 'root' of inequality in biotypically female reproductive capacities. In articulating their position, MacKay and Singer & Wells both rely considerably on the work of de Beauvoir[43] and Firestone,[44] who advocated that oppression was rooted in female reproductive biology.[45] On this view: '[t]he fundamental part that from the beginning of history doomed woman to domestic work and prevented her taking part in the shaping of the world was her enslavement to the generative function.'[46] Commentators use such an account to make the claim that if we remove the generative function from the AFAB body, such people are no longer 'doomed' by the capacity to become pregnant and facilitate gestation.[47] There is longstanding debate in the philosophy and gender studies literature about

[42] Claire Horn, 'Gender, Gestation and Ectogenesis: Self-determination for Pregnant People Ahead of Artificial Wombs' (2020) 46 Journal of Medical Ethics 787–88, 788.
[43] Simone de Beauvoir, *The Second Sex* (C Borde and S Malovany-Chevallier trs, Knopf 1949).
[44] Shulamith Firestone, *The Dialectic of Sex: The Case for Feminist Revolution* (William Morrow and Company 1970).
[45] ibid 74–75.
[46] de Beauvoir (n 43) 117.
[47] eg MacKay (n 4).

the appropriateness of this understanding, and I will not reiterate it in depth here for reasons of space. Scholars working on ectogestation/assisted gestation from feminist perspectives, me included, have primarily chosen to focus on the other premises of the argument (P3 and P4). This is largely because even if P2 is true, there are very compelling reasons to believe P3 and P4 are not.

The importance of understanding the account of the primary biological difference as the capacity to facilitate gestation as the only, or even the primary, source of oppression does have historical roots. That people AFAB sustain pregnancies was the principal reason that throughout time led to women/ people AFAB becoming a subjugated class; how they came to be understood as the 'other' and as vessels for procreation rather than people.[48] It is important to consider, however, that physiological differences form *part* of the reason why people are treated in different ways, but physiological differences are often not the principal reason that persons are oppressed or directly discriminated against. Rather, it is the assumption about what physiological differences a person has, and then specifically *the cultural and social assumptions made about their likely behaviour because of those assertions about physiology*, that result in discrimination against individuals.[49] An employer may be equally likely to fail to promote a person AFAB without a uterus or a trans woman, as they would a person AFAB with a uterus on the basis that the same assumptions are made about their physiology and/or consequently their assumed predicted behaviour. The employer could assume that all these people have the capacity to become pregnant (how would the employer know the exact details of their anatomy and/or associated reproductive capacities?) in combination with the pronatalist assumption that they will want to become a parent through sustaining a pregnancy and birthing. It is not *having* the capacity to become pregnant that makes one a target for workplace discrimination, for example, it is *looking like someone who might.* These assumptions about behaviour still come from the cultural understandings of different physiology and are still subject to considerable social and cultural interpretation.

To focus on 'solving' the capacity to become pregnant (being the physiological difference) as a means of resolving discrimination/oppression against

[48] I am grateful to Dr Dunja Begović for discussions with me on this point.

[49] Drouillard makes the case that oppression is not just about physiology—for example, it is not what kind of genitalia individuals possess, but what genitalia they are assumed to possess, that is used by others to 'justify a certain gendered treatment, a treatment that in turn affects how she views herself within a system of social arrangements'. Drouillard relies on the work of Haslanger (n 20) to explain that gender is constructed externally, though notes that there are some aspects of Haslanger's argument that become circular when trying to explain the disentanglement of gender and sex. Jill Drouillard, 'The King was Pregnant: Reproductive Ethics and Transgender Pregnancy' (2021) 14 International Journal of Feminist Approaches to Bioethics 120–40, 124.

people AFAB and women, seemingly may rest in the idea that biological function assigned female is inferior. More likely, proponents of the argument would suggest not that biological function *is* inferior, but it is that it is *seen as* inferior and altering biological function is the best way to overcome that perception. Such a strategy requires all people AFAB to no longer sustain pregnancies, which seems to be asserting that members of a marginalized group must 'assimilate' for equality,[50] but also might lead to discrimination escalating in some circumstances, for example people who opt for pregnancy. I will explore this problem in more detail later in this chapter. There are some parallels to be drawn with disability here. Focusing on eradicating differently able bodies, rather than on the social constraints that mean those bodies different abilities makes them disadvantaged (per the social model of disability),[51] is clearly harmful in the subjugation of differently abled people, the same must be said to be true of people who can sustain pregnancies—this capacity is not something that makes a body less able, it is rather the social constraints placed on the body that should be of concern.[52]

'Un-sexing' Gestation

P3 holds that AAPT and UTx have the capacity to change one of the most fundamental, and long considered immutable, facts of human procreation: that gestation requires a pregnancy sustained in the body of a biotypical person AFAB. It is seemingly undeniable that UTx and ectogestation could subvert empirical facts of procreation with some radical potential. Gestation facilitated by all bodies, or no body, does enable some reconfiguration of individual reproductive capacities, and our subjective and collective understandings of procreation. While a clear 'ontic injustice',[53] trans men who gestate are, at present, viewed/treated as still conforming to the existing binary. Many nonbinary or trans men people who have carried pregnancies describe being treated by

[50] Giulia Cavaliere, 'Ectogenesis and Gender-based Oppression: Resisting the Ideal of Assimilation' (2020) 34 Bioethics 727–34, 728.

[51] Union of Physically Impaired Against Segregation (1974) <https://disability-studies.leeds.ac.uk/wp-content/uploads/sites/40/library/UPIAS-UPIAS.pdf> accessed 1 September 2024.

[52] I am grateful to Professor Stephen Wilkinson for raising this point with me in discussion.

[53] Katherine Jenkins, 'Ontic Injustice' (2020) 6 Journal of the American Philosophical Association 188–205; Katherine Jenkins, *Ontology and Oppression: Race, Gender, and Social Reality* (OUP 2023). In her book, Jenkins defines ontic injustice as occurring where an individual is 'socially constructed as a member of a certain social kind where that construction consists, at least in part, of their falling under to a set of social constraints and enablements that is wrongful to them' at 35. Trans men or nonbinary people being treated as female or as women because they are gestating is wronging them in assigning them to a social kind that confines their expression of self and identity.

others, including people within gender queer communities, as 'really women' or 'female where it matters'.[54] For some, these social attitudes projected onto their facilitation of gestation generated more dysphoria than the changes to their body resulting from the bodily work facilitating gestation itself.[55] UTx and ectogestation could be used in ways that displace and unsettle the language of procreation structurally because such descriptions of gestation cannot (in ways that misgender or re-sex) revert to binary conceptions of gender and sex. Where cis men (men AMAB) sustain pregnancies, existing social scripts cannot be used to explain away the challenge to cis-heteronormative modes of procreation. Such a pregnancy contributes, like we should understand trans pregnancies as already doing, to understanding how sex as well as gender can be unravelled, unmade, and remade.

Where no person sustains a pregnancy, gendered and sexed terms *need not* be used at all to describe the generative process in procreating. This does not necessarily mean that they would be. There is every possibility that cultural and poetic discourses will gender the artificial placenta.[56] For example, modes of transport like ships and cars are often gendered female as a result of pervasive social scripts. These are things that deliver us to places (from A to B). When people talk of ships they often talk of their 'carriage' and so the gendering here may directly be the result of the analogizing to conceptions of pregnancy (specifically a container model) that takes a conceptus from A (conception) to B (mature fetal physiology and capable of making the transformation to neonatal physiology). Moreover, nationalist discourses often speak of home countries as the 'motherland', which has connotations of gendering in origins. All of this is to say that there is a possibility that AAPT devices are similarly sexed and gendered. Gestation is not necessarily unsexed activity when it is unhumanized.

If non-sexed terms were used for gestation this could have particular importance for challenging the extent to which people's reproductive destinies are deemed dictated by their biosex (eg cis women must reproduce, trans women ought not). There is less attention afforded to the reproductive possibilities for trans women. In some jurisdictions, sterilization of trans women is mandatory for legal transition,[57] and in others limited discussion (if any) is had

[54] Fischer (n 32), 81–82.
[55] ibid.
[56] I am grateful to Professor Suzanne Ost for this point.
[57] eg in Japan. The 2003 law was upheld by the Japanese Supreme Court in 2019. For an account of the geneaology of state-enforced sterilization of trans individuals in Western states (primarily Europe), see Julian Honkasalo, 'In the Shadow of Eugenics: Transgender Sterilisation Legislation and the Struggle for Self-determination' in Ruth Pearce and others (eds), *The Emergence of Trans: Cultures, Politics and Everyday Lives* (Routledge 2019) 17–33.

with transitioning persons about fertility preservation and a fertile future.[58] Cárdenas suggests this has particular harms for trans women of colour and results from a 'trans-misogynist dynamic'[59] within society and within queer communities. This dynamic results from perpetuated notions within feminist and queer theory that desires for procreation in trans women are a mere form of 'heteronormative false consciousness'.[60] Novel technologies enabling gestation could go some way towards enabling transfeminine and nonbinary people AMAB to envision their own procreative futures.

We ought not think of UTx and AAPT as tools to 'de-gender' procreation since persons, whether capable of sustaining pregnancy or not, may consider their gender, as a cultural construct, an important part of how they understand their procreation, and this technology does not introduce gestation outside the gender binary. As noted, this already exists. Rosenblum, in their case for the 'un-sexing' of mothering, emphasizes the importance of the concept of 'un-sexing' in ensuring that analysis is not only focused on the experiences of cis women but also works to challenge the links between biosex and the expectations placed on sexed bodies.[61] UTx and AAPT may be thought of as instruments that 'un-sex' gestation, because they enable people to reproduce by modes not confined to their assigned biological sex. I describe this specifically as a project of 'un-sexing' rather than 'de-sexing' because there may be ways in which people consider their sex as fundamental to their identity[62] and so it is retracting from the complexities of human experience to work towards the complete 'removal' of sex in procreation. 'Un-sexing' instead does the work to signify that sex need not *confine* procreative possibility. It also leaves space for the acknowledgement that sex is not dimorphous. Can it be claimed that replacing or changing the nature of gestation may be able to erode the association between assigned female biology and gestation if it becomes possible for persons of different sexes to more routinely undertake gestational work?

In considering the extent to which UTx and AAPT can 'un-sex' gestation, it is important to understand 'un-sexing' as a *process*. Chadwick explains that imagining how we can un/gender (and, similarly, I suggest, un/sex) 'involves

[58] Shon Faye, *The Transgender Issue: An Argument for Justice* (Allen Lane 2021) 49.

[59] Micha Cárdenas, 'Pregnancy: Reproductive Futures in Trans of Color Feminism' (2016) 3 Transgender Studies Quarterly 48–57, 55.

[60] ibid.

[61] Darren Rosenblum, 'Unsex Mothering: Toward a New Culture of Parenting' (2012) 35 Harvard Journal of Law and Gender 57–116, 59–60.

[62] As Chappell explains it, some individuals will identify more with being a certain sex rather than a gender (and some will identify with a gender more than a sex). Sophie Grace Chappell, 'Transgender: A Dialogue' *Aeon* (2018) <https://aeon.co/essays/transgender-identities-a-conversation-between-two-philosophers> accessed 2 November 2022.

tracing certain kinds of oppressive logics and sociomaterial conditions rather than reiterating a mode of difference that is intrinsic to particular bodies'.[63] Tracing the oppressive logics and socio-material conditions that surround gestation illuminates the extent to which radical possibilities are limited by social forces. The law, though just one instrument in the wider socio-political regulation of procreation, is a significant source of oppressive logics that are fundamentally sexed and thus would likely limit the potential of both UTx and AAPT to 'un-sex' procreation. This occurs both at the level of what is or is not permissible in terms of how each technology can be used and by whom, and at the level of which experiences the law affords recognition to and the language it uses to do so. What I argue here is not that (P3) is incorrect in abstraction, but that the context of oppressive social logics and socio-material conditions will likely limit the radical subversive potential of novel forms of assisted gestation. While imagining the possibilities of UTx and AAPT in a utopian future without binary understandings of sex and gender dictating social conditions is exciting, it does little to illustrate the transformative possibilities of the technology (how we get from here to there). Defenders of the liberal feminist position outlined seemingly, however, assert that it is this technology that has created this future (rendering some of their claims rather circular). It is important to highlight just some of the oppressive forces and socio-material conditions that tell us otherwise. I question the extent to which public attitudes can shift where these technologies are not widely used in ways that challenge, rather than reaffirm, traditional notions of binary biological sex.

Oppressive Forces and Socio-material Conditions

In what follows, I illustrate that the law is consistently used in many jurisdictions to reinforce a binary understanding of procreation and thus it is difficult to imagine the realization of the transformative potential of UTx and AAPT in contemporary socio-material conditions. These conditions, instead, erect clear and complete socio-legal barriers to the subversive potential of novel gestations enabled by technology. Many of these barriers can be claimed to result from the fact that law lags behind scientific possibility. Indeed, some may argue that looking at technologies that do not yet exist in contemporary contexts has limited utility because there will likely be a shift in socio-material

[63] Chadwick (n 39) 246.

conditions by the time that these technologies come to fruition.[64] However, the pace of social, and especially legal, change is much slower than that of scientific advancement. Moreover, as the history of reproductive regulation can attest, even where progressive regulation affords groups marginalized by their sexual or gender identity recognition and protection from some forms of discrimination, the law has not gone so far as to enable procreation outside of the cis-heteronormative archetype even where possible. Sex between men was decriminalized in England and Wales in 1967,[65] but same-sex couples only obtained, by law, the ability to adopt in 2002.[66] The use of assisted reproductive technologies to form families outside of the cis-heteronormative paradigm have historically taken much longer to become lawful, and then (because finally available) subsequently normalized and socially accepted. Despite in vitro fertilization (IVF) becoming routine towards the end of the twentieth century, it was directly prohibited for same-sex AFAB couples (where the pregnant person used their partner's ovum and donor sperm) in France until 2021,[67] and indirectly in England and Wales until 2008.[68] It was only in 2022 that the National Health Service made IVF treatment equally accessible to same-sex AFAB couples.[69] Consideration of the socio-material conditions created by law and other governing structures, and how they interface with these technologies to limit their potential, can also show us what needs to change.

In particular, there exists considerable social and cultural fear surrounding transgender procreation that 'has had a profound impact on the way European jurisdictions recognise gender'.[70] These fears are heavily tied to the discomfort sometimes generated by people engaging in procreative activity that subverts the confines of binary sex roles. While in England and Wales, there has never

[64] Horn describes discussions of ectogestation in 'legal scholarship is frequently preoccupied with accepting the law as it is rather than exploring law as it could be': 'Claire Horn, Gestation Beyond Mother/Machine: Legal Frameworks for Artificial Wombs, Abortion and Care' (PhD thesis, Birkbeck University of London 2020) 152.

[65] Sexual Offences Act 1967.

[66] Adoption and Children Act 2002.

[67] Loi 2021-1017 du 2 août 2021 relative à la bioéthique, Titre ler Élargir L'accès aux Technologies Disponibles Sans S'affranchir De Nos Principes Éthiques (Bioethics Law 2021: Title I, Expand Access to Available Technologies Without Departing from our Ethical Principles).

[68] Because of the requirement in s 13(5) of the Human Fertilisation and Embryology Act 1990 that IVF clinics consider a child's 'need for a father' when determining whether to provide treatment (this was amended by the 2008 Act). See Sally Sheldon and others, '"Supportive Parenting", Responsibility and Regulation: The Welfare Assessment under the Reformed Human Fertilisation and Embryology Act (1990)' (2015) 78 Modern Law Review 461–92.

[69] Tobi Thomas, '"A giant step": charities welcome plan to widen access to IVF on NHS' (2022) *The Guardian* <https://www.theguardian.com/society/2022/jul/20/a-giant-step-charities-welcome-plan-to-widen-access-to-ivf-on-nhs> accessed 6 November 2022.

[70] Peter Dunne, 'Transgender Sterilisation Requirements in Europe' (2017) 25 Medical Law Review 554–81, 555.

been a requirement that people must be sterilized to change their legal gender/sex, such a requirement is commonplace in other jurisdictions. In 2017, *Garçon and Nicot* came before the European Court of Human Rights (ECtHR) in which three French citizens, among other matters related to proper recognition of their sex and gender, submitted that the French state infringed their right to respect for private life[71] in making recognition of their transition contingent on undergoing sterilization or a surgical procedure with a high likelihood of sterility.[72] The Court noted that, at the time they were making this decision, there were twenty-four signatory States (out of the forty-six total) to the European Convention that enforced a legal requirement on gender diverse people to undergo sterilization to obtain legal recognition of their transition.[73] The Court stipulated that, in line with the French government's submission, signatory States have an obligation to recognize gender reassignment. However, States have discretion to determine the conditions a person seeking recognition must meet to establish they have undergone reassignment.[74] The Court found, however, that a condition of sterility, or likely sterility, requires individuals to relinquish full exercise of their physical integrity in a manner that can only be described as a violation of the right to private life.[75]

The *Garçon and Nicot* decision is clearly to be welcomed as a move away from genitocentrism in European jurisprudence,[76] and some scholars have praised the decision as potentially paving the way for the queering of parenthood and having queer family rights protected under the European Convention—for example, recognition for 'the pregnant man or the female father'.[77] I take a more sceptical view, however. The decision is narrow and gives no ground for fuller protections for trans and nonbinary people who view a procreative future as central to their conception of self. This is because of the focus on sterility as one's integrity being *physically* violated, as opposed to a reflection on the deprivation of a procreative future as the harm (potentially, the

[71] Art 8 of the European Convention on Human Rights.

[72] *Garçon and Nicot v France*, Application No 79885/12 (2017).

[73] These countries were Armenia, Azerbaijan, Belgium, Bosnia and Herzegovina, Bulgaria, Croatia, Czech Republic, Finland, France, Georgia, Greece, Latvia, Lithuania, Luxembourg, Montenegro, Norway, Romania, the Russian Federation, Serbia, Slovakia, Slovenia, Switzerland, Turkey, and Ukraine.

[74] Following *Christine Goodwin v the United Kingdom*, Application No 28957/95 (2002); *I v the United Kingdom*, Application No 25680/94 (2002); *Van Kück v Germany*, Application No 35968/97 (2003). NB: The importance of having one's gender recognized as a part of the right to private life was a decades long fight in the ECtHR and there are a considerable number of cases where the argument failed before those listed here resulted in a sea change.

[75] *Garçon and Nicot v France* (n 72) [131].

[76] Damian Gonzalez-Salzberg, 'An Improved Protection for the (Mentally Ill) Trans Parent: A Queer Reading of AP, *Garçon and Nicot v France*' (2018) 81 Modern Law Review 526–38, 532.

[77] ibid 538.

psychosocial harm that results from being *forced* to relinquish the possibility of becoming a genetic parent). Of course, there is a serious violation that occurs where a person is *forced* to undergo a hysterectomy to obtain legal recognition of their being male. However, in focusing wholly on the physical harm in sterility when a person's body is no longer able to procreate with a capacity previously had, there is the danger of not adequately recognizing the harm of being deprived of a procreative future. A finding that European Convention signatory governments may not require sterilization of transitioning individuals does not, I would argue, translate to an empowering statement in support of procreative futures outside biological sex features at birth. The decision does enable trans men and nonbinary people AFAB to retain their generative reproductive function if this is how they envisage becoming a parent. However, this does not prevent State interference in other ways that make procreation impossible for trans men and nonbinary people with a retained capacity to gestate. Many of the States who had passed laws requiring sterilization did so explicitly because they deemed transitioning/transitioned individuals to be incapable of parenting.[78] The transphobic construction of trans/nonbinary people as 'less fit to parent' is not dispelled by this judgment, and thus discrimination instead may manifest in other ways to the same end.[79] As Dunne explains, now '[l]abelling transgender individuals as incapable child-carers may not justify sterilisation, but it can legitimise national rules which withhold custody or reduce employment rights'.[80] Moreover, the decision does not have any implication of a positive right of transitioning persons to assistance in ensuring a reproductive future (eg by cryopreservation of gametes), but is only a negative right to non-state interference with their fertility. The motivations across Europe for sterilization laws were threefold, according to Dunne: certainty in legal parenthood, child welfare, and the preservation of natural procreation.[81] These same conservative logics may also motivate direct and indirect prohibitions on subversive and transformative uses of UTx and AAPT by any person of any sex.

The law in England and Wales, at present, potentially directly prevents both UTx in persons who are legally male and complete ectogestation and is not friendly to procreation outside of the reproductive biosex binary as noted in Chapter 4. The unsuitability of the law to easily accommodate some queer couples/families is reason enough for reform in contemporary contexts.

[78] Dunne (n 70) 569.
[79] ibid 561.
[80] ibid 557.
[81] ibid.

Within the law as written is an undertone of an intention to preserve reproductive binaries in the contemporary legislative regime that may limit the 'un-sexing' capacity of UTx. This could come to limit the possibility of people AMAB becoming pregnant and birthing, never mind its widespread use as a way of 'un-sexing' generative procreative work. In addition to legislation that directly reinforces binary biosex roles in procreation, as discussed in Chapter 4, there are indirect legal mechanisms (such as clinics being required to consider the welfare of future children when providing procreative treatment) by which creative and unsexed modalities of gestation become inaccessible.

Another *directly* oppressive condition by which law genders and sexes procreative roles is in the rules determining categories of parenthood. In England and Wales, people who gestate are 'mothers'[82] regardless of their legal gender.[83] In 2013, proceedings were brought in the German Federal Court of Justice by a trans man who had gestated and birthed and wanted to be recognized on his child's birth certificate as their father rather than their mother.[84] His case was unsuccessful. A similar 2020 challenge to the birth registration system in England by a trans man was dismissed by the Court of Appeal.[85] The judges in the English decision do attempt to assert that their decision is 'gender-neutral' because the label 'mother' serves only to identify a role that a person plays in procreation, rather than signifying their gender.[86] However, these decisions illustrate the sexing and gendering function in law, here reifying sexed and gendered biological determinism.[87] The judgments exemplify the reinforcing of a link between biotypical female reproductive capacities and 'a term that remains gendered in its popular use'.[88] Furthermore, because 'legal language reproduces power structures',[89] these decisions 'exhibit the role of state institutions and officials in regulating family relationships (and, more widely, people's lives)' based on an entrenched ideological commitment to a binary conception of biosex and the cis-heteronormative family.[90]

[82] *Ampthill Peerage Case* [1977] AC 547; Human Fertilisation and Embryology Act 2008, s 33.
[83] Gender Recognition Act 2004, s 12; *R (McConnell and YY) v Registrar General* [2020] EWCA Civ 559.
[84] BGH XXI ZB 660/14.
[85] *McConnell* (n 83).
[86] ibid [279].
[87] Liam Davis, 'Deconstructing Tradition: Trans Reproduction and the Need to Reform Birth Registration in England and Wales' (2021) 22 International Journal of Transgender Health 179–90, 182.
[88] Elizabeth Chloe Romanis, 'Regulating the "Brave New World": Ethico-Legal Implications of the Quest for Partial Ectogenesis' (PhD thesis, University of Manchester 2020) 231.
[89] Zaina Mahmoud and Elizabeth Chloe Romanis, 'On Gestation and Motherhood' (2023) 31 Medical Law Review 109–40, 121.
[90] Alice Margaria, 'Trans Men Giving Birth and Reflections on Fatherhood: What to Expect?' (2020) 34 International Journal of Law, Policy and the Family 225–46, 234.

The current birth registration system might mean that for trans women UTx is appealing because it would be the only way that they could be recognized as the legal mother of a child. However, this is hardly radically subversive since this is requiring trans women to conform to a gestationality requirement to be afforded recognition of their social role in a child's life. Further, gestation determining motherhood deters some trans men from undertaking pregnancy, also a subversive procreative activity, because of dysphoric language describing their relationship to a child. Genetics are used as the primary factor to determine who a 'father' is;[91] and in England, the law is clear this is only a man who has produced sperm.[92] Such rules might also constrain how we come to understand ectogestation if biosex roles are reinforced through gamete contribution. In many ways, therefore, contemporary birth registration systems that determine parentage by both gestation and genetics continue to reinforce the rigidity of biosex roles and also need reform. Parenthood, gestation, and novel technologies enabling gestation is discussed in more detail in Chapter 6.

What this landscape illustrates is that there exists a hostile legal culture towards procreation outside the cis-heteronormative binary, particularly when people seek to break the confines of biosex. As such, technologies that can replace or change the nature of gestation are seemingly unable to sufficiently challenge norms about procreation without accompanying radical reform to social understandings of reproductive roles and of procreation beyond the binary and the legal frameworks that both dictate and enforce them. Even without the legal obstacles to gender/sex parity in procreation, there remain the social pressures that are not just dictated by the law but also social convention and ordering.

The Possibilities from Un-sexing

For Smajdor, there need not be any causative account provided of how 'unsexing' gestation improves gender equality directly; it is simply a matter of justice as fairness. She posits the following, based on Rawls' veil of ignorance:[93]

[91] *Leeds Teaching Hospital NHS Trust v A* [2003] EWHC 259. Note that sperm donors cannot rely on their genetic contribution to be identified as the father where their sperm was donated through a licensed clinic as per the Human Fertilisation and Embryology Act 2008, s 28(6).

[92] Human Fertilisation and Embryology Act 2008, s 3ZA(6); *J v C* [2006] EWCA Civ 551; *X, Y, Z v UK* [1997] ECHR 20.

[93] John Rawls, *A Theory of Justice* (Harvard University Press 1999).

> you are asked whether you would prefer to be born into society A, where women [people AFAB] bear all the risks and burdens of gestation and childbirth, as they do now, or society B, where ectogenesis has been perfected and is routinely used. You do not know whether you will be born as a man or a woman [as a person with or without the innate capacity to gestate]. Which would you choose?[94]

Let us imagine that in society B, UTx has also been perfected for use in any body and is also routinely used. The claim as presented appeals to a natural intuition. I do not seek to deny that ultimately society B is probably preferable to society A for a variety of reasons. In society B, people of all genders and sexes (assuming all other things are equal; note the significant challenges resulting from disparate access to reproductive technologies along the strata of class, socio-economic status, and race in Chapter 4) can seek a procreative experience that matches their particular desires about pregnancy and *gestation*. People who are biologically or socially infertile because of an ability to gestate may find considerable value in these technologies, if available, in facilitating privacy in their reproductive journeys.[95] With the assistance available in the present that requires another party to gestate, there is some sense that reproductive journeys can be fraught with socio-political intervention and feelings of powerlessness.[96] Further, affording people AFAB more control over what physical burdens they are willing to assume in pregnancy allows people who may find the concept of a pregnancy dysphoric, or who are afraid of it or simply see it as bodily work they would rather avoid, to procreate without being pregnant. Simultaneously, people for whom pregnancy is a meaningful experience—whether AMAB or AFAB—can actively seek that experience without biological limitation. However, to say that society B is preferable, and that its conditions better appeal to intuitions of fairness and justice, is not the same as saying that if we lived in society B we would be closer to gender equality. Smajdor herself does somewhat concede this, noting that 'if you are a woman [AFAB], you will be worse off than your male peers. Perhaps not all the disbenefits of being a woman are attributable to childbearing. But alleviating these burdens would surely help'.[97] She goes no further into explaining how.

[94] Smajdor, 'The Moral Imperative for Ectogenesis' (n 4) 343.
[95] Romanis, 'The Equality-Enhancing Potential' (n 11) 640.
[96] ibid 642.
[97] Anna Smajdor, 'In Defence of Ectogenesis' (2012) 21 Cambridge Quarterly of Healthcare Ethics 90–103, 99.

Cavaliere has observed that justifying ectogestation (and presumably also the availability of UTx for people AMAB) 'as a means to end gender-based oppression relies on a bet as to how oppressive social norms will evolve once biological differences have been removed'.[98] Thus, proponents of the original position need to also defend P4 to show some causal connection between the unsexing possibilities of technologies, assuming socio-material conditions do not prevent this, and the elimination of gender-based oppression. Some, including Singer and Wells[99] and Smajdor,[100] make only a causative *assumption*; the mere possibility of persons other than those AFAB undertaking gestation means that a fundamental source of gender-based oppression can be eliminated. Elsewhere with Horn, I noted my concern that these accounts reflect 'a curious paradox: in order to escape "current cultural and social paradigms", the literature tends to leap to a future in which these paradigms have been erased. In so doing, it fails to address the contemporary limitations that make this future ungraspable'.[101] There are, as explored, considerable obstacles to the widespread use of the technology in radically disruptive or transformative ways.

There are two main justifications given for how assisted gestation can enhance gender equality: one relies on a conceptual decoupling of women from pregnancy and gestation in social consciousness, and the other relies on the practical benefits for people AFAB if they are no longer required to gestate to become parents. I argue, however, that neither of these justifications provides a persuasive account of how novel technologies enabling gestation can eliminate or reduce gender-based oppression without significant changes in legal and other socio-material conditions.

Ferreria asserts that ectogestation will 'no doubt decisively contribute to changing society's attitudes to women's perceived traditional roles, decoupling women from the—until then—seemingly indissoluble link between biology and reproduction'.[102] MacKay explains the mechanism for ending gender oppression within gestation outside of the body, and presumably also in bodies AMAB, is in how it 'destabilizes how we conceptualize "woman" as definiendum, and fundamentally removes grounds for a functionalist argument that sees female reproductive capacity as a key definiens'.[103] Ultimately, she explains that despite social progress in recognizing diversity in gender identities,

[98] Cavaliere (n 50) 729.
[99] Singer and Wells (n 6).
[100] Smajdor, 'The Moral Imperative for Ectogenesis' (n 4).
[101] Horn and Romanis (n 10) 236.
[102] Ferreira (n 15) 387.
[103] MacKay (n 4) 347.

'female reproductive function is used to delineate who counts as woman, based on biological features and performances. If it is possible to remove female reproductive work from women's bodies, even theoretically, then this ground for delineation is undermined.'[104] This seems unsubstantiated. There are already pregnancies that subvert these so-called 'key definiens' and yet they are not celebrated and raised as a challenge to a society that shackles by sex and gender. Prevailing social currents continue to otherize these activities as aberrations existing outside the norm. Further, technologies have introduced control over biological function such that people with the capacity to become pregnant can either prevent a pregnancy (contraception) or end a pregnancy (abortion), so that they are no longer confined to a biological destiny of reproducing. There remains, however, a significant undertone of pronatalism to many contemporary societies.

Here, it is pertinent to address the point that the argument of gender equality as it was initially presented is how it is given by scholars who are writing about ectogestation, and not UTx. In fact, Mackay is particularly disparaging of UTx when used by cis women, as she believes it to be a dangerous activity underpinned by a sort of false consciousness instilled by societal pronatalism.[105] UTx in bodies AMAB, I would argue, might have more of the discursive power that these writers claim for ectogestation, because in many ways it goes further to break the link between the cultural understandings of female biological function and gestation. It is easy to imagine the cultural narration about ectogestation being that its use is people AFAB opting out of an activity that is (and always will be) sexed female. Ectogestation could be thus understood as the *unhumanizing* of the generative process, rather than the unsexing of it. In contrast, however, UTx flies in the face of this construction. For Smajdor, the discursive power in ectogestation is enabling 'women to reproduce as men do'[106]—it seems, however, that there is infinitely more discursive potential in a world in which it is normalized for *men to procreate as women do*, that is to undertake bodily, generative work. Even this, however, would require cis men to rise to the challenge, something I am unsure they would do *en masse* because of conscious, or subconscious, subscription to not only the reproductive biosex binary but also the patriarchy (as well as practical reasons about the comparative ease of becoming pregnant and sustaining a pregnancy when born with a uterus versus being born without).

[104] ibid 351.
[105] ibid 349–50.
[106] Smajdor (n 4) 340.

Other commentators have conceptualized gender equality as resulting from the benefit to people who have the capacity to gestate in choosing not to do so when procreating. Kendal explains that the social burden of pregnancy is great; 'pregnancy serves to materially damage women's social lives and limit their future opportunities'.[107] These opportunities are described primarily in relation to the workplace. It is undeniable that women, because they are presumed to have the capacity to gestate (see the example earlier in this chapter), are discriminated against. In jurisdictions with statutory maternity pay, employers attempt to avoid these obligations. People who are thought able to become pregnant are also targeted in other ways (eg not hired because of the potential cost of replacing them if they take unpaid leave). People who carry pregnancies and birth can also often be stereotyped as being less, or not at all, career motivated. Thus, some argue that ectogestation enables people AFAB to no longer automatically be assumed the primary caregiver. MacKay explains how valuable career goods are denied to women, specifically equal pay, equal opportunity for career progression, and particular career options altogether, because they must undertake pregnancy (doing the bodily work in facilitating gestation) to become parents.[108] This is the case despite many jurisdictions having introduced workplace anti-discrimination laws that, in theory, should address these problems.[109] These problems all come, Simonstein advocates, from 'the fact that women (unlike men) are those who bear the child and must slow down'.[110] The biggest strain on the worker who becomes a pregnant is not pregnancy and birthing itself, but the advent of childrearing responsibilities, which pose a significant imposition.[111] Parents who undertook the pregnancy are assumed to need to provide the greater share of care work in childrearing.

Where it is not people AFAB who gestate, it might be argued that care work for resulting children can be more easily redistributed. This may be because gestation outside of the body could normalize a person without female physiology being the primary caregiver. While some have argued that gestation *extra uterum* might lead to men taking on more responsibility for the generative process itself,[112] this position would hold more weight if we talked about

[107] Kendal (n 3) 12. It is important to acknowledge that Kendal's position is more nuanced than most: 'while a lot of social changes are required to combat this problem . . . technological alternatives to physical gestation represent one method of challenging this norm'.

[108] MacKay (n 4) 352.

[109] ibid.

[110] Simonstein (n 4) 182.

[111] ibid.

[112] Iain Brassington, 'The Glass Womb' in Frida Simonstein (ed), *Reprogen-Ethics and the Future of Gender* (Springer 2009) 196–209, 207; Stellan Welin, 'Reproductive Ectogenesis: The Third Era of Human Reproduction and Some Moral Consequences' (2004) 10 Science and Engineering Ethics 615–26, 624.

UTx more seriously since a male body could be expressly connected to the generative function. Even then, I remain unconvinced. Formula milk and breast pumps, as well as shared parental leave,[113] in theory, made it much easier for cis men to become the primary caregiver after birth, allowing birthers to return to work earlier if they wish, and yet such arrangements remain rare. Removing gestation from the body, in particular, does not necessarily mean that thousands of years of societal convention about childrearing are simply displaced. If such shifts did not happen with societal conventions of equal opportunity in employment or equal pay (not that either of these issues should be considered resolved), it is hard to imagine that technology is the silver bullet. Kendal advances a more detailed account of change in that 'the physical incapacitation of gestation lays down the foundation for gender inequality in childrearing responsibilities'.[114] Because people AFAB must physically take the time off from work during a pregnancy, to birth and to recover, this perpetuates an unequal distribution of the burdens of childrearing thereafter. I think this link gets closer to what is at play here, but gendered roles in childrearing seem to go beyond the procreative role in bodily work facilitating gestation. In cis-heteronormative families, a female parent (whether cis-gendered or not) still faces considerable social pressure to undertake the primary burden of childrearing even if they did not gestate, for example, where they used surrogacy or adopted. Much of the social pressure experienced relates to the fact that mothers are consistently assumed to be, or it is reiterated that they should be, the primary caregiver of children. This manifests in the workplace,[115] but also in social settings. In contemporary culture that reiterates the value of 'intensive mothering',[116] Glaser writes '[m]others today are bullied and guilt-tripped into lowering their sights, reining in their ambitions, shelving their pleasures, and putting their own needs last. It's done explicitly, through guidelines: subtly, through the media and public attitudes; and practically, through structural obstacles at every step of the way.'[117] Much of the social pressure around parenting is exerted by people or institutions that do not (and need not) know about how the child was conceived or gestated. 'Good motherhood' narratives can thus impact non-birthing mothers just the same. Maybe at its historical root these pressures exerted on people who did not birth but do mother came

[113] Some examples of countries with comprehensive shared parental leave structures that encourage, incentivize, or mandate fathers taking leave are Finland, Germany, Iceland, Norway, and Sweden.

[114] Kendal (n 3) 14.

[115] Jennifer Berdahl and Sue Moon, 'Workplace Mistreatment of Middle Class Workers Based on Sex, Parenthood, and Caregiving' (2013) 69 Journal of Social Issues 341–66, 343.

[116] See Sharon Hayes, *The Cultural Contradictions of Motherhood* (Yale University Press 1996).

[117] Elaine Graser, *Motherhood: A Manifesto* (4th Estate 2021) 267.

from assumptions that anyone who mothered was assumed to have birthed, but the pressure has since evolved.

Employers, and employment conditions, as they are enabled by the law, are the issue, not pregnancies themselves. As I have argued with Horn elsewhere, the suggestion that social burdens on women to be the primary caregivers 'and gendered oppression in general can essentially be boiled down to the association of pregnancy with women's bodies'[118] fails to capture much of what is happening. This approach 'turns away from more pressing contemporary questions of what issues we need to address in our society if couples are unable to access the resources necessary to share or comfortably distribute the work of parenting'.[119] Further, it fails to appreciate the problems and pressures that such technologies might equally create for people AFAB or anyone who wants to gestate. First, there is the possibility of a 'levelling down' of employment rights[120] where gestation facilitated by bodily work can be framed as a matter of choice. Returning to the potential of UTx in this context, if any person, regardless of how their biosex or gender is perceived by others, was considered a potential gestator, this might do more to protect the rights of gestating persons than a world in which it is considered that no one need gestate. Pregnancy treated as purely a matter of preference (something to which many people attest) may do more harm overall to the objective of gender/sex equality or, more specifically, to equality in the workplace if there is not wide-sweeping reform before such a possibility may come to fruition. There is a real danger of this possibility since employment rights in pregnancy and birthing are legally conceptualized in many jurisdictions (including England and Wales, the European Union, and the US) as protection from discrimination on the basis of sex.

Second, it may be that the framing of employment rights prohibits radical uses of technologies. Decisions of the Court of Justice of the European Union (CJEU) regarding IVF[121] and surrogacies[122] failed to afford pertinent employment protections to putative parents on the grounds that these individuals were not pregnant. In the case of surrogacies, the CJEU has confirmed that employers need not provide maternity leave granted by the Pregnant Workers

[118] Horn and Romanis (n 10) 239.

[119] Elizabeth Claire Horn, 'Artificial Wombs and the Ectogenesis Conversation: A Misplaced Focus? Technology, Abortion, and Reproductive Freedom' (2020) 13 International Journal of Feminist Approaches to Bioethics 174–94, 186.

[120] I am grateful to Dr Victoria Hooton for discussions on this point.

[121] C-506/06 *Sabine Mayr v Bäckerei und Konditorei Gerhard Flöckner* [2008].

[122] C-167/12 *CD v ST* [2014]; C-363/12 *Z v A Government Department, The Board of management of a community school* [2014].

Directive to a putative parent by surrogacy (since the legislation framed access on the biological condition of pregnancy).[123] Member States that want to afford parental leave to parents by surrogacies and adoption must choose to do so with their own domestic legislation. In the case of IVF, the Court found that the EU framework protecting pregnant workers from dismissal did not apply before IVF embryos were implanted—thus creating a window in which an employer could dismiss an employee based on their plans for pregnancy before they are pregnant.[124] Hooton and I have raised concerns about the logic of such decisions being used to limit the employment rights of a person whose fetus is gestating *extra uterum*. It is easy to see how narrow conceptions of employment rights could become coercive (eg people may feel apprehensive about limited employment protections where they use ectogestation). Importantly, we argue that these decisions illustrate the problem in a framework that is overly focused on the fleshiness of procreation. This is not to say that people who get pregnant, sustain pregnancies, and birth should not be afforded protections that are specifically related to these capacities, but to say that employment rights surrounding procreation should not be connected *solely* to this—precisely because this feeds into the notion that it is the biosexed role in procreation that a person undertakes which determines what rights/provisions they are entitled to. This could manifest in a pressure to be pregnant to have guaranteed employment protections for early parenthood.

It may be argued that ectogestation is *the* technology to challenge the narrow formation of existing European employment law. However, the surrogacies and IVF cases are clear examples of injustice, and these technologies have been around for a long time, which illustrates how slow the law is to respond to developments. The law has such engrained notions of biosex roles that change is hard to envisage as a given. Further, many of the accounts of the benefits of ectogestation are precisely that one need not take as much leave from work. This seems to sit against a more radical project that can better protect workplace equality for all: parental leave that goes beyond references to bodily function.[125] The literature that considers ectogestation, therefore, redirects their focus from 'addressing contemporary limitations, such as the absence of support for the work done by caregivers more broadly, or exploring why gestation, as something that historically has been done by women, may be socially

[123] ibid.
[124] *Sabine Mayr* (n 121).
[125] Victoria Hooton and Elizabeth Chloe Romanis, 'Artificial Womb Technology, Pregnancy, and EU Employment Rights' (2022) 9 Journal of Law and the Biosciences 1–33, 26–27 <doi.org/10.1093/jlb/lsac009> accessed 2 September 2024.

devalued' in favour of 'solving pregnancy' without thought to how the consequences might be worse.[126]

Third, there are ways in which employers may also seek exploit procreative alternatives like ectogestation. Social egg freezing (extracting ovum and preserving them as a form of fertility preservation) has come under considerable scrutiny by bioethicists[127] since it has increased in popularity over the last decade. Some companies in the US, for example, have taken to offering social egg freezing as an employee benefit: Google, Apple, and Facebook.[128] While these employers ought not to be assumed to always/all have ulterior motives,[129] for some critics, motive is irrelevant. Employer-funded egg freezing been described as disempowering people AFAB 'by overtly entrenching the otherwise subtle message that women who have babies are not serious about their careers'.[130] It is not far removed from this status quo to imagine that employers might offer incentives for ectogestation or perpetuate an assumption that 'people who choose a complete gestation by pregnancy are less interested in their careers . . . their decision about how to complete a gestation could be seen as a symbolic declaration of their values'.[131] Both Kendal and Simonstein put considerable emphasis on ectogestation as an 'option',[132] but their analysis does not account for the possibility of workplace coercion. All of the highlighted problems will produce greater harm for people who have less bargaining power with their employers (lower-paid or precariously employed workers). Indeed, as has been acknowledged earlier in this book, this would not result in these people being forced to procreate with ectogestation (as they would be unlikely to afford it) but rather in being forced not to procreate.

Many who seek to make the argument that gender equality can result from gestation outside of the body rely on work by Firestone, who did advocate for gestation outside of women's bodies in her feminist manifesto.[133] However, as Murphy observed, arguments about gender equality resulting from technologies capable of gestation *extra uterum* fail to heed her warnings about the

[126] Horn and Romanis (n 10) 239.

[127] Françoise Baylis, 'Left Out in the Cold: Arguments Against Non-medical Oocyte Cryopreservation' (2015) 37 Journal of Obstetrics and Gynaecology Canada 64–67; Lisa Campo-Engelstein and others, 'Freezing Fertility or Freezing False Hope? A Content Analysis of Social Egg Freezing in U.S. Print Media' (2018) 9 AJOB Empirical Bioethics 181–93.

[128] Chris Weller, 'What You Need to Know about Egg-Freezing, The Hot New Perk at Google, Apple, and Facebook' *The Insider* (2017) <https://www.businessinsider.com/egg-freezing-at-facebook-apple-google-hot-new-perk-2017-9> accessed 6 November 2022.

[129] Hooton and Romanis (n 125) 9.

[130] Baylis (n 127) 65.

[131] Hooton and Romanis (n 125) 9.

[132] Simonstein (n 4) 182.

[133] Firestone (n 44) 74–75.

conditions in which the technology has liberating potential.[134] Firestone was adamant that 'in the hands of our current society and under the direction of our current scientists . . . any attempted use of technology to "free" anybody is suspect'.[135] She was explicit that liberation was dependent first, before any singular technological solution, on the abolition of capitalism, racism, sexism, other forms of identity oppression, and institutions that perpetuate that oppression.[136] For Firestone and Lewis, this also means, for example, the abolition of marriage and of the family.[137] AAPT itself only has transformative potential where there is transformation in society.[138] Similarly, I cannot imagine UTx has any more transformative potential as we continue to live under the very conditions Firestone condemned in 1970. As illustrated, current conditions and social orderings limit the use of both AAPT and UTx in transformative ways.

If we treat AAPT and UTx as necessary for equality we perpetuate the notion that equality is impossible now when it could be with radical social and legal reform. As argued in this chapter, how we attribute parenthood and notions of responsibility themselves limit the transformative potential of technologies enabling gestation. This is explored further in Chapter 6.

[134] Murphy (n 8) 38.
[135] Firestone (n 44) 206.
[136] Murphy (n 8) 38.
[137] Firestone (n 44); Sophie Lewis, *Full Surrogacy Now: Feminist Against Family* (Verso 2019).
[138] Murphy (n 8) 38.

6
PARENTHOOD

Gestation and birthing are at the heart of how legal parents are identified in English law. A child can only have a maximum of two legal parents[1] and there are several factors that are deployed and afforded different weight in different contexts to identify these two legal parents.[2] Gestation (the term used by the law to describe the work in pregnancy), however, is the one factor that is *always* determinative at birth. Irrespective of context, the person who facilitated gestation by sustaining a pregnancy is the legal mother.[3] In many circumstances, the legal father/second female parent is defined by their relationship to the person who facilitated gestation via pregnancy.[4] That gestation determines the legal mother is a long-standing legal principle, often traced to the maxim *mater semper certa est* ('it is always certain who the mother is') that is claimed to have its origins in Roman Law.[5] That 'the mother is always certain' is entrenched as a fundamental legal rule in both common law and civil law jurisdictions across the world. Despite significant variance in the cultural, social, and legal meanings of family between jurisdictions, the identification of the person who gestates and births as the legal mother is widespread. Jurisdictions where other factors, such as intention, are used to identify the legal mother at birth are rare exceptions to the prevailing norm.[6]

The attribution of parenthood in English law has been subject to much critique—particularly since the enactment of rules surrounding assisted procreation in the Human Fertilisation and Embryology Acts 1990 and 2008 (HFE Acts 1990 and 2008). This critique has been wide-ranging. Commentators have outlined the limitations of only recognizing two legal parents,[7] revealing

[1] Human Fertilisation and Embryology Act 2008 s 36; s 42.
[2] Emily Jackson, 'What Is a Parent?' in Alison Diduck and Katherine O'Donovan, *Feminist Perspectives on Family Law* (Routledge-Cavendish 2006) 59–74, 60.
[3] *Ampthill Peerage Case* [1977] AC 547; Human Fertilisation and Embryology Act 2008, s 33(1); *R (McConnell and YY) v Registrar General* [2020] EWCA Civ 559.
[4] Jackson (n 2) 65; Julie McCandless and Sally Sheldon, 'Genetically Challenged: The Determination of Legal Parenthood in Assisted Reproduction' in Tabitha Freeman and others (eds), *Relatedness in Assisted Reproduction: Families, Origins, and Identities* (CUP 2014) 61–78, 62.
[5] Rita D'Alton Harrison, *Mater Semper Incertus Est*: Who's Your Mummy?' (2014) 22 Medical Law Review 357–83, 383.
[6] eg California, United States; *Johnson v Calvert* 851 P.2d 776 (1993).
[7] Jackson (n 2).

Biotechnology, Gestation, and the Law. Elizabeth Chloe Romanis, Oxford University Press.
 DOI: 10.1093/9780191986574.003.0006

the inconsistencies between how parenthood is determined in different contexts,[8] accentuating how the rules attributing parenthood are sexed/gendered[9] and reinforce a binary nuclear family model,[10] and highlighting how legal outcomes do not match lived realities in some contexts.[11] Much has been written about the problems associated with gestation defining a legal mother and how it fails to reflect the intentions of the relevant parties to their disadvantage in surrogacies;[12] simultaneously, there has been much written by commentators against surrogacies,[13] specifically against enforceable surrogacy arrangements, implying that pregnancy *should* determine legal motherhood.[14] Though this debate references the role of the/a pregnant person a lot, it is very much *about surrogacies* and not about gestation: it considers a particular technology enabling gestation where one person performs gestational work on the part of another person. Many commentators are explicit that outside of surrogacies, gestation is a legal criterion not worth interrogating, since outside of surrogacies the person who sustains a pregnancy is usually the/a person intending to parent. Jackson describes the criterion as 'unproblematic' with its 'principal defect' being its application only in surrogacies.[15] Most of the critique of gestation as a criterion in the attribution of motherhood focuses on whether the attribution of motherhood in a given context is right. In this chapter, I do something much narrower: exploring why we use gestation to attribute parenthood and whether the reasons to use gestation change if the *nature* of gestation changes. Within the discussion of gestation *qua* legal motherhood, the language used implies that the criterion for the attribution of parenthood is *gestation*, this term is merely a proxy for pregnancy. Where gestation is discussed, it is taken as a given that this means gestation sustained by a pregnant person and this person would be readily identifiable in most cases.

As technologies capable of enabling gestation in different ways come to fruition, some not involving pregnancy and some changing how a pregnancy can

[8] Stuart Bridge, 'Assisted Reproduction and the Legal Definition of Parentage' in Andrew Bainham, Shelley Day Sclater, and Martin Richards (eds), *What is a Parent? A Socio-Legal Analysis* (Hart Publishing 1999) 73–88.

[9] See McCandless and Sheldon (n 4); Zaina Mahmoud and Elizabeth Chloe Romanis, 'On Gestation and Motherhood' (2023) 31 Medical Law Review 109–40.

[10] See Alan Brown, *What is the Family of Law? The Influence of the Nuclear Family* (Hart Publishing 2019).

[11] Kirsty Horsey, 'Fraying at the Edges: UK Surrogacy Law in 2015' (2016) 24 Medical Law Review 608–21.

[12] eg Carmel Shalev, *Birth Power: The Case for Surrogacy* (Yale University Press 1989).

[13] eg Gena Corea, *The Mother Machine: Reproductive Technologies from Artificial Insemination to Artificial Wombs* (HarperCollins 1985).

[14] Mary Lyndon Shanley, *Making Babies, Making Families: What Matters Most in an Age of Reproductive Technologies, Surrogacy, Adoption, and Same-sex and Unwed Parents* (Beacon Press 2001).

[15] Jackson (n 2) 65.

be sustained, *mater est* may no longer be so simple at all. Understanding where '*mater semper incerta est*' comes from and what is, historically and in contemporary terms, taken to be *legally* valuable about gestation and birthing is important in understanding why it is such a pervasive rule and to understand how to think about identifying a legal mother when there is no human-facilitated gestation, or where multiple people/devices undertake different forms of gestational and birthing work. In the first half of this chapter, I illustrate that the justification for treating gestation as determinative of legal motherhood has changed over time. I consider the potential justifications for centring gestation in the attribution of parental status. The logic of these justifications assumes that gestation is a process undertaken in a pregnancy sustained by one person. This sets the scene for considering the specific challenges arising out of novel technologies enabling gestation.

With pregnancy taken as *necessary* for recognition of a person as a legal mother, there are inevitably difficult and complex questions raised by novel technologies enabling gestation. As the Chapter 5 explored, that pregnant people are legally labelled *mothers*, rather than parents, renders invisible the lived experience of trans men and non-binary people who gestate and birth. Pregnancy being labelled as a gendered activity, in addition to one that is biosexed, might prevent the use of uterus transplantation (UTx) by people who want to be recognized as a father or a parent. This chapter looks at further challenges that arise from the potential future *divisibility* of gestational work. Where the law says that the pregnant person is the legal mother, it assumes that there is *one* person who facilitates gestation. Many commentators explain that in UTx the legal mother is clear[16]—in fact, this is one of the reasons why UTx is so attractive to some people.[17] In this way, the law renders the gestational contribution of a donor completely irrelevant. This makes visible that the law does not emphasize any (potentially tenuous) *gestational connection*: but rather *gestational work—pregnancy*. In the context of partial ectogestation, the legal mother would be identifiable as the person who sustained gestation for some period before the fetus was removed for continued gestation *extra uterum*.[18]

[16] Laura O'Donovan and others, 'Ethical and Policy Issues Raised by Uterus Transplants' (2019) 131 British Medical Bulletin 19–28, 20; Laura O'Donovan, 'Pushing the Boundaries: Uterine Transplantation and the Limits of Reproductive Autonomy' (2018) 32 Bioethics 489–98, 490.

[17] Benjamin Jones and others, 'Options for Acquiring Motherhood in Absolute Uterine Factor Infertility: Adoption, Surrogacy and Uterine Transplantation' (2021) 23 The Obstetrician & Gynaecologist 138–47, 142; Alexandra Mullock and others, 'Surrogacy and Uterus Transplantation using Live Donors: Examining the Options from the Perspective of "Womb-givers"' (2021) 35 Bioethics 820–28, 827.

[18] Elizabeth Chloe Romanis, *Regulating the 'Brave New World': Ethico-Legal Implications of the Quest for Partial Ectogenesis* (PhD thesis, University of Manchester 2020) 231.

But in this process there are clearly *two* facilitators of gestation; one human and one machine. Should we ignore a machine's gestational contribution and the associated work (albeit not psychofleshy work) of those involved? Additional challenges arise where there is no human-facilitated gestation at all. In complete ectogestation, does a gestateling 'have [only] a machine for a mother?'[19] In the second half of this chapter, I explore these challenges to consider who is/are the mother/s of children born from technologies enabling gestation.

Being a Legal Parent

Some of the legal consequences of parenting flow from the status of being a legal parent (having legal parenthood), and others stem from having parental responsibility (having legal rights and duties in child rearing).[20] In England and Wales, while only a maximum of two people can have the legal status of parent, more than two people can have parental responsibility[21] and therefore 'all of the rights, duties, powers, responsibilities and authority which by law a parent of a child has in relation to the child'.[22] In contrast, legal parenthood or '*being a parent* is a legal status which has traditionally been associated with a presumed or actual genetic link'.[23] Where parental responsibility gives more than two individuals rights and responsibilities in the day-to-day of child-rearing, the distinction between status and rights/duties might seem relatively unproblematic. Because parental responsibility *can* be afforded to multiple interested parties involved in the social rearing of a child, and because parental responsibility is literally described as the 'rights, duties, powers, responsibilities and authority' that parents have—which many might take to be the most material matter, it might be argued that who has the legal status of parent is of little consequence. However, there are both functional and symbolic reasons why being a legal parent matters to individuals.

First, it is much easier for a legal parent to obtain parental responsibility. Every live birth in England and Wales must be recorded and issued a certificate that identifies the 'mother' and, where apropos, the 'father'/'second parent'.[24]

[19] Jennifer Hendricks, 'Not of Woman Born? Technology, Relationship and Right to a Human Mother' (2011) <http://trace.tennessee.edu/utk_lawpubl/45> accessed 6 March 2023, 49.

[20] Jonathan Herring, *Family Law* (10th edn, Pearson 2021) 498.

[21] Children Act 1989, s 2(5).

[22] ibid, s 3(1).

[23] Andrew Bainham, 'Parentage, Parenthood and Parental Responsibility: Subtle, Elusive Yet Important Distinctions' in Bainham, Day Sclater, and Richards (eds), *What is a Parent?* (n 8) 25–46, 29.

[24] Births and Deaths Registration Act 1953; The Registration of Births and Deaths Regulation 1987.

While legal parenthood can come without parental responsibility,[25] legal parents are often automatically vested with parental responsibility in the birth registration process: all mothers (being the former pregnant person),[26] some fathers (where they are married to the mother, or are named on the birth certificate),[27] and some second female parents (where they are married/civil partnered to the gestational mother or have followed other legal processes during assisted conception at a licensed clinic).[28] While other persons can obtain parental responsibility through legal processes and/or court intervention,[29] such rights and duties are assigned by default to some legal parents, which functionally makes it much easier for those individuals to be social parents.

A social parent that succeeds in obtaining parental responsibility will have the powers/rights that enable them to rear a child, but this will not transform them into the '*legal parent* in the fullest sense'.[30] As Bainham notes, legal parenthood brings with it some 'fundamentals which go beyond everyday decisions involved in upbringing',[31] for example a presumption of contact, liability to financially support a child, creating a legal relationship between the child and the legal parent's existing family, and (where the legal parent also has parental responsibility—as mothers always do) the right to consent/refuse consent to adoption.[32] There are far reaching consequences here for both people who want to be parents, and equally for people who are deemed parents where they do not want to be recognized as such.

There is increasing recognition that the language used in attributing parenthood and recording it on birth certificates has significant expressive and symbolic effect. As Fineman notes, 'the legally constructed image of the family expresses what *is* considered "family"'.[33] Swennen and Crone observe that the law, and more specifically the normative power it has in claiming to explain

[25] eg a biological father might be the legal father but would not have parental responsibility if not married to the gestational mother or named on the birth certificate.

[26] Children Act 1989, s 2(1) and s 2(2)(a).

[27] ibid s 2(1); *Banbury Peerage Case* (1811) 1 Sim & St 153 H.

[28] Children Act 1989, s 4ZA.

[29] eg through a parental agreement with the gestational mother per Parental Responsibility Agreement Regulations 1991, or by obtaining a Child Arrangements Order per Children Act 1989, s 8. It is much easier for an unmarried father to acquire parental responsibility through a Child Arrangements Order because for the child to live with the father they *must* give parental responsibility to the unmarried father. Parental responsibility also endures after the Child Arrangements Order. I am grateful to Dr Dafni Lima for pointing this out.

[30] Bainham (n 23) 35.

[31] ibid 34.

[32] ibid 33; on adoption, a person must both be a legal parent and have parental responsibility. The court can also dispense with parental consent where it is deemed necessary; see Polly Morgan, *Family Law* (OUP 2021) 499.

[33] Martha Alberta Fineman, 'The Neutered Mother', in Richard Merelman, *Language, Symbolism, and Politics* (Westview Press 1992) 169–84, 176 (emphasis added).

how 'things stand in reality', has considerable power in providing a 'description' of what counts as family. This description, they explain, 'operates like a sieve that makes certain relationships sociopolitically visible, and thus speakable, and confines others to the realm of political (and to some extent social) inexistence'.[34] In legitimating some kinship groups as 'families' (based around identified parents), while failing to recognize others (by not recognizing some people as parents) people involved in the care of children are treated differently legally. For those who do not have their 'parenthood' recognized legally, this might constitute a form of psychological oppression in that these individuals are subject to a wrongful constraint of labelling: they are not recognized as having an attribute (being a particular person's parent) that they consider an essential attribute of their sense of self.[35] Being legally recognized as a *parent*, rather than someone able to make decisions about a child day-to-day, has identity implications for individuals. There are identity implications both for people who believe themselves to be the parent of a particular child in the (lack of) legal recognition for how they see themselves in relation to a particular child and for children in a (lack of) legal recognition that they are a particular person's child.

There are numerous examples of judicial reasoning emphasizing the identity implications for children in who their legal parents are.[36] As Theis J observed, determinations of legal parenthood reach 'far beyond the strict application of the law . . . it has emotional, psychological and social significance, as well as being at the core of the child's identity'.[37] Despite recognition of the importance of identity for children in who parents are, there are substantive problems in the operation of the law. As Brown and Wade argue that 'there is no coherent concept of identity from which the rules attributing legal parenthood flow; rather, the concept is invoked to provide a veneer of normative support for decisions as to who the parents should be in the different legal contexts'.[38] While there has been some recognition of the identity implications of parental status for the adult(s) surrounding a child, these implications often

[34] Frederik Swennen and Mariana Croce, 'The Symbolic Power of Legal Kinship Terminology: An Analysis of "Co-motherhood" and "Duo-motherhood" in Belgium and the Netherlands' (2016) 25 Social & Legal Studies 181–203, 189.

[35] Sandra Bartky, *Femininity and Domination: Studies in the Phenomenology of Oppression* (Routledge 1990) 30.

[36] *Re X (A Child) (Parental Order: Time Limit)* [2014] EWHC 3135 (Fam), per Munby P at [54]; *M v W* [2019] EWHC 648 (Fam), per Theis J at [64]; *A v J* [2022], per Morgan P at [34].

[37] *M v W* [2019] EWHC 648 (Fam), per Theis J at [35].

[38] Alan Brown and Katherine Wade, 'The Incoherent Role of the Child's Identity in the Construction and Allocation of Legal Parenthood' (2022) Legal Studies <doi:10.1017/lst.2022.21, 16> accessed 3 September 2024.

are not asserted in such forceful terms nor referenced as determinative considerations (in different ways in different contexts) in the attribution of parenthood. *R (McConnell and YY) v Registrar General*[39] concerned a trans man seeking to change his status from being the legal mother of his child to the legal father (discussed in Chapter 5). In the Court of Appeal, there was explicit recognition that being recorded as a mother on a birth certificate interfered with Mr McConnell's gender identity and that there was an interference with his right to family life[40] 'because the state describes [his] relationship [with his child] . . . as being that of mother and son; whereas, as a matter of social life, their relationship is father and son.'[41] Despite this, however, the Court determined that the law is clear that Mr McConnell is his son's mother. This case clearly illustrates that identity claims of parents in their specific relationships to children are not taken to carry much weight. This is also exemplified when we consider that little space is made for non-binary parental identities.[42] While in some instances persons can be named as parent 1/parent 2, this is only in specific cases (following a parental order in surrogacies/adoption) and not where an individual performs a specific biological role in the conception/gestation of a new human entity or in their relationship to a pregnant person,[43] as is explored in the next section.

Legal parenthood clearly has broad reaching implications; we all have an interest in the institution of parenthood and the ways in which it is determined that some experiences of being a parent are legally recognized and others are not. As Munby J put it, the attribution of legal parenthood is 'of the most fundamental gravity and importance.'[44] Investigation of the attribution of legal parenthood in the context of technologies enabling gestation is, therefore, of critical importance. In this chapter, I focus on gestation and the attribution of parenthood as an identity status—why does gestation denote being a mother? And what does this mean where the nature of gestation changes?

[39] *R (McConnell and YY)* (n 3).
[40] ibid, per Lord Burnett of Maldon CJ, King, Singh LJJ at [55].
[41] ibid.
[42] I am grateful to Dr Anna Nelson for discussions on this point.
[43] Mahmoud and Romanis (n 9) 118.
[44] *Re Human Fertilisation and Embryology Act 2008 (Cases A, B, C, D, E, F, G and H)* [2015] EWHC 2602 (Fam), at [53].

The Attribution of Legal Parenthood in England and Wales

In ascribing parenthood, the law follows a strict set of defined rules. The attribution of legal parenthood begins with the mother: identified as the person who is pregnant (facilitating gestation) and births.[45] This rule is a long-standing principle in the common law,[46] codified in the HFE Acts 1990 and 2008.[47] A legal mother can abdicate their parental status to another only though adoption[48] or where the court hands down a parental order,[49] both of which cannot occur until a minimum of six weeks post-birth. Following either of these processes, a child has no legal mother, only one (or two) legal parents: 'motherhood' is reserved only for formerly pregnant people.[50]

Identifying the legal father/second female parent of a child[51] is much more complex. In contrast to legal motherhood—determined solely by one attribute—there are several relevant factors taken into consideration and these are applied in different ways in different contexts. Where procreation was 'natural' (conception occurred following sexual intercourse), the marital presumption applies; where the person who sustained the pregnancy is married/in a civil partnership at the time of giving birth, their husband/male civil partner is the legal father.[52] Where the legal mother is unmarried/not in a civil partnership, the legal father is the person named as such on the birth certificate.[53] Finally, where there is a dispute about parentage and/or where the mother is unmarried and there is no father is named on the birth certificate, the genetic progenitor will be the legal father.[54] In 'natural' procreation the law, in the first instance, ranks the factors in the following way: (1) relationship with the pregnant person; (2) genetic contribution.

An adapted set of rules is used to identify the legal father or second female parent where procreation involves assisted conception (in vitro fertilization (IVF) or artificial insemination). Where the person who sustains the pregnancy is married or in a civil partnership at the time of insemination/embryo

[45] *Ampthill Peerage Case* (n 3).
[46] ibid.
[47] s 33(1).
[48] Adoption and Children Act 2002, s 52(3).
[49] Human Fertilisation and Embryology Act 2008, s 54.
[50] Mahmoud and Romanis (n 9).
[51] As noted, these are the only category of parental roles outside of adoption and surrogacy where parental orders are issued.
[52] *Ampthill Peerage Case* (n 3).
[53] Adoption and Children Act 2002, s 111.
[54] *Leeds Teaching Hospital NHS Trust v A* [2003] EWHC 259.

transfer, the legal parent is their spouse or civil partner unless it can be shown that this person did not consent.[55] Where the spouse/civil partner is male, this person is recorded as the legal father, where they are female, they are recorded as the second female parent. Where the person who sustains the pregnancy is unmarried/not in a civil partnership, the legal father is the man who consented to be treated as the legal father provided there is also consent from the person who sustains the pregnancy that this same man is to be treated as the legal father.[56] Equally, there is a second female parent (as opposed to a father) where a woman consented to be treated as the second female parent and the intended pregnant person consents that this same woman is to be treated as the second female parent.[57] In the context of assisted conception, genetic contribution is expressly given no weight (unlike in the context of sexual procreation where it can matter). The HFE Act 2008 emphasizes that the pregnant person is the mother irrespective of whether donor oocytes were used[58] and that a sperm donor is not the legal father.[59] While intention has no formalized role in the law surrounding natural procreation, intention is very clearly centred in the attribution of parenthood where conception is assisted (except, of course in cases where assisted conception is followed by surrogacy). This happens literally in that when undergoing fertility treatment, patients and their partners are provided with forms to consent to parenthood while consenting to treatment.[60]

In setting out the rules for attributing legal parenthood, what becomes immediately evident is that considerable thought went into determining how to identify fathers/second female parents in different contexts. I make no comment on whether these rules provide the right answers,[61] but wish to highlight the discrepancy in the fact that varied factors are taken to be material in determining fatherhood/second female parenthood, but motherhood is 'stagnant' and treated as 'innate' to pregnancy facilitating gestation by the law. In contrast to the large body of academic literature that explores the

[55] Human Fertilisation and Embryology Act 2008, s 35 (on legal fathers); s 42 (on second female parents).
[56] ibid s 37.
[57] ibid s 44.
[58] ibid s 47.
[59] Human Fertilisation and Embryology Act 1990, s 28(6); *Leeds Teaching Hospital NHS Trust v A* (n 54).
[60] These forms embody the agreed fatherhood/second female parenthood conditions in the Human Fertilisation and Embryology Act 2008.
[61] There is a considerable body of literature that critiques how these factors are against each other. Some commentators eg Bridge (n 8) argue that the little recognition afforded to genetic contribution runs counter to most people's intuitions.

conceptual foundations of legal fatherhood,[62] Willekens and Scheiwe point out that '[s]ince motherhood for a long time was seen as "natural" and self-evident ("*mater semper certa est*"), no theoretical debate about the foundations and justifications of the legal assignment of motherhood emerged'.[63] While procreation might be a natural phenomenon, and procreative work indisputable in gestation facilitated by pregnancy, 'the fact that procreators are responsible for rearing their children is not'.[64] So where did *mater semper certa est* come from? It is important to ask this question to track the lineage of this legal maxim and understand its meaning and evolution. It is often put that gestation is the natural source of legal motherhood *because it always has been*. However, the characterization of legal motherhood as innate in a single biological fact of origin, and the values behind this determination, have changed over time. Without tracing the evolution of the value placed in gestation by the law, the fact that the law is making a value judgement about what makes a mother is obscured. The assertion pervasive in accounts of where the 'gestation determines motherhood' requirement comes from perpetuates an authoritative diagrammatic account of the origin of legal rules, which has come to limit thinking in contemporary contexts.

What follows is not a complete historiography of legal motherhood across different social contexts, but rather, an account of the possible origins and meanings of '*mater semper certa est*' in English law and how these have evolved. This is useful in revealing some of the power given to the rule attributing legal motherhood due to its consistent reinforcement as being historically rooted.

A Critical History of *Mater Semper Certa Est*

Where referenced, the maxim '*mater semper certa est*' is cited to the following passage in the sixth century Digest of Justinian:

> *quia semper certa est, etiam si uologo conceperit: pater vero is est, quem nupitae demonstrant.*[65]

[62] eg Sally Sheldon, 'Fragmenting Fatherhood: The Regulation of Reproductive Technologies' (2005) 68 Modern Law Review 523–53; Richard Collier and Sally Sheldon, *Fragmenting Fatherhood: A Socio-Legal Study* (Hart Publishing 2008).

[63] Harry Willekens and Kirsten Scheiwe, 'Motherhood and the Law: Introduction' in Harry Willekens, Kirsten Scheiwe, Theresa Richarz, Eva Schumann (eds), *Motherhood and the Law* (Universitätsverlag Göttingen 2019) 9–22, 10.

[64] Susan Kennedy, 'Willing Mothers: Ectogenesis and the Role of Gestational Motherhood' (2020) 46 Journal of Medical Ethics 320–27, 320–21.

[65] *Justinian's Digest*, Liber Secundus, iiii, 5 (d. 2.4.5 Paulus).

This passage is difficult to translate; it engages the ablative case and several relative clauses and thus has several potential literal meanings. A rough literal translation would be: 'For/because it/she is always certain, even if she conceives illegitimately, the father is without doubt him to whom the marriage points'.[66] However, the terms that are acknowledged as potential alternatives here 'for/because' and 'it/she' are significant and change the entire meaning of the maxim. *Quia semper certa est* could translate to 'For it is always certain' or 'Because she is certain'. If the former, the maxim is reiterating the marital presumption in identifying a legal father, which does, of course, have the *inference* that a biological mother is easily identifiable, but that a mother is certain is not given as a matter of law (a legal status is not conferred on her). Though this might seem a small detail, the language is revealing, and it is unclear that this passage should be used as authority for the statement that the *legal* mother is always certain even if there is the implication of who a 'natural' mother is within the statement. Moreover, as Willekins posits, it is notable that throughout history law has 'remained silent (and yet crystal clear) as to the basis on which the maternal status is assigned, so silent that one might be tempted to conclude that we are not at all dealing with a social norm here, but with a pre-legal, natural "given" not subject to differentiated human decision-making'.[67] It is arguably misleading to describe the maxim as explaining the attribution of legal motherhood: it is simply giving power to silence and conflating an implication of biological motherhood with a legal status.

Even if the latter translation is preferred, 'because she is certain', it is still significant that the maxim does not use the language of 'mother'. That 'she' is not called 'mother' is revealing about the objective of the maxim and the greater scheme of Roman family law. Roman law had no interest in codifying who a mother was because it was of little consequence. Roman mothers were afforded no formal legal rights over their children;[68] rather persons who gestated and birthed were treated as a functional means of identifying fathers. Fathers mattered because the oldest male relative in a familial structure had executive authority over all family members until his death (*paterfamilias*):[69] mothers had no authority whatsoever. It is untrue, therefore, to say that *legal motherhood*

[66] I am grateful to Dr Sindre August Horn and Hannah Philp for their help translating this phrase.

[67] Harry Willekens, 'Motherhood as a Legal Institution: A Historical-Sociological Introduction' in Harry Willekens, Kirsten Scheiwe, Theresa Richarz, Eva Schumann (eds), *Motherhood and the Law* (Universitätsverlag Göttingen 2019) 21–52, 29.

[68] Andrew Riggsby, *Roman Law and the Legal World of the Romans* (CUP 2010) 182.

[69] Judith Evans-Grubbs, *Women and the Law in the Roman Empire: A Sourcebook on Marriage, Divorce and Widowhood* (Routledge 2002) 20.

has been determined by gestation since Roman law because legal motherhood *did not exist* in the sense that we know it today.

A 2014 decision of the Supreme Court of Ireland acknowledged that '[t]here does not appear to be any evidence that the maxim mater semper certa est formed part of the Common Law'.[70] The decision surveyed legal writings on Common Law ranging from 1658 to 1939 and concluded there was no 'stream of reference to *mater semper certa est*' within them that would have indicated it was a maxim of common law, while the marital presumption of fatherhood was consistently elucidated.[71] The *Ampthill Peerage Case* in 1977 was the first case to, *obiter*, state with conviction that a mother is certain: '[m]otherhood, although a legal relationship, is based on a fact, being proved demonstrably by parturition'.[72] This statement, unlike the oft-cited Roman law maxim,[73] actually provided an account as to what it was that made a mother certain: 'parturition'. From this eventually, the maxim '*mater est quam gestatio demonstrat*' (by gestation the mother is demonstrated) begins to appear in academic writings about parenthood.[74] Baldassi credits the convention *by gestation the mother is demonstrated* to a textbook by Mason and McCall Smith in 1983.[75] She is critical of the failure of many scholars to notice the more recent origins of 'gestation equals motherhood', instead perpetuating the principle as if *it had always been there*. Dickens, writing from Canada, is a notable exception: '[t]he legal maxim *mater est quam gestatio demonstrat,* while necessarily of more recent origin than the Latin form may suggest, accords to established understanding' that legal motherhood is determined by gestation and birth.[76]

That both Roman Law and Common Law were likely not explicit about the certainty of a legal mother, and definitely not explicit that pregnancy facilitating gestation was determinative of motherhood, does not mean, for some commentators, that 'the rules determining the maternal status *do not have a history*'.[77] Willekins, for example, accepts that in most legal orders *mater*

[70] *MR and DR & ors v An t-Ard-Chláraitheoir & ors* [2014] IESC 60, at [70] per Denham CJ

[71] ibid at [73], see [74]–[77].

[72] *Ampthill Peerage Case* (n 3), per Lord Simon o'Glaisdale at 577.

[73] If one surveys Roman law, there are other places where the inference is much clearer that a mother is the person who births, for example, in the law surrounding citizenship sources say things like a person is a citizen where 'born of a Roman mother', eg Edward Poste, *Gai Institutiones* (4th edn, OUP 1904) §32.

[74] Cindy Baldassi, '*Mater est quam gestatio demonstrat*: A Cautionary Tale' (2006) <https://papers.ssrn.com/sol3/papers.cfm?abstract_id=927147> accessed 6 March 2023, 6.

[75] ibid, 4; J Kenyon Mason and Alexander McCall Smith, *Law and Medical Ethics* (Butterworths 1983).

[76] Bernard Dickens, 'Reproduction Law and Medical Consent' (1985) 35 The University of Toronto Law Journal 255–86, 283.

[77] Harry Willekens, 'Motherhood as a Legal Institution: A Historical-Sociological Introduction' in Harry Willekens, Kirsten Scheiwe, Theresa Richarz, Eva Schumann (eds), *Motherhood and the Law* (Universitätsverlag Göttingen 2019) 21–52, 29.

semper certa est was not 'explicitly formulated' but still 'the basic rule for assigning the legal status of motherhood has always and everywhere been the same . . . it is only recently that it has come to be deemed necessary to write down the rule'.[78] However, this statement is illusory about 'legal motherhood'. It has long been taken as a given that a pregnant person facilitating gestation/the birth-giver was a *biological* parent, however it is relatively recently in legal history that such a person was afforded a legal status that meant *any* recognition, never mind any rights.[79] Until 1839, married women who birthed had no right to custody of or visitation with their children if they divorced their husbands.[80] In stark contrast, in today's legal context, legal motherhood has come to conscript. Hendricks asserts that the law should value pregnancy and birth as creating the relationship between 'mother' and 'child' without 'stereotyping'.[81] However, as I have argued with Mahmoud elsewhere, it is significant that 'law affords those who do not gestate and birth the freedom to make social determinations about their legal parental status, whereas biological determinism inhibits the freedom of gestating people to make such arrangements'.[82] In contemporary social contexts, 'the motherhood penalty' now imposes a completely different social, economic, and political tax on people who (can) gestate and birth (predominantly women).[83] The rule that birthers are 'naturally' legal mothers and thus have a status that affords them rights over and responsibilities for their children historically helped rectify an injustice, but today it propagates one in essentializing the female body for motherhood (and stereotyping people who can become pregnant as mothers).[84]

Furthermore, even if we take it that rules determining maternal status have a history, some commentators have observed the significant ambiguity as to the values behind the content of these rules. As Bridge explains, before the advent of IVF, '[t]he genetic mother was the gestational mother and was the legal mother. Nothing else was biologically possible, or therefore legally necessary'.[85] As Martin puts it, '[i]t was not necessary for the law to define motherhood, for it was evident from the fact of childbirth'.[86] Birth has always been an obvious means of identifying a person's connection to a new human being

[78] ibid.
[79] Fineman (n 33) 171.
[80] Custody of Infants Act 1839.
[81] Jennifer Hendricks, *Essentially a Mother: A Feminist Approach to the Law of Pregnancy and Motherhood* (University of California Press 2023) 3.
[82] Mahmoud and Romanis (n 9) 119; see also Jackson (n 2) 66.
[83] Elaine Glaser, *Motherhood: A Manifesto* (Fourth Estate 2021) 4.
[84] See Mahmoud and Romanis (n 9).
[85] Bridge (n 8) 75.
[86] Morgan (n 32) 455.

since that entity literally emerges from being a part of their body to become a part of the world. The connection between a birther and a resulting child is thus an easy marker by which to ground consideration of who a new human entity exists in relation to. Before the advent of any reproductive technology and genetic testing, indeed, this was the only marker.[87] What is interesting, however, is how that marker is conceptualized.

First, the link between baby and legal mother is consistently described by commentators as one of *gestation*, rather than *of birth*. This is presumably because they are not being attentive to the difference between pregnancy and gestation. Legal sources elucidate some conceptual confusion in that the common law refer to motherhood being demonstrated 'by parturition'[88] (a synonym for birth), whereas the HFE Acts 1990 and 2008 stipulate a legal mother as the person 'carrying or has carried a child'[89] (a synonym for gestation facilitated by pregnancy in common parlance). This might seem like it is of little consequence, after all a pregnant person (beyond a certain duration of pregnancy) is necessarily also a birther.[90] However, as I argue later in this chapter, novel technologies enabling gestation give us reason to seek conceptual clarification. Second, the biological connection in gestation/birth clearly has significant value placed in it by the law. However, there remain questions about *what* it is that is being valued. As Hill explains:

> This principle [that the person who sustains pregnancy/births is the legal mother] reflects the ancient dictum mater est quam gestation demonstrat (by gestation the mother is demonstrated). The phrase, by its use of the word 'demonstrated' has always reflected an ambiguity in the meaning of the presumption. It is arguable that while gestation may demonstrate maternal status, it is not the sine qua non of motherhood. Rather, it is possible that the common law viewed genetic consanguity as the basis for maternal rights. Under this latter interpretation, gestation simply would be irrefutable evidence of the more fundamental genetic relationship.[91]

[87] eg there are multiple cases throughout history before reproductive technology whereby men seek to a claim that a child was not theirs based on the length of gestation vs their last sexual intercourse with their wife. See *Alsop v Bowtrell* (1619) 79 ER 464; *Wood v Wood* [1947] P 103; *Glenister v Glenister* [1945] P 30; *Clark v Clark (No 1)* [1939] P 228.

[88] *Ampthill Peerage Case* (n 3).

[89] s 33(1).

[90] In making this comment, I do not wish to diminish experiences of pregnancy that do not end in live birth, but merely highlight that after the fetus attains a particular size delivery is necessarily a birth.

[91] John Hill, 'What does it mean to be a "Parent?" The Claims of Biology as the Basis for Parental Rights' (1991) 66 New York University Law Review 353–420, 370.

The question is, as Jackson put it: '[i]s it gestation itself that is decisive [of legal motherhood], or does gestation merely *demonstrate* or offer proof that the woman who gives birth is the *genetic* mother of the child?'[92] Before the advent of IVF, there was no separability of genetics and gestation in those assigned female at birth (AFAB),[93] thus it is unsurprising that we cannot find the answer in Roman family law perhaps because they thought the question was easy to answer, though more likely because they did not ask the question at all. On the advent of IVF, however, the gestational and genetic role of a person AFAB in procreating could be severed. It became possible for a person AFAB capable of becoming pregnant to become pregnant using an oocyte donated by another person AFAB. Some people will become pregnant using a donor oocyte because they want to become a mother but do not have (good quality) oocytes of their own. Some people in a same-sex relationship gestate using the oocyte of their partner so that both parties can be biologically connected to the resulting child. Other people are gestational surrogates, performing gestational work using the oocyte of another person AFAB (with or without a partner/family network) who intends to parent it. As such, it is critical to ask the question of *why* we value gestation/birth and *what* we value in it as the determinative factor of legal motherhood.

If we continue to embolden *mater semper certa est* as historically rooted, and reiterate that this means that motherhood is innate in sustaining pregnancy/birthing, we give it considerable power. However, the reality is, this rule has not been enshrined for thousands of years—both in the sense that the rule was not expressly given in the formulation now known to be so familiar, but also in that we are not clear what it encompasses. In the story often told, the mother as a legally defined person in relation to her child was just so obvious that it did not need reiterating in express terms; this tells us a story about the 'naturalness' of motherhood and negates the conceptual challenges in what is heralded as a simple rule. However, if we recognize that motherhood was not legally defined and this was often the case because mothers had no rights in relation to their children, a different story is revealed.

92 Jackson (n 2) 65.
93 ibid.

Contemporary Meaning in *Mater Semper Certa Est*

Despite the confusing history, English law is clear that the legal mother is the person who sustains a pregnancy and births. This is not just the position of English law, but in fact, it is the case in much of Europe. The European Court of Human Rights noted in 1980 that:

> [T]he Court cannot but be struck by the fact that the domestic law of the great majority of the member States of the Council of Europe has evolved and is continuing to evolve, in company with the relevant international instruments, towards full juridical recognition of the maxim *mater semper certa est.*[94]

Even in jurisdictions with more progressive regulation enabling two female people to be recognized both as 'mothers' (which is not possible in England and Wales), such as 'co-mothers' in Belgium or 'duo-mothers' in the Netherlands,[95] motherhood remains tethered to gestation; the person who facilitates gestation by undertaking pregnancy is the mother and another person can *also* be a mother.

The system of '[f]amily law cannot help but reflect the society's values and choices'.[96] While traditionally western societal convention and law treat parenthood as 'a question of fact rather than judgment', the reality is that 'parenthood is not a fact waiting to be discovered' and the law is consistently making normative judgments about the comparative significance of differing claims to parenthood.[97] As Johnson explained, '[b]iology does not give an answer to the question: what is a parent'[98] unless we make the normative decision to value biology above other factors. The law makes a value assessment in determining that gestation is the most important aspect in determining parenthood. McCandless and Sheldon explain that 'it has been seen that motherhood is firmly grounded in gestation and, while some speculate that historically this merely stood as a proxy for a genetic link, today it clearly holds significance per se'.[99] But what is this significance? There is a tendency to afford this biological

[94] *Marckx v Belgium* (1979–80) 2 EHRR 330 at [39].

[95] Frederik Swennen and Mariano Croce, 'The Symbolic Power of Legal Kinship Terminology: An Analysis of "Co-motherhood" and "Duo-motherhood" in Belgium and the Netherlands' (2016) 25 Social & Legal Studies 181–203.

[96] Elizabeth Paul, *Taking Sides Clashing Views on Controversial Issues in Sex and Gender* (McGraw-Hill 2001) 260.

[97] Jackson (n 2) 67.

[98] Martin Johnson, 'A Biomedical Perspective on Parenthood' in Bainham, Day Sclater, and Richards (eds), *What is a Parent?* (n 8) 47–72, 68.

[99] McCandless and Sheldon (n 4) 67.

account significance, but we must take the time to scrutinize the potential motivations, presented as a continuation of a natural long-existing biological rule, rather than a value judgement. In what follows, I consider the justifications for the leading role of gestation in the attribution.

A meaningful biological tie? ('Best interests of the child')?

In *Re G*, Baroness Hale famously opined that 'the process of carrying a child and giving him birth . . . brings with it, in the vast majority of cases, a very special relationship between mother and child, a relationship which is different from any other'.[100] The emphasis of a 'maternal tie based on presumed *in utero* bonding' exemplifies the assumption that it was in the best interests of a child to be raised by the person who birthed them irrespective of the circumstances.[101] In Norway, commentators suggested that the *mater semper certa est* rule is favoured to prevent interference with nature ('tukle med naturen').[102] In Spain, the report of a special Commission into assisted reproduction concluded that:

> [t]he more important than the genetic one, as the gestating mother bears the child within her for nine months and protects the child physiologically and psychologically . . . the biological preponderance of gestational motherhood over the genetic one is considered and that the legal mother is always the gestating woman, even in the case where egg donation is involved.[103]

There are some scholars that support the gestation *qua* motherhood rule on these grounds; for example, Hendricks explains that '[a]t birth, the only existing, tangible human relationship on which a child can draw is with the woman from whom she has just separated'.[104] She describes pregnancy as 'caretaking'[105] and argues that where pregnancy is not seen as determinative of motherhood, as she shows is the case in some jurisdictions within the United

[100] *Re G (Children)* [2006] UKHL 43, per Baroness Hale at [34].
[101] Mahmoud and Romanis (n 9) 125.
[102] Marit Melhuus, 'Sperm, Eggs and Wombs: The Fabrication of Vital Matters through Legislative Acts' in Penny Harvey, Christian Krohn-Hansen, and Knut G Nustad (eds), *Anthropos and the Material* (Duke University Press 2019) 122–42, 123.
[103] Miguel Palacios Alonso, *Informe de comisión especial de estudio de la fecundación 'in vitro' y la inseminación artificial humanas* (Madrid 1986): translation from Itziar Alkorta, 'Surrogacy in Spain: Vindication of the *Mater Semper Certa Est* Rule' (2020) 26 The New Bioethics 298–313, 302.
[104] Hendricks, 'Not of Woman Born?' (n 19) 49.
[105] Hendricks, *Essentially a Mother* (n 81) 3.

States, then there is a concerning propagation of problematic genetic essentialism.[106] She retorts that when there is argument about changing how gestation is valued in the law (especially where there is reflection on equality for biological progenitors) this 'equates biological motherhood with biological fatherhood, as if gestating and ejaculating are the same thing'.[107] There are two claims at work in these arguments: first, the idea that there is a special bond between a person who facilitated gestation with bodily work and the fetus that needs recognition (both for the welfare of a resulting child and for the welfare of the birthing person) and second that if pregnancy is not seen as determinative of parental status then there is the risk of devaluing the bodily work that pregnant people undertake.

These first claim is essentially stipulating that 'social bonds are grounded biologically in pregnancy'[108] however, as Lewis suggests, 'what some call the "nine-month head start" to a relationship—is ultimately incomplete'.[109] Though many pregnant people and birthers conceive of themselves as undertaking a form of care work, this is not a universal experience. Many see pregnancy and birthing as intimately connected to their desire to become a parent (for some, specifically to be a mother) and describe a feeling of prenatal bonding, others describe feelings of prenatal bonding though unrelated to being a mother after birth,[110] and others describe having no experience of prenatal bonding at all.[111] Furthermore, as Hill has pointed out, 'the implications [of any prenatal bonding, however understood] for parental-rights arguments are unclear'.[112] As Mahmoud and I have argued, gestation is not parenting work, since parenting is a relational activity and a fetus is a part of a pregnant person, pregnancy facilitating gestation is a precursor to parenting.[113] As such it is rather odd that we perpetuate gestation and birthing as the 'natural' sources of parental status. It is clear in the law that gestation is considered a meaningful biological tie, and with the move towards recognition of informing children about their origins,[114] the way that gestation is described as above makes the case for

[106] ibid 63.
[107] ibid 99.
[108] Sophie Lewis, *Full Surrogacy Now: Feminist Against Family* (Verso 2019) 14.
[109] ibid.
[110] For example, some surrogates refer to themselves as 'babysitters': Zsuzsa Berend, '"We Are All Carrying Someone Else's Child!": Relatedness and Relationships in Third-Party Reproduction' (2016) 118 American Anthropologist 24–36.
[111] Gregory Pence, 'What's so Good about Natural Motherhood? (In Praise of Unnatural Gestation' in Scott Gelfand and John Shook (eds), *Ectogenesis: Artificial Womb Technology and the Future of Human Reproduction* (Rodopi 2006) 84–85.
[112] Hill (n 91) 398.
[113] Mahmoud and Romanis (n 9) 111–15.
[114] Culminating in the Human Fertilization and Embryology Authority (Disclosure of Donor Information) Regulations 2004 which permit individuals who were conceived through gamete or

the recognition of gestational origins being as important in origin stories as genetics but does not necessarily explain why pregnant people ought to be definitively *always* the legal mother.

After birth, when a new human entity exists, there is a clear moment of transformation—not just in the emergence of a new person, but in the 'becoming' of new parents. There are visible social and biological relationships between childrearers and children, and these people may not necessarily be those involved in their creation or gestation. Some commentators have thus argued the clear delineation between biological and social parenthood often perpetuated in Western culture and in the law is not so clear-cut because 'many of the processes and relationships involved in childrearing—particularly of very young children—are shaped by biology'.[115] Examples include chestfeeding[116] (a person need not have been pregnant to chestfeed),[117] feeding in general, and the physical intimate relationship that a child can have with a parent to regulate biological parameters (eg skin to skin contact can regulate temperature and heartbeat).[118] These are all biological activities that last much longer than the duration of pregnancy. Despite this, however, the law privileges the biological relationship in gestation.

Undoubtedly, pregnancy and birth are significant bodily work. However, if we take the approach Hendricks takes, in her concern for avoiding genetic essentialism, we end up reifying *gestational essentialism*. Essentially in her work, she criticizes one form of biological essentialism to justify the propagation of another form of biological essentialism. One does not need to say gestation is *the* determinative factor in attributing parental rights in order to hold the position that gestational work is significant work, encompassing of greater physical and emotional labour of a wholly different nature, that is not equivalent to ejaculating. Importantly, if we hold that pregnancy always identifies a mother we are not respecting the intentions of the person undertaking gestational work (and all it involves) because we are not respecting any negative intentions

embryo donation after April 2005 and are eighteen years old or older to request the identity of their donor from the Human Fertilisation and Embryology Authority.

[115] Teresa Baron, *Pregnancy, Procreation, and Moral Parenthood* (PhD thesis, University of Southampton 2020) 20.

[116] eg Tonse Raju, 'Breastfeeding Is a Dynamic Biological Process—Not Simply a Meal at the Breast' (2011) 6 Breastfeeding Medicine 257–59.

[117] Gemma Cazorla-Ortiz and others, 'Methods and Success Factors of Induced Lactation: A Scoping Review' (2020) 36 Journal of Human Lactation 739–49.

[118] eg Ann Bigelow and Michelle Power, 'Mother–Infant Skin-to-Skin Contact: Short- and Long-Term Effects for Mothers and Their Children Born Full-Term' (2020) 11 Frontiers in Psychology <doi.org/10.3389/fpsyg.2020.01921>(accessed 3 September 2024).

they may have including not wanting to mother.[119] The work that the person has done in sustaining a pregnancy (that which Hendricks calls 'caretaking' that demands respect), as Ruddick writes, is not compromised where they decide to transfer 'to others the responsibility for the infant she has birthed'.[120]

Legal certainty

While feminists have long distinguished between 'giving birth and being a mother',[121] English law recognizes no such distinction.[122] As birth is completed, the birther becomes a legal mother with serious practical ramifications, as this person has parental responsibility from birth.[123] This has particularly harmful effects for persons who undertake pregnancy but who do not wish to parent.[124] This construction means, however, that routinely there is always an identifiable person responsible for a human entity from the moment of its existence in the world.[125] This might be considered important for the welfare of the child. Concealment of birth and abandonment of an infant under two years are both criminal offences in England and Wales,[126] reiterating the insistence of the law that the person who sustains gestation and births must always identify themselves and be responsible for the child after birth[127] (and if they do not want to parent they are responsible for initiating adoption). Though a compelling motivation, it remains unclear why the person who sustained a pregnancy *must* be recorded as the legal mother where another person is willing to be recorded as such (and thus to take responsibility for the child).

In the *McConnell* case, the High Court decision reiterated *obiter* the importance of certainty as a matter of clear and consistent record keeping in birth registration.[128] Though, as Fenton-Glynn observed, no clear rationale was provided for the importance of homogeneity in birth registration, especially over the specific harms to people who sustain pregnancies being recorded as

[119] Dafni Lima, 'Legal Parenthood in Surrogacy: Shifting the Focus to the Surrogate's Negative Intention' (2024) 46 Journal of Social Welfare and the Law 245–66, 250.

[120] Sara Ruddick, *Maternal Thinking: Towards a Politics of Peace* (Beacon Press 1989) 51.

[121] Adriene Rich, *Of Woman Born: Motherhood as Experience and Institution* (WW Norton & Company 1995).

[122] Mahmoud and Romanis (n 9).

[123] Children Act 1989, s 2(1) and s 2 (2)(a).

[124] Mahmoud and Romanis (n 9) 138.

[125] Morgan (n 32) 458.

[126] Offences Against the Person Act 1861, s 60 (concealment); s 27 (abandonment).

[127] Mahmoud and Romanis (n 9) 123.

[128] *R (on the application of TT) v The Registrar General for England and Wales* [2019] EWHC 2384 Fam, per Sir Andrew McFarlane P at [234], [243], [244].

legal mothers where it is not their intention to parent.[129] The determination of legal parenthood and the birth registration process were historically of importance to settle inheritance and succession. However, in more recent years, birth certificates are considered more a matter of specifying a child's origins.[130] As noted, recording origins is something potentially facilitated independently to determining legal parents, thus, the certainty of birth registration does not appear sufficient justification for *mater semper certa est.*

A surrogacies deterrent/Preventing the exploitation of people sustaining pregnancies

In Europe, it is interesting that the *mater semper certa est* rule operates both in jurisdictions that have banned surrogacies and those that have not. It is arguable, however, that pregnancy *qua* legal motherhood operates as a deterrent in all jurisdictions—just to different degrees. Alkorta, writing from the Spanish context in which surrogacies are unlawful,[131] asserts the importance of the 'gestational-model of motherhood' on the grounds that it 'not only deters surrogacy malpractice but is also a fair principle by which to protect birth mothers and their children from the abuses of reproductive market force'.[132] I will not go into detail about prohibitions on surrogacies here, but I raise this to note that in jurisdictions that prohibit surrogacies, there is more consistency in *mater semper certa est* as an additional deterrent for surrogate-seekers. What is confusing is the maintenance of this rule in jurisdictions permitting surrogacies (in some circumstances). In England and Wales, surrogacies are permissible for altruistic reasons only, with commercial surrogacies prohibited,[133] though there is a lack of clarity related to compensated arrangements.[134] Johnson, critiquing the apparent contradiction in the HFE Acts ignoring genetics in the

[129] Claire Fenton-Glynn, 'Deconstructing Parenthood: What Makes a Mother?' (2020) 79 The Cambridge Law Journal 34–37.

[130] See Edward Higgs, 'A Cuckoo in the Nest? The Origins of Civil Registration and State Medical Statistics in England and Wales' (1996) 11 Continuity and Change 115–34; Liam Davis, 'Deconstructing Tradition: Trans Reproduction and the Need to Reform Birth Registration in England and Wales' (2021) 22 International Journal of Transgender Health 179–90, 180.

[131] Assisted Reproduction Technologies Act of 1988 (Law 35/1988, 22nd November) Art 10.

[132] Alkorta (n 103) 299.

[133] Surrogacy Arrangements Act 1985, s 2.

[134] Per the Human Fertilisation and Embryology Act 2008, s 54(8) surrogates can be compensated for 'expenses reasonably incurred'. However, sometimes the line between reasonable expenses and payment is not always clear-cut. Moreover, because this is considered by the Courts as part of the process of making a parental order, expenses are considered retrospectively and often approved even where they look like they may exceed 'reasonable expenses': *Re Q (Parental Order)* [1996] 1FLR 369; *Re X and another (Children) (Parental Order: Foreign Surrogacy)* [2008] EWHC 3030.

context of surrogacies, implies that the purpose of the law may be to deter these sorts of arrangements. He writes, '[c]ouples are almost challenged by the law not to risk entering unenforceable surrogacy agreements by giving them little or no control over their own genetic material'.[135] The European Court of Human Rights acknowledged that UK law maintains a deterrent against surrogacies in the attribution of legal motherhood:

> [T]he legislature has chosen to confer parenthood on the gestational mother and her husband. This choice appears to have been influenced both by the need to prevent gamete donors from being recognised as legal parents at birth and the desire to prevent surrogacy agreements from being enforceable so as not to encourage the removal of babies from their gestational mothers against the mothers' wishes.[136]

So why permit surrogacies but pass laws that may deter it? As discussed in Chapter 4, the Warnock committee's recommendations, resulting in the Surrogacy Arrangements Act 1985, had sought to capture the permissibility of surrogacies where intended parents have a compelling medical need.[137] Most of Warnock's members hoped that surrogacies would just go away by constructing a regulatory regime that would not encourage its use.[138] In making surrogacies more legally complex, the surrogacy journey is limited to people who *need* assisted gestation, rather than those who might want to outsource gestation.[139] These legal complexities, however, have not completely undermined demand for surrogacies,[140] since there are many biological, psychosocial, and/or social factors affecting a person's ability to become pregnant that contribute to their being involuntarily childless without surrogacies, or, indeed, novel technologies enabling gestation.[141]

One of the key concerns that Warnock raised that has been built into the fabric of the regulation surrounding surrogacies; the prevention of the exploitation of pregnant people. While much of the report's concerns are about

[135] Johnson (n 98) 66.
[136] *H v United Kingdom*, Application No 32185/20 (2021) at [55].
[137] Margaret Brazier, 'Regulating the Reproduction Business?' (1999) 7 Medical Law Review166–93, 169.
[138] ibid 179.
[139] The report described people 'with compelling medical need' as deriving medical need. On the complexity of determining need where people seek out assisted/assistive gestation see Elizabeth Chloe Romanis, 'Assisted Gestative Technologies' (2022) 48 Journal of Medical Ethics 439–46, 444.
[140] Kirsty Horsey, 'Not Withered on the Vine: The Need for Surrogacy Law Reform' (2016) 4 Journal of Medical Law and Ethics 181–96, 182.
[141] Romanis, 'Assisted Gestative Technologies' (n 139).

exploitation in commercial surrogacies, they also indicate they had concerns about exploitation in altruistic arrangements too.[142] For some, there remains an 'inherent exploitation' in the altruistic pregnancy-facilitated gestation of a child that is to be parented by others.[143] Such an account assumes that there is something in the biological nature of the work of gestating that makes one not raising the resulting child a harm to the person who sustained the pregnancy. A holder of this belief would advocate that there is some protection for the pregnant person in *mater semper certa est* because it gives them the opportunity to use the law to ensure they have custody of a born child, and there are legal mechanisms that enable them to give up their parental status if this is still what they want *after* pregnancy.

However, this position—that *never* allows the person who sustained the pregnancy to be anything other than the legal mother, and to remain as the legal parent for the first six weeks after birth even if they mean to have the child adopted or to be given to its intended parents[144]—is a form of biological essentialism that is also exploitative. Presuming that a person who has been pregnant and births *must* feel a biological need 'to mother the resulting baby is a relic of a time when it was biologically impossible and socially unacceptable for people not to "mother" their biological children'.[145] Indeed, it is exploitative to co-opt the identity of a person who has facilitated gestation with bodily work and birthed by labelling them 'a mother'—and potentially enforcing care responsibilities—where they did not see this as their intention in undertaking pregnancy. Some may argue that starting legal motherhood from gestation may conscript, but it is the only way to protect pregnant people from exploitation since intention-based accounts of parenthood negate the fleshy-ness of the contribution of the person who was pregnant; it 'ignores the months she has spent *in a relationship with a* developing human being'.[146] This continues to promulgate essentialism and one way of understanding gestation and pregnancy. Moreover, it creates a false dichotomy in possible intention-based accounts. As I have argued with Mahmoud elsewhere:

> [An] intention-based parenthood model does not necessarily displace the gestating individual's central role in the creation of a new human entity.

[142] Department of Health and Social Security, *Report of the Committee of Inquiry into Human Fertilisation and Embryology* (Cmnd 9314, 1984) [8.17].

[143] Ingvill Stuvøy, 'Troublesome Reproduction: Surrogacy under Scrutiny' (2018) 7 Reproductive Biomedicine and Society Online 33–43, 38.

[144] Adoption and Children Act 2002, s 52(3); Human Fertilisation and Embryology Act 2008, s 54(7).

[145] Mahmoud and Romanis (n 9) 116.

[146] Shanley (n 14) 116.

> We see no reason why an intention-based model would not start from the gestating person's intention [to ensure some recognition of the bodily labour a gestator does in a way that does not conscript them].[147]

I am not denying that there are and will be circumstances where surrogacies can be exploitative—where a person is pressured or coerced—but we should not take from this that the law should be structured in a way that reinforces the idea that surrogacies—assisting another to become a parent by undertaken gestation—are *innately* exploitative. Rather, as Begović highlights, specificity is important; we must carefully 'identify in what ways it can be exploitative, and how this can be avoided'.[148] The law offering no flexibility about who the mother is does not prevent exploitation; it can sometimes enable it if we look at the biological essentialism it propagates. This seemingly indicates the motivation as concern about the fabric of the nuclear family where a third person plays a crucial role in a family's procreation[149] indicating the contemporary meaning of *mater semper certa est* is a legal deterrent against surrogacies for the protection of the nuclear family.

As this section has explored, there are several potential contemporary rationales for *mater semper certa est* that are clearly distinct from the (questionable) origins of this maxim. I have also illustrated why these rationales do not stand up to scrutiny. Understanding the potential rationales behind the rule that gestation is determinative of motherhood/parenthood is important context for thinking about the novel conceptual problems that are raised by novel gestations.

Novel Gestations; Novel Conceptual Problems

In a recent study, I asked reproductive rights advocates about novel technologies enabling gestation and the problems and pressures arising from their availability.[150] Overwhelmingly, participants stressed that the law surrounding

[147] Mahmoud and Romanis (n 9) 137.

[148] Dunja Begović, *Upholding Women's Autonomy in Pregnancy: Responding to the Challenges of New Reproductive Technologies* (PhD thesis, University of Manchester 2021) 138.

[149] Lewis stresses that surrogacy is considered problematic because it is 'antithetical to so-called traditional family values': Sophie Lewis, 'Defending Intimacy against What? Limits of Antisurrogacy Feminisms' (2017) 43 Signs: Journal of Women in Culture and Society 97–125, 100.

[150] Elizabeth Chloe Romanis, '"The Law is Very, Very Outdated and Not Keeping Up with the Technology": Novel Forms of Assisted Gestation, Legal Challenges, and Perspectives of Reproductive Rights Advocates in England and Wales' (2023) 10 Journal of Law and the Biosciences <doi.org/10.1093/jlb/lsad027> accessed 3 September 2024.

the attribution of parenthood was flawed but its conceptual failings would become even more evident with novel technologies enabling gestation.[151] As Brown explains, 'this choice to privilege gestation . . . reflects UK law's construction of motherhood as a *"natural", indivisible, process*'.[152] However, technologies enabling gestation have and will introduce challenges to this framing. Pregnancy-facilitated gestation is not necessarily an entirely 'natural' process where its inception follows assisted conception (in surrogacies because there need not be any genetic relation between the person sustaining the pregnancy and the conceptus), where it takes place in a transplanted uterus, or where it is facilitated (partially) by a machine. Moreover, it may no longer be an 'indivisible' form of work where another person contributes material to make the gestation possible—as in UTx—or where a machine takes over gestation in place of a person continuing a pregnancy (partial ectogestation). In what follows, I consider who the legal mother is where novel forms of gestation are used in the creation of new human entities. I highlight three serious conceptual challenges to the way that gestation and birthing are understood in the legal framework surrounding the attribution of parenthood. First, I look at the challenges where gestation becomes divisible work. Second, I consider the complexities of gestation beyond the confines of biosex. Finally, I examine the difficulties in attributing parental status where gestation takes place entirely ex utero. I argue that *mater semper certa est* makes little sense in many of these contexts: it is not clear who the legal mother is or should be.

Divisible gestation

Scholars have highlighted the many benefits UTx provides for people who want to become parents and gestate themselves, specifically that it 'not only enables the experience of gestation, but allows biological, social and legal parenthood, thereby avoiding some of the potential problems with surrogacy'.[153] Throughout the commentary on UTx, the person who gestates after a transplant is consistently identified as the legal mother.[154]

While UTx aligns intention to parent with gestation (the person who gestates does so because they want to parent) it also symbolizes a gestation where there are multiple people needed to make it possible. Mitochondrial Replacement

[151] ibid.
[152] Brown (n 10) 116 (emphasis added).
[153] Jones and others (n 17) 142.
[154] ibid; O'Donovan and others (n 16) 20.

Techniques (MRTs) (the process by which the mtDNA of the oocyte used to create an embryo is replaced with mtDNA from another person who produces ovum),[155] though a technique of assisted conception, is an interesting parallel with UTx. MRTs involve genetic contributions from three people (rather than the usual two) and there is a body of literature probing how this affects how we think about parenthood.[156] Some philosophers have been clear that the contribution of genetic material by donors in MRTs must clearly be understood as also denoting genetic parenthood in the philosophical sense,[157] though the genetic contribution from the mtDNA donor is deemed too small to be of note in the attribution of *legal* parenthood.[158] UTx, similarly, might involve a gestational contribution from two people (rather the one); one provides the organ that makes gestation possible and the other sustains the gestation with their bodily work. As explored in Chapter 2, in a pregnancy a fetus is a part of a pregnant person, a fetus is linked to and a part of the pregnant person's physiology and metabolism; it is functionally integrated.[159] In this sense, the gestational contribution of a pregnant person is the creation and sustaining of the environment in which a fetus can develop—it is the being of all that the fetus needs to be created.[160] This gestation, however, is mediated through the uterine wall, and in this way we might come to understand the donor as having making some gestational contribution too, as the donated material creates the means by which the gestation can occur in the first place. While no genetic material from the donor is passed to the fetus, the placenta is connected to the uterus endometrium (the inner lining of the uterus) and material from

[155] Marni Falk and others, 'Mitochondrial Replacement Techniques — Implications for the Clinical Community' (2016) 374 The New England Journal of Medicine 1103–06, 1104.

[156] McCandless and Sheldon (n 4); Johnson (n 98); I Glenn Cohen and others, 'The Regulation of Mitochondrial Replacement Techniques Around the World' (2020) 21 Annual Review of Genomics and Human Genetics 565–86; Rebecca Dimond, 'Social and Ethical Issues in Mitochondrial Donation' (2015) 115 British Medical Bulletin 173–82; César Palacios-González, 'Does Egg Donation for Mitochondrial Replacement Techniques Generate Parental Responsibilities?' (2018) 44 Journal of Medical Ethics 817–22; Catherine Mills, 'Nuclear Families: Mitochondrial Replacement Techniques and the Regulation of Parenthood' (2021) 46 Science, Technology, & Human Values 507–27.

[157] Palacios-González (n 156) 818.

[158] Department of Health, 'Mitochondrial Donation: Government response to the consultation on draft regulations to permit the use of new treatment techniques to prevent the transmission of a serious mitochondrial disease from mother to child' <https://assets.publishing.service.gov.uk/government/uploads/system/uploads/attachment_data/file/332881/Consultation_response.pdf> accessed 26 March 2023, 29; The Human Fertilisation and Embryology (Mitochondrial Donation) Regulations 2015 make no changes to the rules concerning legal motherhood in the Human Fertilisation and Embryology Acts 1990 and 2008.

[159] Elselijn Kingma, 'Were You a Part of Your Mother?' (2019) 128 Mind 609–46, 626.

[160] Michael Power and Jay Schulkin, *The Evolution of the Human Placenta* (Johns Hopkins University Press 2012) 74.

this endometrium constitute an important part of the placenta; blood vessels from the endometrium 'grow into' placental tissue,[161] penetrating it to facilitate the functional integration of fetus and pregnant person, which thus enables and impacts on the gestation. We should recognize that there is some gestational contribution on the part of the donated uterus, even if we do not think that would be sufficient to determine that the donor is a parent by virtue of a *gestational* contribution. Indeed, it is not a clear gestational connection—the contribution of a uterus donor is really no different from a kidney donor in enabling a person to gestate (a person cannot safely become pregnant with no working kidneys).[162] In the MRT literature a persuasive case has been made for the availability of MRTs to same-sex female couples wanting to reproduce in a way in which they have both made genetic contributions[163] (even if they are not both recognized as the *legal* mothers). One could imagine a scenario in a same-sex female couple where *both* want to contribute to the generative labour in procreation (particularly if one of the pair does not have a uterus—though this need not necessarily be the case). One of these contributions in terms of the gestation of a new entity is far more significant than the other (the person who is pregnant facilitates gestation, whereas the other person does not gestate but makes that gestation possible), it is interesting, nevertheless, that there has been limited reflection about the operation of the role affording the status of legal mother where the gestation is enabled by donor material.

While for the most part motherhood applying current rules here is self-evident, it is cases like UTx that require us to ask what it is about gestation that denotes the attribution of legal motherhood. It is the language of the HFE Acts 1990 and 2008 that made it clear that the person who sustains a pregnancy is the legal mother: 'the woman who is carrying or has carried a child as a result of the placing in her of an embryo or sperm and eggs'.[164] While a donated uterus sustains the 'carrying of' a fetus in a person's body, it is the person who is pregnant who is actually 'carrying' a fetus. Further, the reference to birthing ('parturition') in the common law also makes it very clear that it is the person who *births* that is the legal mother; since the new human entity emerges from the pregnant person's body, it is the pregnant person that must be the legal

[161] Neil Gude and others, 'Growth and Function of the Normal Human Placenta' (2004) 114 Thrombosis Research 397–407, 398.

[162] I am grateful to Dr Nicola Williams for this analogy.

[163] Giulia Cavaliere and César Palacios-González, 'Lesbian Motherhood and Mitochondrial Replacement Techniques: Reproductive Freedom and Genetic Kinship' (2018) 44 Journal of Medical Ethics 835–42.

[164] Human Fertilisation and Embryology Act 1990, s 33(1).

mother under the current framework. This is the answer that best promotes the contemporary rationales for *mater semper certa est* except perhaps concerns about exploitation. While thinking about exploitation about gestational labour would favour the mother claim of the pregnant person, if the motivation of the law is to prevent the exploitation of persons involved in the process of gestation, the uterus donor should surely be more visible?

Partial ectogestation more visibly makes gestation into divisible work. Similarly to UTx, there is not much written on how legal motherhood is attributed in *partial* ectogestation, because there is a person who sustains a pregnancy for a period before the developing human entity is extracted for continued gestation *extra uterum*. Thus, the person who facilitates gestation for that period is, under the current legal framework, the legal mother.[165] However, this only seems like a partly satisfactory answer. The gestation is partly undertaken inside a human body, rather than completely, allowing us some recourse to revisit how we conceptualize of gestation/birthing in the attribution of motherhood. Depending on how *extra uterum* gestation is designed and conceptualized, there may be additional people that believe they have built a biological gestational bond with a developing gestateling that would suffice to say they also had a gestational connection to it (eg they engaged with features of the artificial placenta that produce changes in the gestational environment, such as, recording their voice), even if that is not an embodied one. The criterion of gestation thus becomes less clear if different people were to make claims that 'gestation' (distinguishable from pregnancy) supported their claim to legal motherhood. It would certainly impact on the certainty that gestation as a criterion is thought to attribute. However, since the law at present has so deeply embedded within it the assumption that what attributes legal motherhood is 'parturition' or the 'carrying' of a fetus, it is likely the embodied gestational claim that would be favoured. This is a result of the fact that the law does emphasize the biological tie of gestation—the physical oneness where a fetus is a part of a pregnant person. Gestation being meaningful in the attribution of motherhood in the physical biological tie raises its own conceptual challenges in a slightly different set of circumstances. This illustrates the shaky foundations of the *mater semper certa est* maxim when we consider its contemporary meaning and try to apply it in the context of novel technologies enabling gestation.

[165] Romanis, *Regulating the 'Brave New World'* (n 18) 231.

Disembodied gestation

Complete ectogestation 'is unprecedented in that it creates a human being who has no "birth mother" in the usual sense'.[166] Alghrani writes that a machine capable of ectogestation clearly cannot be a 'mother'.[167] Several commentators have thus asked the question, who is the legal mother where no person has gestated?[168] As Hendricks explains:

> The claim that the gestator should be the legal parent assumes human gestation. That is, if parental status must vest in the gestator, then the gestator must be human; we are not going to assign parental rights to . . . mechanical incubators.[169]

Unlike partial ectogestation, where ectogestation is complete there is never a human person who sustains the generative process and/or physically brings the new human entity into the world from their flesh. Embodied gestation as the definitive attribute of legal motherhood cannot function as the sole and irrebuttable presumption in this context. Moreover, the potential contemporary justifications for *mater est*, whether any or all of legal certainty, recognition of a meaningful biological tie, preventing the exploitation of people who sustain pregnancies, do not point us to any obvious or clear answers where gestation is disembodied.

How the current legal framework might respond were such a problem to arise imminently is difficult to anticipate. On the one hand, the law has emphasized the importance of biology in the insistence that the pregnant person is the legal mother, and in much of the law surrounding natural procreation. Against this backdrop, one could speculate that the law would 'fall back' onto genetics to identify the legal parents as the genetic progenitors of a resulting child from complete ectogestation. As Sander-Staudt explains, children born of complete ectogestation 'would have no actual "birth mother" but only a "genetic mother"'.[170] In many ways, this seems likely since the law, as I have illustrated in Chapter 5, tends to reinforce biosex roles in procreation. Moreover, it seems

[166] Maureen Sander-Staudt, 'Of Machine Born? A Feminist Assessment of Ectogenesis and Artificial Wombs' in Scott Gelfand and John Shook (eds), *Ectogenesis: Artificial Womb Technology and the Future of Human Reproduction* (Rodopi 2006).
[167] Amel Alghrani, *Regulating Assisted Reproductive Technologies: New Horizons* (CUP 2018) 259.
[168] Natasha Hammond-Browning, 'A New Dawn? Ectogenesis, Future Children and Reproductive Choice' (2018) 14 Contemporary Issues in Law 349–73, 370.
[169] Hendricks, 'Not of Woman Born?' (n 19) 53.
[170] Sander-Staudt (n 166) 124.

plausible that many people's intuitions would jump to genetics where there is no person sustaining gestation by being pregnant; indeed, many people's intuitions favour genetics[171] even where there is assisted gestation involving a third person (eg surrogacies).[172]

However, equally, the law has, in the context of assisted *conception*, been very clear that genetics are of less importance than an intention to be treated as the parent of a new human entity.[173] Any inconsistency with the law surrounding assisted conception might be rather alarming, especially considering there may be some people who need to use both assisted conception techniques and complete ectogestation to procreate, for example a same-sex male couple may need an oocyte donor. It is plainly confusing that an oocyte donor (who has no intention to parent) could be recognized as the legal mother because of their genetic contribution where ectogestation was used, but not where they used surrogacy. The example exemplifies how people AFAB have little freedom to shape how their biological contributions to procreation are recognized. Similarly, a trans man or non-binary person who produces ovum and does not want to be pregnant because it would potentially be dysphoric or because they *do not want to be recognized as the legal mother* may welcome the opportunity of ectogestation to procreate where their partner cannot gestate, their partner does not want to gestate, or they do not have a partner. Again, it seems baffling that such an individual could be identified as the legal mother because of a genetic contribution where they would not in any other context (if their partner or a surrogate had gestated). Both examples exemplify how LGBTQ+ families are excluded by a legal order that continually emphasizes a biological connection (whether gestational or genetic) in the attribution of parenthood.[174]

How might intention play out in the context of *extra uterum* gestation? In the context of surrogacies, Horsey has explained:

> [B]ecause the intended parents initiate, plan and prepare for the birth of the child, they should be legally recognised as the parents of that child that, *but for them, would not exist.* It is they who choose to use assisted conception, thus choosing whether to use a donor of genetic material or a surrogate. They

[171] Avery Kolers and Tim Bayne, '"Are You My Mommy?" On the Genetic Basis of Parenthood' (2001) 18 Journal of Applied Philosophy 273–85, 274.

[172] This is reflected in the law to some degree eg the conditions for a parental order require a genetic link between at least one of the intended parents and the resulting child per the Human Fertilisation and Embryology Act 2008, s 54(1)(b). I am grateful to Dr Zaina Mahmoud for discussions on this point.

[173] Brown (n 10) 121.

[174] Romanis, '"The Law is Very, Very Outdated"' (n 150).

are the 'first cause' of the child and as such are of prima facie importance in the procreational relationship.[175]

This way of conceptualizing of intention centralizes factors beyond gestation, which is exactly to make the point that, for Horsey, the role of a gestational surrogate performing the work is of less importance when considering how to attribute parenthood. Intention-based accounts tend to think about the broader social facts of parenting that exist far beyond gestation.[176] Where embodied gestation is no longer a potential factor, it might be possible to adapt our thinking slightly to include thinking about who was involved in forms of gestational work while the entity is *ex utero* as a part of this notion of the intended parents as the 'first cause' of the child, for example, who records their heartbeat for the machine to play, who speaks into the artificial placenta device, etc? These behaviours might feed into broader exploration of the intention to become parents. How would a claim from a person who has involved themselves here with an intention to parent weigh up against someone else who expresses an intention to parent but cannot demonstrate that they took part in the gestation even though it was *extra uterum*? These might be important considerations, but it is important to also think about how this might stratify access to legally recognized parenthood.

As I explored in Chapter 4, access to procreative assistance in the form of complete ectogestation as a choice is likely to be more difficult for people marginalized based on class and/or race, and people with limited economic resources. The way that thinking about expectations of caring relationships during ectogestation, and taking this into account in assigning parental rights, might be another way of further cementing that ectogestation is a technology of the privileged. Spending time involved in the gestation of an entity in an artificial placenta is different from undertaking gestation. While no longer a form psychofleshy work, the work of visiting a medical facility to 'spend time with'[177] the gestateling is now a demand of a different nature: one of time and resources (eg for getting to the facility). This is simply more challenging for people who work demanding jobs, or do low-paid work,[178] and/or have limited parental leave and need to save this for when there is a baby (post-ectogestation) that

[175] Kirsty Horsey, 'Challenging Presumptions: Legal Parenthood and Surrogacy Arrangements' (2010) 22 Child and Family Law Quarterly 439–74, 472.

[176] Jonathan Herring, *Caring and the Law* (Hart 2013) 200.

[177] See Chapter 2 on the distinction between the gestateling and neonate and the extent to which the gestateling can be interacted with.

[178] Romanis, 'Assisted Gestative Technologies' (n 139) 645.

needs physical care.[179] For families with more income and/or no existing children, attending a facility to be involved in ectogestation is a much more realistic ask. Those who would be least likely to struggle are more likely to be those who have existing and entrenched social privileges: being from a higher social class, being white, and having resources like a car, or the ability to not work, or the ability to hire childcare for any existing children.

The neonatal intensive care unit (NICU) makes for an interesting comparison here—though it is important to note the degree of difference in the physical care a parent could provide to a neonate and a prospective parent to a gestateling. I point this out because it is even more understandable why people who might struggle to get time off work/arrange childcare for existing children/afford travel to a medical facility are even less likely to achieve attending regularly *before* their child is born. Davis illustrates how, in the American NICU, health professionals are known to construct motherhood and enforce their perceptions of maternal failure through various mechanisms (eg calling or threatening to call social services).[180] She uses the response to people who are unable to attend the NICU everyday (mostly because of resources) as a particular example and emphasizes the 'power medical professionals had in referring Black women and men's worth and status as parents. Black women, in particular, have not been respected as mothers'.[181] It is easy to see how, even if a gestateling cannot be interacted with in the same physical sense, putative parents who turn up every day—likely to be those with class privilege and those who do not experience the systemic social effects of racism—will be treated by health professionals as the 'better parents'. Thus, there are clearly negative implications of thinking about behaviour during the ectogestation period as proof of an intent to parent in the attribution of legal parenthood.

With ectogestation, there is not just the matter of how to determine parental status where there is only a partial pregnancy or no pregnancy at all; there is also the question of *when* one becomes a legal parent.[182] Singh, and subsequently Mahmoud and I, have made the case that parenthood is a relational status and thus one becomes a parent once an entity has been born into the world.[183] Thus, Mahmoud and I argue gestation is not mothering, and

[179] Victoria Hooton and Elizabeth Chloe Romanis, 'Artificial Womb Technology, Pregnancy, and EU Employment Rights' (2022) 9 Journal of Law and the Biosciences <doi.org/10.1093/jlb/lsac009> accessed 3 September 2024, 1–33, 18–19.

[180] Dána-Ain Davis, *Reproductive Injustice: Racism, Pregnancy, and Premature Birth* (New York University Press 2019) 77.

[181] ibid.

[182] Romanis, 'Assisted Gestative Technologies' (n 139).

[183] Prabhpal Singh, 'Fetuses, Newborns & Parental Responsibility' (2020) 46 Journal of Medical Ethics 188–93; Mahmoud and Romanis (n 9).

highlight the problem with the HFE Act 2008 describing a mother as a person 'carrying' a pregnancy.[184] Horsey and Jackson concur, legal motherhood is afforded 'at birth'.[185] As I explained in Chapters 2 and 3, in partial ectogestation, a pregnant person has *birthed* but their product of conception has not *been born*.[186] It seems intuitive that parental rights and responsibilities kick in at birth, when there is an entity to be cared for, though where that entity is still undergoing gestation (albeit no longer a part of a pregnant person) that gestateling does not have the same relational needs. However, if we do not afford parental rights over entities in the artificial placenta, there is the potential for excessive medical control where intended parents have little say over clinical decisions made about their gestateling.[187] It seems intuitive that a person who has *birthed* even if their intended future child is not yet born because it is the subject of *extra uterum* gestation attain the rights and responsibilities of the legal mother—they had carried the entity and *birthed* it: and it will need a legal parent in relation to decisions made about it. The same logic in theory could be applied to complete ectogestation. A gestateling gestated entirely *extra uterum* would need legal parents to make decisions for it. What would be important to emphasize, however, is the importance of the distinction between a gestateling and a fetus, to emphasize that there are no parental rights over fetuses, even if there are parental rights over gestatelings, to protect the rights of pregnant people. Who these people are, however, remains confusing where there is no person who gestates. The legal mother (and therefore) the father is not certain.

Unsexed gestation

As explored in Chapter 5, novel technologies enabling gestation—particularly UTx—have the capacity to 'unsex' procreative capacities and enable people assigned male at birth (AMAB) to undertake generative, procreative work. Horsey and Alghrani have both raised the question of UTx enabling trans men or cis men to gestate and what this might mean for the attribution of

[184] ibid.

[185] Kirsty Horsey and Emily Jackson, 'The Human Fertilisation and Embryology Act 1990 and Non-Traditional Families' (2023) 86 Modern Law Review 1472–88, 1478.

[186] Elizabeth Chloe Romanis, 'Artificial Womb Technology and the Significance of Birth: Why Gestatelings are Not Newborns (or Fetuses)' (2019) 45 Journal of Medical Ethics 728–31.

[187] This might be a concern even if there are parental rights afforded since ectogestation will likely be a highly medicalized process: Victoria Adkins, 'Impact of Ectogenesis on the Medicalisation of Pregnancy and Childbirth' (2021) 47 Journal of Medical Ethics 239–43.

parenthood.[188] The HFE Act 2008 specifies that 'the *woman* who is carrying or has carried a child as a result of the placing in her of an embryo or of sperm and eggs, and no *other woman*, is to be treated as the mother of the child'.[189] Alghrani, writing in 2018, questioned whether a child born following male gestation (whether trans man or cis man) would therefore be legally motherless, since no woman 'carried' the pregnancy.[190] The *McConnell* case, however, has made it clear that a man gestating does not mean the resulting child is motherless, finding that a person who gestates is a mother, irrespective of their gender identity.[191] The judgment is insistent that mother is a gender-neutral term, and although it did recognize the imposition on trans men who gestate, this could not change the fundamental legal definition of who a mother is.[192] Would the same determination would have been made if a cis man were to gestate and birth? The law has consistently continued to reinforce a traditional, nuclear family model; a child has two parents—usually a mother and a father.[193] Indeed, on paper a family where there is a mother and a father fits the nuclear model in some ways, but such a family also challenges the fabric of the cis-heteronormative assumptions behind the nuclear family where both the mother (person who sustained the pregnancy) and father (sperm contributor) are male. Further, would a court continue to reify the same 'parental labels are gender neutral' in a circumstance where the male person who undertook pregnancy was raising the child with a woman? This leads us into a deeper exploration of the additional questions about the attribution of parenthood where cis men gestate. If they are the mother, who is the other parent?

Where a person has a transplanted uterus, conception would be assisted, and so rules would be dictated by the HFE Acts. Where the male person who undertook pregnancy is married or in a civil partnership their husband/wife/civil partner will be the father/second female parent unless it is shown they do not consent.[194] However, the law does not accommodate the possibility of the pregnant person being a man, it specifies 'where a woman is married to . . . or civil partner of a man at the time of treatment'[195] or where the case of a 'woman in civil partnership or marriage to a woman at time of treatment'.[196] In

[188] Alghrani (n 167) 255; Kirsty Horsey, 'Legal Parenthood and Parental Responsibility' in Ruth Lamont (ed), *Family Law* (OUP 2022) 325.
[189] s 33(1).
[190] Alghrani (n 167) 255.
[191] *McConnell* (n 3).
[192] ibid at [35].
[193] Brown (n 10) 7.
[194] Human Fertilisation and Embryology Act 2008, s 35 and s 42.
[195] ibid s 35.
[196] ibid s 42.

such a circumstance, if the statute were to be interpreted literally, this marital/civil partner presumption would not apply. Another person would be the father/second female person only where both they, and the person who will sustain the pregnancy, consented to them being the father/second female parent during treatment and the agreed fatherhood/second female parenthood conditions are met.[197] Where the pregnant person is a man (with a transplanted uterus), much like where the pregnant person is a woman who has undergone assisted conception, what genetic contributions had (or had not) been made are irrelevant. Thus, if the other person contributed the ovum,[198] and the person who sustains the pregnancy had also contributed the sperm, the pregnant person would still be the mother and their partner the second female parent. Here, there may be another huge conceptual and linguistic challenge to the nuclear family model—effectively an inversion. The man would be referred to legally as the mother because of their role in gestation and the woman legally described as the second female parent (even though there is no 'first' female parent). This is something that lawmakers and courts would be likely to take more seriously as a challenge to the scheme of regulation around parenthood because of the tendency at present to focus on procreation as a biosexed activity (and thus render trans reproduction invisible). In *McConnell*, gestation by a trans man was treated as a technical matter, rather than a conceptual challenge to the entire scheme of legal rules.[199] Procreation beyond the limitations of biosex—embodied in a heterosexual man AMAB gestating and being labelled a mother—is something that is far more likely to spark fundamental reform surrounding the attribution of parenthood since it strikes at the heart of cis-heteronormative conceptions of the family. This challenge is likely to give more pause to the notion that *the mother is always certain* by virtue of being the person who gestates.

Finally, as has been explored in Chapter 5, there are those who have advocated that disembodied gestation is effectively unsexed gestation where there is a conceptual decoupling of bodies AFAB and gestation.[200] I explained that UTx in cis men was likely to have far more transformative potential to socially engrained ideas about who 'mothers' and 'fathers' are than ectogestation. This applies just as much to how we *identify* and *define* these roles in legal terms as

[197] ibid s 37 and s 44.

[198] This person could produce their own ovum if they are biotypically AFAB, or ovum could be generated through *in vitro gametogenesis*.

[199] Alan Brown, 'Trans Parenthood and the Meaning of "Mother", "Father" and "Parent"—*R (McConnell and YY) v Registrar General for England and Wales* [2020] EWCA Civ 559' (2021) 29 Medical Law Review 157–71, 169.

[200] See Chapter 6.

it does in thinking about how social expectations are placed on persons identified as mothers and fathers. Ultimately, novel forms of gestation pose important conceptual challenges to the way that gestation is legally understood and centralized in the attribution of parenthood—both mothers and fathers. At present, the law's insistence that the mother is the person who facilitates gestation is the mother perpetuates sexed, embodied, and 'whole' accounts of gestation that simply no longer make sense where we pay proper attention to technologies enabling gestation, particularly UTx and ectogestation. We need to revisit more carefully, and free from biosexed essentialism and assumptions about gestation and pregnancy and how they are understood by individuals, whether mediated by (AFAB) bodies or not, 'what is it that makes a parent?'

Disembodied gestation also raises broader questions of procreative rights in relation to bodily work. This is discussed in Chapter 7.

7
ABORTION

Much like procreating itself, pregnancy is an experience that many value,[1] but no person should be forced to undertake gestational work unwillingly.[2] As Overall puts it, 'pregnancy is such a demanding, all-enveloping, potentially transformative physical and psychological process that no woman[/person] should have to go through it against her[/their] will.'[3] I believe this to be an intuitive and simple claim, and further, I would argue that novel procreative technologies, including technologies enabling gestation, have no bearing on the morality of abortion whatsoever. Unwilling pregnancy is never justifiable. As I argue in this chapter, abortion decisions are about more than bodily autonomy (as they can encompass decisions beyond whether to end a pregnancy), however, since pregnancy is bodily work matters of bodily integrity will always be pertinent and must remain in the foreground of our thinking about the importance of access to abortion into the future (encompassing novel technologies enabling gestation). The right to end a pregnancy always belongs to the person undertaking pregnancy (whether they are an intended parent or not).

The literature on *ectogestation* is dominated by work questioning the ethics of abortion if gestation beyond bodies becomes possible. Many scholars have argued that if the justification for abortion is that persons should not be forced to facilitate gestation with bodily work unwilling, Artificial Amnion and Placenta Technology (AAPT) ought to be welcomed as a means of freeing people from the burden of forced pregnancy without this necessarily resulting in fetal death.[4] In response, there is a growing body of feminist

[1] See Chapters 2 and 3.
[2] Judith Jarvis Thomson, 'A Defense of Abortion' (1971) 1 Philosophy & Public Affairs 47–66; David Boonin, *A Defense of Abortion* (CUP 2003); Maggie Little, 'Abortion, Intimacy, and the Duty to Gestate' (1999) 2 Ethical Theory and Moral Practice 295–312, 303.
[3] Christine Overall, 'Rethinking Abortion, Ectogenesis and Foetal Death' (2015) 46 Journal of Social Philosophy 126–40, 127.
[4] Peter Singer and Deane Wells, 'Ectogenesis', in Scott Gelfand and John Shook (eds), *Ectogenesis: Artificial Womb Technology and the Future of Human Reproduction* (Rodopi 2006) 9–25; Eric Mathison and Jeremy Davis, 'Is There a Right to the Death of the Foetus?' (2017) 31 Bioethics 313–20; Christopher Kaczor, *The Edge of Life: Human Dignity and Contemporary Bioethics* (Springer 2005); Christopher Kaczor, *The Ethics of Abortion: Women's Rights, Human Life, and the Question of Justice* (Taylor & Francis 2010); Christopher Kaczor, 'Ectogenesis and a Right to the Death of the

Biotechnology, Gestation, and the Law. Elizabeth Chloe Romanis, Oxford University Press.
 DOI: 10.1093/9780191986574.003.0007

literature that challenges the strength of this claim.[5] The focus on abortion in the ectogestation literature detracts attention from considering the possibilities of what this technology, and indeed other novel technologies enabling gestation, have the potential to do. The focus on how ectogestation 'diminishes' the justifications for abortion (as defenders of this view would put it) exemplifies how procreative technologies can be used to structurally oppress and abuse people. I believe the arguments against abortion in the advent of this technology are a distraction,[6] and that such claims embody a nefarious use of ectogestative technologies. This chapter offers a summary of the arguments and the reasons why they are unpersuasive. I consider the implications of how we frame a defence of abortion in light of AAPT and what this might mean in other contexts. Most importantly, I reflect on *why* the literature is dominated by theorizing about abortion, the problems this focus causes, and feminist legal futures for abortion and procreative justice.

In this chapter, I first explain the importance of abortion as a basic tenet of procreative justice and offer arguments explaining why the development of novel technologies enabling gestation has no bearing on the importance of abortion access. Second, I outline the claims made in the bioethics literature that ectogestation is an 'alternative' or 'solution' to abortion, or that it can offer a 'compromise' position on abortion, as well as the feminist responses to these arguments. The arguments presenting ectogestation as 'the end of abortion',

Prenatal Human Being: A Reply to Räsänen' (2018) 32 Bioethics 634–38; Bruce Blackshaw and Daniel Rodger, 'Ectogenesis and the Case Against the Right to the Death of the Foetus' (2019) 33 Bioethics 76–81; William Simkulet, 'Abortion and Ectogenesis: Moral Compromise' (2020) 46 Journal of Medical Ethics 93–98; Christopher Stratman, 'Ectogestation and the Problem of Abortion' (2021) 34 Philosophy & Technology 683–700; Christopher Kaczor, 'The Artificial Womb and the End of Abortion' in N Colgrove, BP Blackshaw, and D Rodger (eds), *Agency, Pregnancy and Persons: Essays in Defense of Human Life* (Routledge 2022); Michal Pruski and Richard Playford, 'Artificial Wombs, Thomson and Abortion – What Might Change?' (2022) 19 Diametros 35–53.

[5] Christine Overall, *Human Reproduction, Principles, Practices, Policies* (OUP 1993); Leslie Cannold, 'Women, Ectogenesis and Ethical Theory' (1995) 12 Journal of Applied Philosophy 55–64; Amel Alghrani, 'The Legal and Ethical Ramifications of Ectogenesis' (2007) 2 Asian Journal of WTO & International Health Law and Policy 189–212; Sarah Langford, 'An End to Abortion? A Feminist Critique of the "Ectogenetic Solution" to Abortion' (2008) 31 Women's Studies International Forum 263–69; Emily Jackson, 'Degendering Reproduction?' (2008) 16 Medical Law Review 346–68; Claire Horn, 'Ectogenesis is for Feminists: Reclaiming Artificial Wombs from Antiabortion Discourse' (2020) 6 Catalyst: Feminism, Theory, Technoscience 1–15; Claire Horn, *Gestation Beyond Mother/Machine: Legal Frameworks for Artificial Wombs, Abortion and Care* (PhD thesis, Birkbeck University of London 2020); Elizabeth Chloe Romanis and Claire Horn, 'Artificial Wombs and the Ectogenesis Conversation: A Misplaced Focus? Technology, Abortion, and Reproductive Freedom' (2020) 13 International Journal of Feminist Approaches to Bioethics 174–94; Evie Kendal, 'Pregnant People, Inseminators and Tissues of Human Origin: How Ectogenesis Challenges the Concept of Abortion' (2020) 38 Monash Bioethics Review 197–204.

[6] I had thought, to avoid contributing to the distraction, that I would not include a chapter about abortion in this book at all. It came to be on the insistence of reviewers.

I argue, are premised on several excessive abstractions and misconceptions. As Patterson-Brown and Watson recently put it, proposing ectogestation 'as a substitute for abortion is a dangerous waste of time'.[7] Third, following on from this argument, I reflect on why and how abortion has come to dominate the thinking around ectogestation and the harms that this propagates. I draw inspiration from the feminist philosophy of science literature[8] to demonstrate the problematic operative background assumptions within the debates on ectogestation, leading to an excessive focus on abortion. Finally, I reflect on what debates about abortion and ectogestation mean for legal frameworks, considering that abortion is criminalized in *most* jurisdictions. While it is evident in England and Wales that novel forms of assisted gestation pose no direct threat to abortion access within the contemporary legal framework (because of how the law is constructed),[9] this is not as clear in other jurisdictions. This matters against the context of the echo chamber of arguments and campaigning against abortion in the ectogestation context and in the contemporary climate. I explore how we must orient towards better legal futures that are properly attentive to the importance of abortion. This is all in recognition of the fact that pregnancy is bodily work.

Abortion and Abstraction

Debates about abortion in the philosophical literature situate themselves in abstraction, treating decisions about continuing a pregnancy similarly to other hypothetical moral dilemmas. Some degree of abstraction is taken to be necessary in analytical philosophical method. Ruddick writes that 'philosophical discussion is of course abstract and is meant to be'.[10] However, there is increasing recognition of the importance of abstracting *appropriately*—particularly in applied ethics. As Basu has explained, '[i]t is naïve and irresponsible to think that philosophy takes place in a vacuum, and not in a society rich with real-world consequences and practical import'.[11] Abortion, specifically the question whether it is justified and under what circumstances, remains a

[7] Benjamin Patterson-Brown and Katie Watson, 'No Substitute: The False Promise of Artificial Womb Technology as an Alternative to Abortion' (2023) 23 American Journal of Bioethics 87–89, 88.

[8] I am grateful to Dr Eric Bayruns García for pointing me in the direction of this literature and acknowledge that he will find it irritating that I have done so in a footnote.

[9] This will be demonstrated in the last section of this chapter.

[10] Sara Ruddick, *Maternal Thinking: Towards a Politics of Peace* (Beacon Press 1989) 96.

[11] Rima Basu, 'Risky Inquiry: Developing an Ethics for Philosophical Practice' (2023) 38 Hypatia 275–93, 277.

matter of philosophical fascination, with multitudes of papers rehashing the same ground published every year. Against this intellectual echo-chamber, the real-world context is rather jarring.

Abortion is common. One in three women* in England and Wales[12] and one in four women* in the United States[13] have an abortion by the time they are forty-five. In 2020, there were 18.6 (legal) abortions per 1,000 women* in England and Wales,[14] and 11.2 (legal and recorded) abortions per 1,000 women* in the United States.[15] Furthermore, for abortion-seekers, abortion is a *necessity*. As Janiak and Goldberg have observed, despite the tendency for abortion to be categorized as a choice or an option in the face of unwanted pregnancy, most abortion-seekers do not feel that their abortion is a matter of choice at all; 'the notion of continuing this particular pregnancy is absolutely out of the question for them'.[16] Abortion is generally supported by the public in Western high-income economies. In the UK, a YouGov poll (reporting in 2023) suggests that 88 per cent of adults believe that women* should have the right to abortion.[17] The Pew Research centre estimates that 61 per cent of Americans are in favour of abortion being legal in all or most cases.[18]

Legal context is also important: abortion rights and access remain illusory and fragile in many places. Across the UK, abortion access is improving, but it remains a crime in England and Wales under the relevant legislation.[19]

[12] Genevieve Edwards, '1 in 3 women has an abortion, and 95% don't regret it – so why are we so afraid to talk about it?' (2015) *The Independent* <https://www.independent.co.uk/life-style/health-and-families/features/1-in-3-women-have-an-abortion-and-95-don-t-regret-it-so-why-aren-t-we-talking-about-it-10392750.html> accessed 15 August 2023. The term woman is used in the source of the data and so I have used it here.

[13] Rachel Jones and Jenna Jerman, 'Population Group Abortion Rates and Lifetime Incidence of Abortion: United States, 2008–2014' (2017) 112 American Journal of Public Health 1225–1345, 1288. The term woman is used in the source of the data and so I have used it here.

[14] Department of Health and Social Care, 'Abortion statistics, England and Wales: 2021' <https://www.gov.uk/government/statistics/abortion-statistics-for-england-and-wales-2021/abortion-statistics-england-and-wales-2021> accessed 14 August 2023. Statistics in England and Wales are reasonably accurate because registered medical practitioners are required (per the Abortion Act 1967) to notify the Chief Medical Officer of every abortion. The word women is used in the source and so I have used the same language.

[15] Katherine Kortsmit and others, 'Abortion Surveillance—United States, 2020' (2022) 71 Surveillance Summaries 1–27 <https://www.cdc.gov/mmwr/volumes/71/ss/ss7110a1.htm?s_cid=ss7110a1_w.html> accessed 14 August 2023. It is important to note that these statistics are likely to be an underestimate given the difficulty many people have accessing abortion through formal channels in the United States. The word women is used in the source and so I have used the same language.

[16] Elizabeth Janiak and Alisa Goldberg, 'Eliminating the Phrase "Elective Abortion": Why Language Matters' (2016) 93 Contraception 89–92, 91.

[17] YouGov, 'Should women have the right to an abortion?' <https://yougov.co.uk/topics/politics/trackers/should-women-have-the-right-to-an-abortion> accessed 14 August 2023.

[18] Pew Research Center, 'Public Opinion on Abortion' <https://www.pewresearch.org/religion/fact-sheet/public-opinion-on-abortion/> accessed 14 August 2023.

[19] Elizabeth Chloe Romanis, 'Abortion Access and the Benefits and Limitations of Abortion-Permissive Legal Frameworks: Lessons from the United Kingdom' (2023) 32 Cambridge Quarterly of

There is public support for decriminalization,[20] but political attempts to decriminalize in England and Wales have fallen short.[21] In the United States, the constitutional abortion right was dismantled by the Supreme Court in 2022[22]—stripping people with the physiology to become pregnant of a right that had existed, at least in name, for the past fifty years.[23] The last two years have seen increasingly hostile attempts by state legislatures across the United States to enact restrictions on abortion access.[24] In many states, these attempts have not greatly restricted access, since it had already been all but impossible.[25] In those places where abortion is criminalized, the effects of the criminal law (invasive investigation and punitive consequences) are borne disproportionately by marginalized populations.[26] Abortion access is a pressing issue, even in US States that have not taken steps to prohibit abortion, as well as in other jurisdictions with abortion-permissive legal regimes.[27] For people who need access to abortion, the mainstream philosophical literature is often not speaking to the problems they are facing.

Basu argues that:

> in a world where transmisogynistic violence is rampant, to contribute to a philosophical discourse that would further encourage such violence carries with it high moral risks and those risks ought to constrain how we conduct philosophical inquiry on such matters.[28]

Against the abortion context outlined, that the philosophical literature continues to focus on the justifications for abortion, as opposed to issues of access

Healthcare Ethics 378–90, 380; abortion is criminal per the Offences Against the Person Act 1861, ss 58 and 59 and Infant Life (Preservation) Act 1929, s 1.

[20] Anne Marie Gray and Kaye Wellings, 'Is Public Opinion in Support of Decriminalisation?' in Sally Sheldon and Kaye Wellings (eds), *Decriminalising Abortion in the UK: What Would it Mean?* (Policy Press 2020) 17–36.

[21] There was a successful *partial* decriminalization of abortion in Northern Ireland with the repeal of the relevant sections of the Offences Against the Person Act 1861, but the same provisions remain in force in England and Wales. In Scotland, abortion is a crime by virtue of the common law.

[22] *Dobbs v Jackson Women's Health* 597 US 215 (2022).

[23] See Elizabeth Chloe Romanis, 'The End of (Reproductive) Liberty as We Know It: A Note on Dobbs v. Jackson Women's Health 597 USC (2022)' (2023) 23 Medical Law International 71–87.

[24] ibid 79–84; Emily Ottley and others, '*Dobbs v Jackson Women's Health Organization* (2022): Consequences One Year On' (2023) 31 Medical Law Review 457–68.

[25] See Jordan A Parsons and Elizabeth Chloe Romanis, *Early Medical Abortion, Equality of Access, and the Telemedical Imperative* (OUP 2021) Ch 3.

[26] Michele Goodwin, *Policing the Womb: Invisible Women and the Criminalization of Motherhood* (CUP 2020) 11.

[27] Romanis, 'Abortion Access' (n 19) 382–83.

[28] Basu (n 11) 279.

and the related ethical problems,[29] epitomizes the moral risks that Basu describes. Boonin, in the preface to his famous philosophical defence of abortion, wrote that it is 'distasteful . . . to think of abortion as purely a theoretical issue . . . grappled with only in the abstract and impersonal terms'.[30] He continues, 'abortion is not like other intellectual puzzles where little is at stake beyond the mere display of philosophical acumen, and it is objectionable to think of it as if it were'.[31] In academic discussion, determining what is an ethical issue for debate, and the terms on which the debate is engaged in, is a political choice. As I have argued with Horn elsewhere, suggesting that the morality of abortion provision is a thorny philosophical problem is political in that 'it passes judgment on whether the community should allow the availability of a choice that many pregnant persons would consider a personal and private matter'[32] and that is certainly a matter of (medical) necessity. There is a clear potential for translational harm from the focus in the debate as 'ethical argumentation is often translated directly to political argumentation'.[33]

Even setting this issue of the influence of ethical argumentation aside, some academic questions, or ways of posing a question, can be seen to inherently demean or dehumanize the persons about whom the question/s are asked.[34] There is a tendency in the argumentation around abortion, and especially surrounding ectogestation, to ignore people with the physiology to become pregnant and to negate their experiences of unwanted pregnancy. At times, the complete decentralizing of pregnant people in the discussion verges on dehumanization. These individuals, and the material knowledge generated from their experience/s, are abstracted from the inquiry in the way that abortion is predominantly discussed—most obviously in that abortion is described as the problem, rather than *unwanted pregnancy*. There is also disregard for the necessity of legal abortion to evade the negative health consequences associated with criminalizing the practice.[35]

In the philosophical literature, the conversation around abortion has been dominated by two strands of debate. The first, and most dominant until recently, centres around the question of whether a fetus is a person. Most scholars who focus on this question take the position that the permissibility of abortion

[29] Margaret Matthews, Aashna Lal, and Danielle Pacia, 'The Role of Epistemic Injustice in Abortion Access Disparities' (2022) 22 American Journal of Bioethics 49–51; Romanis, 'Abortion Access' (n 19).
[30] Boonin (n 3) xiv.
[31] ibid.
[32] Romanis and Horn (n 5) 181.
[33] ibid.
[34] Basu (n 11) 278.
[35] See Fiona De Londras and others, 'The Impact of Criminalisation on Abortion-related Outcomes: A Synthesis of Legal and Health Evidence' (2020) 7 BMJ Global Health e010409.

is determined by the answer to this question.[36] Work that takes the status of a fetus as the material matter is an example of this abstraction from real-world considerations taken too far. As Little explains, centring this question of fetal personhood means that:

> we can end up thinking of fetuses, not just as persons, but as persons *atomistically situated*, as physically individuated and separate—as though the bundle of specified rights at issue for the fetus are the same bundle we commonly face walking down the street in everyday life.[37]

To focus on fetal status and fetal attributes is to abstract away the most crucial aspect of its existence: that it is a part of a pregnant person.[38] Disappointingly, however, authors who take the approach that I advocate are routinely asked to provide a detailed defence of the position that the fetus is not a person[39] (a task that some feminist philosophers have risen to),[40] whereas scholars who make the opposite assumption seemingly are not challenged to justify their starting positions in this way.

The second dominant framing of the philosophical debate about abortion sets aside the question of fetal personhood (taking it to be irrelevant) and instead focuses on the matter of whether any person[41] has the right to demand the use of another's body for survival.[42] While this approach does have the advantage of centring the pregnant person, it too has suffered from some problems resulting from abstraction. First, while this discussion (including the famous violinist analogy by JJ Thomson)[43] does emphasize the bodily work involved in sustaining a gestation, this is often in a narrow sense. For example, where people make arguments about an obligation to sustain a pregnancy, they mostly neglect the social—in addition to the physical—consequences of pregnancy. They abstract away material conditions that make pregnancy a huge ask, for example, rising maternal mortality rates in high-income economies[44]

[36] This is the position of some scholars who believe the fetus is a person as well as scholars who do not eg Kate Greasley, *Arguments about Abortion: Personhood, Morality and Law* (OUP 2017) 86.

[37] Little (n 3) 299.

[38] See Chapter 2.

[39] Romanis and Horn (n 5) 185.

[40] Mary Anne Warren, 'On the Moral and Legal Status of Abortion' (1973) 57 The Monist 43–61; Mary Anne Warren, 'The Moral Significance of Birth' (1989) 4 Hypatia 45–65.

[41] Scholars making this argument often assume that the fetus is a person to strategically show the strength of the argument.

[42] Thomson (n 3).

[43] ibid.

[44] Birthrights, 'Systemic Racism, Not Broken Bodies: An Inquiry into Racial Injustice and Human Rights in UK Maternity Care' (2022) <https://www.birthrights.org.uk/wp-content/uploads/2022/05/Birthrights-inquiry-systemic-racism_exec-summary_May-22-web.pdf> accessed 28 November 2023.

(embedded institutional racism means this particularly impacts racialized groups)[45] and the economic costs of pregnancy (in a capitalist world in which discrimination against pregnant people, particularly from the working classes, is rife). Further, it abstracts away from the fact that unwanted pregnancy is experienced only by a subset of people;[46] people with the physiology to become pregnant, who are often discriminated against in other contexts based on *assumptions about* their sex assigned at birth and corresponding assumptions about gender. As many feminist scholars have recognized, the importance of having access to abortion is not just in the preservation of bodily autonomy, but in that there can be no *meaningful* equality for people with the physiology to become pregnant without the availability of abortion.[47]

Absent the ability to end a pregnancy, anyone who is or *can* become pregnant is denied that their body (and conception of self) is their own.[48] There are objectors to abortion who may not follow this line of reasoning on the basis that they believe there is moral responsibility for the creation of a fetus where persons engage in consensual penis-in-vagina sex.[49] Their argument would suggest that persons with the capacity to become pregnant have individuation: they can refuse to engage in activity that risks them becoming pregnant or they can use contraception. This position is steeped in the responsibilization of people who can become pregnant for the consequences of sexual activity, to the exclusion of the responsibility of people who can inseminate.[50] Power dynamics around sexual activity can mean that, even where sex is consensual, people with the capacity to become pregnant (gendered as women) are burdened with contraceptive responsibility, but it can be hard for them to assert that people with penises (gendered men) also exercise responsibility. What I mean by this is that the gender dynamics around sex, accompanied by social norms and expectations, often mean that it is hard for people being penetrated

[45] See Dána-Ain Davis, *Reproductive Injustice: Racism, Pregnancy, and Premature Birth* (NYU Press 2019); Keisha Ray, *Black Health: The Social, Political, and Cultural Determinants of Black People's Health* (OUP 2023).

[46] David O'Brien, 'Fairness, Care, and Abortion' (2023) 40 Journal of Applied Philosophy 658–75.

[47] Drucilla Cornell, *The Imaginary Domain: Abortion, Pornography and Sexual Harassment* (Routledge 1995) 33; Rosemary Nossiff, 'Gendered Citizenship: Women, Equality, and Abortion Policy' (2007) 29 New Political Science 61–76; Elizabeth Chloe Romanis, 'Abortion & "Artificial Wombs": Would "Artificial Womb" Technology Legally Empower Non-gestating Genetic Progenitors to Participate in Decisions about How to Terminate Pregnancy in England and Wales?' (2021) Journal of Law and the Biosciences <doi:10.1093/jlb/lsab011> accessed 4 September 2024.

[48] Cornell (n 47) 47.

[49] Timothy Kirschenheiter, 'Responsibility Arguments in Defence of Abortion: When One is Morally Responsible for the Creation of a Fetus' (2023) 29 The New Bioethics 340–51.

[50] Arianne Shahvisi, 'Towards Responsible Ejaculations: The Moral Imperative for Male Contraceptive Responsibility' (2020) 46 Journal of Medical Ethics 328–36.

to demand use of a condom.[51] Other contraceptive methods for people with physiology assigned female at birth (AFAB) place emphasis on altering (temporarily or longer-term) that person's fertility by altering their hormonal profile and/or physicality (eg altering cervical mucus). The side effects of such measures ought not be downplayed: they can fundamentally change a person's mood, appetite, appearance, and consequently, for many, sense of self. The (un)acceptability of contraceptives is a highly individuated matter contingent on individual embodied experience.[52] Moreover, the chorus that people ought to protect themselves from pregnancy by 'just using long term contraception' is ignorant of the context in which they are made. Marginalized and racialized populations have long been coerced into the use of long-acting reversible contraceptives with eugenic undertones.[53] Whatever contraception is used, where the individuals involved are fertile, there is *never* a zero chance of becoming pregnant when engaging in penis-in-vagina sex. Moreover, as the most important response to this line of argumentation, it is not being able to undo a pregnancy that results in a lack of control over one's body once pregnancy is established. Insisting that a pregnancy could have been prevented in the first place is of little utility to person's experiencing the *dysphoria* of unwanted pregnancy. As Tongue has described this dysphoria, bodily changes in pregnancy (where unwanted) that are 'experienced subjectively by each pregnant person, can represent estrangement from . . . one's body'.[54]

A final critique is not an issue with abstraction but rather with framing and the story that is told in describing pregnancy as 'sustaining' the life of another entity. Much work frames continuing a pregnancy as a 'rescue', or aiding a more vulnerable entity that cannot survive on its own. As such, some scholars have deployed care-based feminist challenges to abortion, arguing that there can be a duty to rescue.[55] I argue that such arguments are also flawed because of an inaccurate framing of pregnancy, which continues to neglect the material conditions I highlighted earlier in this section.

As Pattinson explains of thought experiments in general, '[s]ome of the most demanding ethical and legal challenges are presented by the very complexity

[51] Leah East and others, 'Condom Negotiation: Experiences of Sexually Active Young Women' (2019) 67 Journal of Advanced Nursing 77–85, 78.

[52] Jenny Higgens and Nicole Smith, 'The Sexual Acceptability of Contraception: Reviewing the Literature and Building a New Concept' (2016) 53 The Journal of Sex Research 417–56.

[53] Krystale Littlejohn, *Just Get on the Pill: The Uneven Burden of Reproductive Politics* (University of California Press 2021).

[54] Zoe Tongue, 'Locating Abortion and Contraception on the Obstetric Violence Continuum' (2024) 17 International Journal of Feminist Approaches to Bioethics 1–24, 14.

[55] Gina Schouten, 'Fetuses, Orphans, and a Famous Violinist: On the Ethics and Politics of Abortion' (2017) 43 Social Theory and Practice 637–65.

and uncertainty that it is so tempting to ignore'.[56] In trying to find the 'purest' form of ethical problems, it is often the case that detail that makes the problem messy, complex, and puzzling is removed, and as such the answer produced by ethical reasoning is of little utility where these details are added back in. Abstract discussions about abortion (of which the ectogestation debate is one example) have failed to centre pregnant persons, their needs, and what is at stake when making procreative decisions.[57] Much, if not most, philosophical reasoning about abortion is abstracted from the material conditions in which people experience the need to end a pregnancy. The literature that has emerged about ectogestation is no exception. Stratman writes that 'the possibility of ectogestation will radically transform the problem of abortion'.[58] Similarly, Hopkins asks 'would such technology [ectogestation] actually fix the social problem of abortion by giving everyone what they want?'[59] These statements exemplify that much (if not most) speculative work about AAPT embodies the same issues as scholarship about abortion in contemporary context by describing abortion as the problem, rather than recognizing it as *a solution* to an unwanted pregnancy.

The Ectogestation-Abortion Debate

As long as there has been a bioethical and legal literature about ectogestation, it has focused on the putative implications of this technology for abortion. This literature centres around the claim that that, with AAPT available, it will become possible to, conceptually and practically, separate 'the termination of pregnancy and the death of the fetus'.[60] As Freitas put it in 1980, if ectogestation were available, 'unwilling pregnant women have an alternative to feticide or unwanted childbirth'.[61] From these observations comes the central claim, recurring in the literature, that:

[56] Shaun Pattinson, *Law at the Frontiers of Biomedicine* (Bloomsbury Publishing 2023) 4.
[57] Katrina Kimport and Monica McLemore, 'The Problem with "Justifying" Abortion: Why Real Reproductive Justice Cannot Be Achieved by Theorizing the Legitimacy of Abortion' (2022) 9 Women's Reproductive Health 27–31, 29.
[58] Stratman (n 4) 683.
[59] Patrick Hopkins, 'Can Technology Fix the Abortion Problem?' (2008) 22 International Journal of Applied Philosophy 311–26, 315.
[60] Mathis and Davidson (n 4) 313–14; Blackshaw and Rodger (n 4) 77–78; Stratman (n 4) 684.
[61] Robert Freitas, 'Fetal Adoption' (1980) 40 The Humanist 22–23.

> Freedom to choose what is to happen to one's body is one thing; freedom to insist on the death of a being that is capable of living outside's one body is another.[62]

Essentially, the argument goes: a pregnant person has the right to end an unwanted pregnancy but does not have the right to the death of the fetus.[63] This position is also put in terms that clearly indicates what they are taking the central problem to be. Ectogestation has been described as an 'alternative to',[64] a 'compromise' in place of,[65] a 'solution for',[66] and 'the end to'[67] abortion. Most people who take this position state it thus, with little defence, and attention directed rather to counterarguments, rather than substantiating the case for moral or legal interference with the private choice to seek abortion.[68] These arguments have not gone unanswered. There has emerged a body of feminist literature defending a moral right to abortion in the advent of ectogestation,[69] and imagining legal frameworks that might best protect access to abortion.[70] Much of this work serves to ground the analysis by highlighting material conditions and explanations as to why we should not ignore them. Thus, this work removes some of the unjustifiable abstraction around ectogestation and abortion that has become so common.

Bodily autonomy and ending a pregnancy

Kaczor advocates that the disagreement about abortion in the context of ectogestation comes down to what abortion is taken to mean. If abortion is defined as 'the right not to be pregnant' then partial ectogestation, he writes, 'would solve the problem'.[71] He claims that since most scholarship (mostly that by philosophers and medics) defends abortion as a right of evacuation at present, this at least changes the nature of the abortion conversation. A defence

[62] Singer and Wells (n 4) 12.
[63] Perry Hendricks, 'There is No Right to the Death of the Fetus' (2018) 32 Bioethics 395–97.
[64] Simkulet (n 4) 93.
[65] Hopkins (n 59) 312.
[66] ibid.
[67] Singer and Wells (n 4); Kaczor, 'The Artificial Womb and the End of Abortion' (n 4).
[68] Indeed, at least one philosopher who made the case against abortion in the advent of this technology—see Stratman (n 4)—has since published a piece explaining why there ought to be no legal interference with the choice to seek abortion.
[69] See (n 5).
[70] Claire Horn, 'Abortion Rights after Artificial Wombs: Why Decriminalisation is Needed Ahead of Ectogenesis' (2021) 29 Medical Law Review 80–105; Horn, *Gestation Beyond Mother/Machine* (n 5).
[71] Kaczor, 'The Edge of Life' (n 4) 107.

of abortion must, he argues, shift to an explicit defence of the right to fetal death.[72] This framing seeks to treat the matter of a person's bodily autonomy as now entirely irrelevant. In this conceptualization, bodily autonomy is sufficiently realized in the ending of a pregnancy, such that moral demands can be made of persons in *how* that ending of the pregnancy is undertaken. However, such an understanding fails to appreciate both the material differences between extraction for ectogestation and abortion,[73] and the proper substance of a right to bodily autonomy.

Describing ectogestation and abortion as simply two forms of ending a pregnancy, however, is to significantly abstract away from what each process involves. This is a strategy that is common amongst those making the argument against abortion in light of ectogestation. For example, Stratman postulates that:

> It is not incoherent or implausible to think that fetal transfer would involve a surgery that is at least equally or, perhaps, even less invasive and risky than current lethal forms of terminating one's pregnancy.[74]

Similarly, Kaczor writes:

> Ex hypothesis, partial ectogenesis, as imagined in the future, would not be dangerous for women. Many procedures that were dangerous and invasive 40 years ago, now are safe. Even so, the choice would presumably not be between no danger and danger, but between the dangers of abortion, the dangers of ectogenesis, and the dangers of later term childbirth.[75]

Extraction for ectogestation is simply *not* the same procedure as an abortion, nor is it one that harbours comparatively similar risks. Fetal transfer to AAPT could feasibly not occur before the entity had obtained fetal physiology,[76] which, at the very earliest, would be thirteen weeks gestation[77] (though in all likelihood, because of the size of AAPT, it would be much later in gestation that an entity could be supported).[78] Yet, most abortions in high-income economies

[72] ibid.
[73] Romanis, 'Abortion & "Artificial Wombs"' (n 47).
[74] Stratman (n 4) 688.
[75] Kaczor 'The Edge of Life' (n 4) 108.
[76] Seppe Segers and Elizabeth Chloe Romanis, 'Ethical, Translational, and Legal Issues Surrounding the Novel Adoption of Ectogestative Technologies' (2022) 15 Risk Management and Healthcare Policy 2207–20, 2209.
[77] Romanis, 'Abortion & "Artificial Wombs"' (n 47) 7.
[78] This fact of how the device functions was discussed at a recent meeting of the US Food and Drug Administration Pediatric Advisory Committee Meeting about artificial wombs on 19 and 20 September

like England and Wales take place before nine weeks' gestation.[79] Thus, any requirement to undergo fetal transfer as one's means of securing freedom from pregnancy amounts to placing upon pregnant people an obligation to remain pregnant for a period against their will. Even if this were not the case, however, the nature of the processes of extraction versus an abortion are illustrative of how they should not be considered comparable in the way that the abstracted argument makes them seem.

A transfer to AAPT is complex and intricate, since interventions are necessary to ensure that there is no fetal-to-neonatal physiology transition during extraction and transfer.[80] This means a caesarean section,[81] and it would likely be a more technical and elaborate surgery since it would be undertaken earlier in gestation.[82] Studies on animal models have thus far attempted only to undertake transfer by caesarean section to maintain as much control as possible over the entity during the process. A caesarean section involves the pregnant person being administered anaesthesia, after which an incision is made through both the abdominal wall and the uterine wall to extract the fetus.[83] As a major surgery, it poses substantial risks to the pregnant person including those associated with the use of anaesthetics, blood loss, surgical injuries to the bowel and/or bladder, and an increased likelihood that any future pregnancies would have to be delivered surgically.[84] By way of contrast, most abortions in high-income economies like England and Wales are medication abortions,[85] which involve the administration of two medications orally/vaginally in a twenty-four to forty-eight-hour window.[86] The World Health Organization (WHO) recommends medication methods of abortion until twelve weeks' gestation.[87] Possible side effects from these medications are mild; stomach

2023, see < https://www.fda.gov/advisory-committees/pediatric-advisory-committee/2023-meeting-materials-pediatric-advisory-committee> accessed 16 November 2023.

[79] Department of Health and Social Care (n 14).

[80] M Beatrijs van de Hout-van der Jagt and others, 'Interprofessional Consensus Regarding Design Requirements for Liquid-Based Perinatal Life Support (PLS) Technology' (2022) 9 Frontiers in Pediatrics <doi.org/10.3389/fped.2021.793531> accessed 4 September 2024.

[81] Seppe Segers and others, 'The Ethics of Ectogenesis-aided Foetal Treatment' (2020) 34 Bioethics 264–370, 367. Though some have hypothesized that a vaginal delivery may not be wholly impossible if the physiological challenges can be overcome see ibid.

[82] Romanis (n 47).

[83] I am grateful to Dr E Joanne Verweij for discussion of this process.

[84] See National Health Service, 'Risks – Caesarean Section' <https://www.nhs.uk/conditions/caesarean-section/risks/> accessed 20 November 2023.

[85] 87% of abortions in England and Wales in 2021 were medication abortions: Department of Health and Social Care (n 14).

[86] World Health Organization, 'Abortion Care Guideline' <https://www.who.int/publications/i/item/9789240039483> accessed 6 November 2023, 68.

[87] ibid.

pain, indigestion, diarrhoea, vomiting, and headaches.[88] Medication abortions (in which a miscarriage is triggered by drugs) are thus clearly far less invasive, enable a person a greater degree of personal privacy (in many jurisdictions, the medications can be lawfully administered at home),[89] and involve a much lesser degree of risk to the pregnant person's health and life than a caesarean section for fetal transfer.[90] Where medication abortion is not appropriate or an alternative is preferred, abortion-seekers can have a surgical termination, such as vacuum aspiration or dilation and evacuation. Sometimes these procedures can necessitate local or general anaesthetic, or conscious sedation, but in comparison to caesarean section are both a much briefer and less complex procedures (vacuum aspiration can take between three and ten minutes; dilation and evacuation between ten and thirty minutes).[91] While these procedures carry some risks associated with surgical intervention, they are much lesser than a fetal transfer surgery would be because of the lower level of complexity, how routine these procedures are, and because they are less invasive (not involving incision through muscle and then an organ).

The risks associated with abortions, whether medication or surgical, are so much lesser that we should consider Kaczor's comparison between 'the dangers of ectogestation' and 'the dangers of abortion'[92] to be clearly disingenuous. In response to these comparisons, he has since claimed that technological possibilities ought not to be discounted; '[g]iven the advancements of the last 100 years, I would hesitate to rule out technical possibilities' of fetal extraction becoming comparable methods of abortion' Kaczor argues.[93] Such a position is plainly fanciful, and a clear move back into unjustifiable abstraction,[94] given the reality that a fetus is a part of a pregnant person (it is embedded into the uterine wall), and the necessity of the entity to be extracted to have developed sufficiently (so that it has fetal physiology) before extraction.

Bohn posits that, where a pregnant person wants to end their pregnancy, '[n]o one mandates that she have a procedure; they merely restrict which procedures she[/they] may choose'.[95] The argument she is making is that where

[88] British Pregnancy Advisory Service, 'Pills by Post – Abortion Treatment at Home: Expected Effects of Treatment' <https://www.bpas.org/abortion-care/abortion-treatments/the-abortion-pill/remote-treatment/> accessed 20 November 2023.
[89] Parsons and Romanis (n 25) 89.
[90] Romanis, 'Abortion & "Artificial Wombs"' (n 47) 12.
[91] For a full description see Parsons and Romanis (n 25) 2–3.
[92] Kaczor 'The Edge of Life' (n 4) 108.
[93] Kaczor, 'The Artificial Womb and the End of Abortion' (n 4) 181.
[94] It is unclear how Kaczor imagines an entity might be extracted non-invasively.
[95] Jessalyn Bohn, 'The Feminists' Dilemmas' in Colgrove, Blackshaw, and Rodger (eds), *Agency, Pregnancy and Persons* (n 4) 201.

ectogestation is available—pregnant persons would not be mandated to remain pregnant, or to end their pregnancy, but if they do choose to end that pregnancy they would just have the one available option of doing so. What this fails to recognize is that decisions about *how* to end a pregnancy are as much a matter of person's bodily autonomy as the matter of deciding to end the pregnancy. As Kendal explains, proper recognition of bodily autonomy means a pregnant person 'has a right to choose from among her[/their] treatment options' including those that are conducive to transfer to AAPT and those that are not.[96] Given the varying impact that the termination choices above have on person's bodies, and in different ways, the decision a person may want to make in this situation will be personal, based on their preferences about physical risks as well as their sense of physical self. The argument given against abortion in favour of fetal transfer as sufficient to protect bodily autonomy only recognizes a narrow conception of bodily autonomy;[97] as a matter of, in this context, only deciding to not be physically pregnant, rather than as a matter of making decisions about one's physicality. Forcing someone to have an invasive surgery must be considered to be as serious as forcing them to continue a pregnancy unwillingly and, of course, would go against norms of consent and constitute a major human rights violation. It is for this reason that some (though, sadly, few) proponents of ectogestation as an alternative to abortion recognize that fetal extraction cannot be morally *required* of pregnant people, because people must be permitted to choose less invasive procedures.[98]

Beyond bodily autonomy

Horn argues that continuing to focus on a defence of abortion rights on the basis of bodily autonomy 'leaves abortion rights contingent on the degree to which a convincing argument can be made that a procedure is physically invasive'[99] and thus 'on its own is insufficient'.[100] Such a move is also one into abstraction, since it, to some degree, is negating some of the material physicality of abortion that I have argued it is problematic to abstract from. However, recognition that abortion is a matter of bodies *and* of imagined futures does

[96] Kendal (n 5) 199.
[97] This is very clear in work by Bohn in which she suggests that offering an ectogestation-compatible procedure in place of abortion, or induced labour in place of a requested caesarean section, is respectful of people's bodily autonomy. See Bohn (n 95) 200.
[98] Mathison and Davis (n 4).
[99] Horn 2020 (n 5).
[100] Horn, 'Ectogenesis is for Feminists' (n 5) 7.

make visible that abortion embodies other meanings and sources of importance for people experiencing unwanted pregnancy. Many commentators have emphasized that in the 'perverse daydream' of ectogestation in place of abortion[101] there is a lack of consideration of the abortion-seeker's rights *not* to reproduce.[102] As Langford explains, for many, '[t]erminating a pregnancy is but a means to an end. The end is preventing motherhood'.[103] Similarly, Jackson has observed that few abortion-seekers want to simply avoid pregnancy and labour; their aim is to evade biological parenthood.[104]

Objectors to this line of argumentation assert that the choice to abort should not be recognized as rejecting biological parenthood, because they subscribe to the misconception that once pregnant, a person is already a parent.[105] I have already fully refuted this conceptualization of pregnancy and parenthood in Chapter 2.[106] The reality is that termination of pregnancy (and not the coerced use of AAPT) is the only way for persons to conclusively reject the social burdens of motherhood that, through both social and legal mechanisms,[107] are strongly imposed on those who gestate and birth.[108] Bringing an unwanted child into the world is something that is deeply distressing to birthing people.[109] Kaczor has suggested that 'if we consider psychological burdens, then abortion may be (all things considered) more burdensome than partial ectogenesis'.[110] This position, however, is based on the dubious claim that abortion causes psychological harm to pregnant people,[111] as opposed to the concrete psychological harms of being forced to procreate.

Critics of the argument that pregnant people must be entitled to reject procreating (and thus may have an abortion rather than having to opt for ectogestation to end their pregnancy) often espouse a chorus of 'but what about men [or the non-gestating genetic progenitor] too?'[112] The argument

[101] Patterson-Brown and Watson (n 7).
[102] ibid.
[103] Langford (n 5) 265.
[104] Jackson, 'Degendering Reproduction?' (n 5) 362.
[105] Christopher Kaczor, 'The Artificial Womb and the End of Abortion' in Colgrove, Blackshaw, and Rodger (eds), *Agency, Pregnancy and Persons* (n 4) 183.
[106] See also Zaina Mahmoud and Elizabeth Chloe Romanis, 'On Gestation and Motherhood' (2023) 31 Medical Law Review 109–40.
[107] Such as how gestation is determinative of parentage at birth (see Chapter 6) and a number of criminal offences that make anonymous birth unlawful in England and Wales.
[108] Romanis, 'Abortion & "Artificial Wombs"' (n 47).
[109] Cannold (n 6).
[110] Kaczor, 'The Artificial Womb and the End of Abortion' (n 105) 181.
[111] EM Dadlez and William Andrews, 'Post-Abortion Syndrome: Creating an Affliction' (2010) 24 Bioethics 445–52.
[112] Iain Brassington, 'The Glass Womb' in Frida Simonstein (eds), *Reprogen-Ethics and the Future of Gender* (Springer 2009) 197–210.

is that we cannot afford respect to a pregnant person's right not to procreate without violating the other genetic progenitor's right to procreate. While a person does not have a right to use another person's body to fulfil their desire to procreate, some argue that the ectogestation context is different: that it allows one to respect pregnant person's bodily autonomy and the other genetic progenitor's right to procreate simultaneously.[113] As I have set out, forcing ectogestation as the only means of ending an unwanted pregnancy does not actually respect pregnant persons' bodily integrity and autonomy in a meaningful way and is overly abstracting. For argument's sake, however, let's engage in abstraction from the body to illustrate how this argument remains flawed when contemporary social conditions are taken duly into consideration. Gendered and sexed socially enforced norms of parental responsibility mean that the implications of unwanted procreation are much greater for people who have birthed (predominantly women). As Jaggar has explained, social conditioning, reinforced by law,[114] means 'most women's lives are totally changed as the result of the birth of a child, while men can choose how much they wish to be involved'.[115] Moreover, the law constructing motherhood from gestation in a way that is practically immutable[116] entrenches the centrality of the person who gestated in a born child's life. Consequently, those who gestate but do not parent are socially vilified as not only 'bad mothers' but 'bad people', whose behaviour is unexplainable by reference to traditional notions of gender.[117] A potential mother must always, therefore, have the responsibility for deciding whether to continue a pregnancy (and they, of course, can consult the other genetic progenitor if they wish).[118] Such conditions are deeply socially-engrained.[119]

Abortion is not only about bodily autonomy and procreative autonomy, but it is also a basic tenet of equality for people who have the capacity to become pregnant. Without recognition of the moral right to abortion, Cornell explains, 'there can be no meaningful equality for women'[120] (and other people with the capacity to become pregnant). Where a person is denied the ability to make decisions about becoming or remaining pregnant, they are denied the ability

[113] ibid.
[114] For example, with the passing of policies that result in people who birth being the primary care giver of a child.
[115] Alison Jaggar, 'Abortion and a Woman's Right to Decide' in Alison Jagger (ed), *Living with Contradictions: Controversies in Feminist Social Ethics* (Routledge 1994) 283.
[116] See Chapter 6; Mahmoud and Romanis (n 106).
[117] Romanis, 'Abortion & "Artificial Wombs"' (n 47) 33.
[118] Jaggar (n 115) 283.
[119] See analysis in Chapter 6.
[120] Cornell (n 47) 22.

to think of themselves as an integrated self with (through their decisions) some control over their selfhood and its boundaries.[121] Without the ability to make choices about pregnancies, their biological capacity for pregnancy becomes thus cemented as a fundamental aspect of that person's being; should they become pregnant, they cannot end that state of being. The State is enabled to 'conscript women [and people with the capacity to become pregnant] to give their bodies against their will to deliver children at its legal demand'.[122] This has the effect of reducing people who can become pregnant to only that capacity, and consequently, treating them as 'second-class citizens'.[123] Abortion enables people with the capacity to become pregnant to engage in sexual activity without feeling defined and restricted by the possibility of pregnancy. Without it, procreation is state-mandated in a manner that reinforces biological essentialism (around 'biological' procreative destiny).

Kaczor has disputed abortion as necessary for equality by posing the following question:

> If half of all CEOs in Fortune 500 companies are not female, doesn't this show that women are not yet equal to men? In the United States, we've had abortion on demand since January 1973.[124]

Setting aside the obvious inaccuracy in describing the *Roe* era in the United States as 'abortion on demand', when there were such severe problems with access across much of the country[125] (and the nonsense notion that the number of female CEOs is indicative of equality across society), Kaczor misunderstands that abortion is necessary but not sufficient for social equality. Abortion is important to ensure that we recognize the individuation of people who can become pregnant, but it does nothing to address systemic sexism and racism in capitalist structures (and no one was claiming that it did). The United Nations Committee on the Elimination of Discrimination Against Women concluded in 2018 that criminalization of abortion, and denying abortion, amounted to discrimination because it denied a service that some need (only people with the physiology to become pregnant).[126] Denial of abortion, of course, can

[121] ibid 47.
[122] Rebecca Cook and Bernard Dickens, 'Human Rights Dynamics of Abortion Law Reform' (2003) 25 Human Rights Quarterly 1–59, 44.
[123] ibid.
[124] Kaczor, 'The Artificial Womb and the End of Abortion' (n 4) 190.
[125] See Parsons and Romanis (n 25) Chapter 3.
[126] They used the language of woman here, I have adjusted this to better reflect who can become pregnant: United Nations Committee on the Elimination of Discrimination against Women, 'Inquiry concerning the United Kingdom of Great Britain and Northern Ireland under article 8 of the Optional

exacerbate the inequalities embedded in capitalist societies, because unwanted pregnancies can have serious social, economic, health, and cultural consequences,[127] and denying abortion can therefore enforce on people life conditions (motherhood) that often result in structural discrimination.[128] There is no reason to suppose that coerced uses of AAPT to end pregnancies would result in a different outcome than that forced pregnancy already has in contemporary conditions—including entrenching social scripts rooted in misogyny (about the role of bodies assigned female at birth).[129]

The substance of the abortion right

I agree that the substance of the moral right to abortion encompasses more than a recognition of a pregnant person's bodily autonomy, not least because the reproductive justice framework highlights how entangled any notion of bodily autonomy is with context: that is the safe environment, resources, and other support a person must have to make decisions.[130] It is insufficient for the State to refrain from interference with the moral right to abortion, for the right to abortion to have real meaning there must be 'the establishment of conditions in which safe abortions are available to women[/people] of every race, class and nationality'.[131] Horn has argued that conceptualizations of the abortion right in the ectogestation debate which continue to centre bodily autonomy leave 'abortion rights contingent on the degree to which a convincing argument can be made that a procedure is physically invasive'.[132] She continues that the right constructed in this way is therefore always precarious and lacks any care for pregnant persons.[133] However, to decentre bodily integrity as a crucial aspect of the abortion right is, again, a move into abstraction that could have significant implications. I am not arguing that we should return to thinking of abortion rights as *strictly* a matter of bodily autonomy and nothing else, but

Protocol to the Convention of the Elimination of Discrimination against Women: report of the Committee on the Elimination of Discrimination against Women' <https://digitallibrary.un.org/record/1480026?ln=en> accessed 16 November 2023.

[127] Kate Hunt and Mike Gruszczynski, 'The Ratification of CEDAW and the Liberalization of Abortion Laws' (2019) 15 Politics & Gender 722–45, 730–31.

[128] See Cook and Dickens (n 122) 44.

[129] Patterson-Brown and Watson (n 7) 89.

[130] Loretta Ross and Rickie Solinger, *Reproductive Justice: An Introduction* (University of California Press 2017) 9.

[131] Cornell (n 47) 33.

[132] Horn, *Gestation Beyond Mother/Machine* (n 5) 99.

[133] ibid.

rather that in broadening the recognition of what abortions are for, bodily integrity ought not to be completely disregarded. Not least because of the centrality of this concept in both legal and medical frameworks.

The physicality of the work of gestation sustained by pregnancy is not something that can or should be set aside in thinking about abortion rights. First, it sets aside some of the important aspects of decision-making about abortion that will be material to pregnant people. For many who wish to have an abortion, the desire is not just to have one, but to have it *as soon as possible*. Our bodies are fundamentally tied to our sense of physical integrity and of being. The physicality of pregnancy, where that state of being is unwelcome (because of the awareness that abortion is necessary/the pregnancy is unwanted), can cause serious distress and discomfort for individuals. For some, it may be distressing because it changes their boundaries of being. It is for this reason that delays in accessing abortion can be a serious affliction; persons are forced to remain in a dysphoric state where their conception of themselves and their being are misaligned with their embodiment. Once we recognize the central problem as unwanted pregnancy, these bodily harms—in addition to the reproductive and social harms of forced pregnancy—become visible. Even where arguing for abortion rights, reasoning that does not start from the body can perpetuate the same notion of the fetus as atomistically situated which I highlighted earlier in this chapter as having substantive harms.[134]

Second, disregarding the centrality of bodily autonomy opens up the possibility of persons other than the pregnant person making claims that they are entitled to participate in decision-making about abortion. Some persons, such as the sperm contributor, may argue that they are equally impacted, in terms of their psychosocial wellbeing, by the existence of a child and consequently, that they should have a say in abortion decisions.[135] While the availability of novel forms of assisted gestation, alongside surrogacies, should not be considered to have a significant impact on the availability of abortion, there are some instances where there are multiple people who might believe they have a stake in abortion decisions. The social harms of forced reproduction are significantly impacted by gendered and sexed norms, and this can to some extent account for differences between persons making claims about abortion. After all, the social implications of persons understood to be 'mothers' choosing not to

[134] Barbara Katz Rothman, *The Tentative Pregnancy: Prenatal Diagnosis and the Future of Motherhood* (Viking 1986); Rosalind Pollack Petchesky, 'The Power of Visual Culture in the Politics of Reproductions' (1987) 13 Feminist Studies 263–92; see also Ch 2.

[135] Joona Räsänen, 'Ectogenesis, Abortion and a Right to the Death of the Fetus' (2017) 31 Bioethics 697–702.

parent are far greater than for persons understood to be 'fathers'.[136] However, the reality remains that being attentive to the geography of gestation is critical in explaining who can make decisions about continued gestation. Where gestation is sustained by a pregnant person, any decision about continued gestation impacts primarily on their bodily boundaries and selfhood and, as a consequence, that decision must be theirs. While disagreements about abortion in surrogacies are rare,[137] where these occur the decision (and the consequences) must belong to the surrogate. Similarly, they would be entitled to refuse to end a pregnancy. This is also relevant in the case of UTx. Surgeons undertaking the procedure have noted that complications from rejection could arise and observed that 'the life and health of the recipient should always be the priority, even when threatened during a pregnancy before expected neonate viability'.[138] It is important that pregnancy termination remains lawful because it will be necessary to terminate pregnancies, even where a person has undertaken UTx because they really wanted to be pregnant, to save pregnant person's lives. Surgeons have also noted the possibility that in such cases regnant people may refuse hysterectomy (and the ending of the pregnancy) and in such cases, they note, 'the medical team must thoroughly counsel the patient concerning the consequences' and provide psychological support and immune suppression treatment.[139] Such an approach is important because forcing the end of a pregnancy where a person refuses should be as of much concern as forcing a person to remain pregnant.

The relevance of bodily integrity thus explains why a person cannot be forced to continue an unwilling pregnancy or undergo extraction for ectogestation, but also why decisions about continued gestation where the entity is being gestated in AAPT might reasonably involve more than one person.

The Focus on 'Abortion Solutions'

New procreative technologies often raise questions about abortion. Acknowledging the ectogestation and abortion conversation as 'another disheartening example of bioethicists' obsession with high-tech

[136] Romanis, 'Abortion & "Artificial Wombs"' (n 47) 34.

[137] Deborah Forman, 'Abortion Clauses in Surrogacy Contracts: Insights from a Case Study' (2015) 49 Family Law Quarterly 29–54, 30–31.

[138] Mats Brännström and others, 'Uterus Transplantation: From Research, through Human Trials and into the Future' (2023) 29 Human Reproduction Update 521–44, 534.

[139] ibid.

hypotheticals',[140] Patterson-Brown and Watson declare that '[e]thicists should be clear and consistent in delineating the appropriate use of' ectogestation, rather than looking at it as an abortion alternative.[141] That the focus has, nevertheless, been primarily on abortion justifications is telling; fetal extraction is argued for as a reasonable alternative to abortion procedures precisely because the wrong 'problem' is consistently identified by scholars in procreative ethics. Lloyd observes that 'background assumptions and values can play a role in specifying the very object of inquiry'.[142] While she was writing about science rather than ethics, her observation is just as true of ethics and of law as academic disciplines. What is identified as the pertinent or pressing ethical or legal question is revealing about the background assumptions and values of the thinker situated within their discipline, or even of the discipline itself. The bioethics/ethico-legal literature's echo chamber questioning the permissibility of (or, in response, reiterating the permissibility of) abortion has become damaging in that it is distracting us from the appropriate moral and legal questions.

The language used to describe ectogestation, as the 'solution' or 'compromise' to abortion, and also to describe abortion itself in the ectogestation literature, is emblematic of the background assumption at play: that abortion always needs explanation and justification. This reiteration of abortion as the problem has become so normal that it is seemingly accepted as objective to approach unwanted or dangerous pregnancies as questions about the permissibility of abortion, rather than how these conditions can be alleviated (with the most obvious *answer* being abortion). This way of thinking about abortion is highly pervasive. The permissibility of abortion is treated as one of the fundamental problems in applied ethics: it is the subject of as many books and is featured on every applied ethics/bioethics syllabus. As I have observed with Horn elsewhere:

> [A]uthors who take the position that abortion is in need of some greater justification beyond that of respecting the importance of a private choice of termination are less frequently subject to challenge for their starting position than those who approach ethico-legal issues from the starting point of abortion as healthcare.[143]

[140] Patterson-Brown and Watson (n 7) 88.
[141] ibid.
[142] Elisabeth Lloyd, *The Case of the Female Orgasm: Bias in the Science of Evolution* (Harvard University Press 2005) 242.
[143] Romanis and Horn (n 5) 185.

With the starting point of abortion needing justification being so widespread, it can consequently be difficult for scholarship that centralizes the problem of *unwanted pregnancy* (eg looking at abortion access) to be published[144] or seriously engaged with. This is because it starts from a fundamentally different premise. This leaves us with the question of how and why the literature on ectogestation (and abortion more generally) has come to be dominated by the premise that abortion is the moral problem to be addressed.

What is taken to be a suitable starting assumption for inquiry is, inevitably, the result of disciplinary practices, which are, in turn, contingent on who makes up the community and constructs the dominant culture of the discipline. Where marginalized groups are excluded from recognition as 'qualified' researchers within a discipline, it is inevitable that the social values, interests, and agendas that might better reflect their experience are excluded from determinations about the 'objective approach' to identifying problems in need of investigation.[145] Traditionally, philosophy (and applied ethics) paid little attention to those issues impacting on the lives of people with the physiology to become pregnant. This can be related both to the historical exclusion of women from the discipline, but also to the way in which women have been (and often are still) characterized as 'less qualified thinkers' within philosophy.[146] Where a group of people (women and/or people with the physiology to become pregnant) are excluded or taken less seriously, there is the exclusion of knowledge rooted in their (range of) life experiences. This necessarily means that how certain contexts are understood lacks the benefit of the knowledge generated from the experiences, and the interpretations of, women/people with the physiology to become pregnant. In this way, thinking about pregnancy is easily abstracted from context. Finn has noted that in bioethics and philosophy, pregnancy and birth have not been considered issues of significant philosophical value, with the comprehensive body of literature on abortion being a 'glaring anomaly'.[147] She explains, however, that this seeming anomaly actually makes perfect sense; philosophy has historically had consistently little interest in persons

[144] My paper with Claire Horn was rejected by a number of prominent bioethics journals before finding its home in the International Journal of Feminist Approaches to Bioethics. One editor at a leading journal commented that we should 'try a feminist journal': this experience solidifies how feminist scholarship in ethics is often siloed into narrow spaces with limited engagement outside those who are already interested in feminist perspectives.

[145] Sandra Harding, 'Rethinking Standpoint Epistemology: What Is "Strong Objectivity"?' (1992) 36 The Centennial Review 437–70, 459.

[146] This second point is especially important because of the distinction between descriptive and substantive representation. See analysis on this distinction in the context of women in philosophy see Suki Finn, 'Being-from-Birth: Pregnancy and Philosophy' (2023) 19 European Journal of Analytic Philosophy S7–S32, 13.

[147] ibid S19.

undertaking pregnancy and their experiences—but a focus on abortion is not actually on these people, rather it is a focus on the fetus.[148] In centring the fetus, and simultaneously excluding people with experiences of pregnancy, it is easy to see how abortion was centred as the matter for investigation, rather than there being recognition of the impact of *unwanted pregnancy* and this being the starting point from which to reflect on the ethical issues surrounding pregnancy. The disciplinary norm is analysis based on an androcentric centring of the fetus—ethical conversation centres reflection about the fetus. Theorizing about ectogestation with a focus on abortion emerges naturally as the continuance of the side-lining of the experiences of pregnant people in place of the focus on the fetus. In so doing, the literature consistently systematically contributes to the continued marginalization of people who have, will, or could experience unwanted pregnancy.

I would argue that there is a need for a course correction in the literature: we should stop problematizing abortion itself by stepping back and starting from the point of centring the experience of unwanted pregnancy.[149] A focus on abortion as the problem has led to an excessive focus on the permissibility of abortion as we debate novel forms of assisted gestation in cases like ectogestation, rather than considering how we might provide alternative procreative experiences (as has been the primary focus of this book). Further, it has contributed to problematizing abortion provision in circumstances where it is, and ought to be recognized as, routine. Once we recognize that abortion remains necessary notwithstanding technological developments including novel forms of assisted gestation, the law as a barrier to abortion access becomes a more visible part of the philosophical conversation about the regulation of pregnancy.

Legal Futures

There has, in the last decade, been a general trajectory across the globe towards liberalization of abortion,[150] recognition of abortion as a human right,[151] and acceptance of the importance of abortion access.[152] Yet the two jurisdictions

[148] ibid.
[149] See also Horn, 'Abortion Rights after Artificial Wombs' (n 70).
[150] See Lisa Remez and others, 'Global Developments in Laws on Induced Abortion: 2008–2019' (2020) 46 International Perspectives on Sexual and Reproductive Health 53–65, 58. There are some countries, such as the United States, that are obvious outliers in recent regression.
[151] eg United Nations Committee on the Elimination of Discrimination against Women (n 126).
[152] See World Health Organization (n 86).

in which I have lived while writing this book (the United States and England and Wales) have been different stories. In 2022, the Supreme Court of the United States, overruling fifty years of established precedent, ruled that the US Constitution conferred no right to abortion,[153] which has had a devastating impact.[154] In England and Wales, abortion access has improved in the years since 2020 as a result of the legalization of telemedical abortion care pathways.[155] However, abortion remains criminalized and there is a growing trend of prosecutions of abortion-seekers who have their abortions outside the heavily medicalized circumstances in which it is legal.[156] Against this context, there might reasonably be concerns about the introduction of novel technologies enabling gestation (especially ectogestation) because of the impact they may have on the legal availability of abortion in contemporary legal frameworks. In jurisdictions where abortion is criminalized, technologies like ectogestation pose a greater threat to abortion access in a number of ways. Indeed, even some commentators who have advocated that abortion is morally questionable in light of AAPT have argued that criminalization and infringements on legal access are harmful and propagate 'systematic misogyny'.[157] Thus, I argue, building on the work of Horn,[158] that for a future with both novel technologies enabling gestation and reproductive justice, decriminalization of abortion is a necessity. Decriminalization alone, of course, is not *sufficient* to ensure access to abortion care,[159] but the point is that where there is criminal regulation of abortion, the potential for novel developments to come to limit abortion access is much greater.

Criminal law, to varying degrees, remains at the heart of abortion regulation almost universally (Canada being the only jurisdiction in the world where abortion is *fully* decriminalized),[160] though the nature and degree of that criminalization varies. In its construction, the criminalization of abortion in

[153] *Dobbs* (n 22).

[154] Elizabeth Chloe Romanis, 'The End of (Reproductive) Liberty as we Know It: A Note on Dobbs V. Jackson Women's Health 597 USC __ (2022)' (2023) 23 Medical Law International 71–87; Emily Ottley and others, 'Dobbs v Jackson Women's Health Organization (2022): Consequences One Year On' (2023) 31 Medical Law Review 457–68.

[155] Parsons and Romanis (n 25).

[156] Sally Sheldon and Jonathan Lord, 'Care not Criminalisation; Reform of British Abortion Law is Long Overdue' (2023) 49 Journal of Medical Ethics 523–24, 523; Elizabeth Chloe Romanis, '*R v Foster*: Exemplifying the Urgency of the Decriminalisation of Abortion' (2023) 31 Medical Law Review 606–14.

[157] Christopher Stratman, 'Ectogestation and the Good Samaritan Argument' (2023) Journal of Law and the Biosciences <doi.org/10.1093/jlb/lsad012> accessed 4 September 2024.

[158] See Horn (n 5).

[159] Romanis, 'Abortion Access' (n 19) 385–86.

[160] Following the Supreme Court decision in *R v Morgentaler* [1988] 1 SCR 30.

England and Wales is one of the strictest on paper in Europe,[161] and most convoluted in terms of the disjuncture between law and practice.[162]

In England and Wales, abortion is a criminal offence. Unlawful procurement of miscarriage, carrying a maximum penalty of life imprisonment, is committed where a pregnancy is intentionally ended.[163] The Abortion Act 1967 has amended the parameters of the offence (the actus reus) in dictating that unlawful procurement of miscarriage is lawful under certain conditions dictating why, when, and where the abortion takes place.[164] These conditions are heavily proscriptive, and disproportionate given the safety and efficacy of abortion, particularly as concerns medication abortions at earlier gestations.[165] In practice, the majority of abortions are conducted under the 'socio-medical' ground[166] for abortion: where the pregnancy is less than twenty-four weeks' gestation and continuing the pregnancy is a greater risk to the physical or mental health of the pregnant person or any existing children of their family than termination.[167] This ground has come to be interpreted broadly by the health profession and dedicated abortion service-providers: effectively, every pregnancy is legally terminable before twenty weeks' gestation.[168] While this is the case, a person having an abortion must still comply with the conditions set out in the Act—they must have medical permission,[169] and they must administer abortion medications at their legally recognized home address[170] or a licensed clinic,[171] or where the abortion is surgical, in a licensed clinic.[172] Where they do not comply with legal requirements, abortion-seekers face all of the difficulties of a criminal investigation, trial, and potentially imprisonment.[173]

There have been longstanding calls to decriminalize abortion in England and Wales[174] because the criminalization of abortion is in disjuncture with the

[161] Sally Sheldon, 'British Abortion Law: Speaking from the Past to Govern the Future' (2016) 79 Medical Law Review 283–316.

[162] Romanis, 'Abortion Access' (n 19).

[163] Offences Against the Person Act 1861, ss 58 and 59.

[164] Abortion Act 1967, s 1; Elizabeth Chloe Romanis and others, 'The Excessive Regulation of Early Abortion Medication in the UK: The Case for Reform' (2022) 30 Medical Law Review 4–32.

[165] See ibid.

[166] While this is sometimes termed the 'social' ground for abortion, 'socio-medical' is more accurate since the termination must still be justified in medical terms: Parsons and Romanis (n 25) 17.

[167] Abortion Act 1967, s 1

[168] Emily Jackson, *Regulating Reproduction: Law, Technology and Autonomy* (Hart Publishing 2001) 80.

[169] Abortion Act 1967, s 1(1).

[170] Abortion Act 1967, s 1 (3D) as inserted by Health and Social Care Act 2022, s 178(4).

[171] Abortion Act 1967, s 1 (3).

[172] ibid.

[173] See n 156.

[174] International Federation of Gynecology and Obstetrics, 'FIGO Calls for the Total Decriminalisation of Safe Abortion' <https://www.figo.org/resources/figo-statements/figo-calls-total-decriminalisation-safe-abortion> accessed 14 August 2023.

necessity of abortion and no longer serves the purpose it was originally designed for: to address safety concerns about abortion when performed by unskilled persons.[175] Horn has argued that the need to decriminalize abortion is particularly pressing in the wake of new technologies: most especially, that of AAPT.[176] As I have outlined elsewhere, it is unlikely that as the law is currently constructed in England and Wales (the AA 1967) the advent of AAPT would pose a direct threat to abortion access. The 'socio-medical' ground still renders lawful early pregnancy termination,[177] and there is no requirement that a pregnant person eligible for lawful termination should consider or be required to choose any method of ending a pregnancy (including opting for use of APPT).[178] This is not the case in plenty of other jurisdictions, however, where the legality of abortion is tied directly to determinations about fetal viability.[179]

Even in jurisdictions like England and Wales where there is not a direct threat to abortion access in the current construction of the law, this does not mean that the criminalization of abortion does not pose a threat to abortion access. Where abortion is part of the criminal code this inherently emboldens restrictions. As Baehr explains, 'if you repeal something from the law, you take it out of the law entirely. If you legalize something, you grant control to the state'.[180] Indeed, in England and Wales the underlying criminal offences are broad and can be broadly construed and the AA 1967, which has narrowed the boundaries of criminality, could be amended. In England and Wales, the two greatest threats to abortion access following ectogestation are in how health professionals interpret abortion legislation, and in any potential parliamentary intervention to create new restrictions.[181]

In the United States, how state legislators will respond is of great concern. With the overturning of the constitutional right to abortion, meaning States have the ability to legislate on abortion however they see fit, it is a scary prospect. In terms of what might be anticipated, while many commentators imagine

[175] Jackson, *Regulating Reproduction* (n 168) 84; Sally Sheldon and Kaye Wellings, 'Introduction', in Sheldon and Wellings (eds), *Decriminalising Abortion in the UK* (n 20) 9.

[176] Horn (n 70).

[177] Amel Alghrani, *Regulating Assisted Reproductive Technologies: New Horizons* (CUP 2018) 148; Emily Jackson, 'Degendering Reproduction' (2008) 16 Medical Law Review 346–68, 362; Elizabeth Chloe Romanis, 'Challenging the "Born Alive" Threshold: Fetal Surgery, Artificial Wombs, and the English Approach to Legal Personhood' (2020) 28 Medical Law Review 93–123, 116.

[178] Romanis, 'Abortion & "Artificial Wombs"' (n 47) 10.

[179] For example, the Netherlands, see explanation and critique: Sam Halliday and others, 'The (mis) use of fetal viability as the determinant of non-criminal abortion in the Netherlands and England and Wales' (2023) 31 Medical Law Review 538–63.

[180] Ninia Baehr, 'Deregulating Abortion' in Alison Jaggar (ed), *Living with Contradictions: Controversies in Feminist Social Ethics* (Routledge 1994) 272.

[181] Romanis, 'Challenging the "Born Alive" Threshold' (n 177) 117.

that abortion would not be banned but that use of AAPT would be mandated in place of 'conventional' abortion, this is plainly fanciful. As Paterson-Brown and Watson have observed, 'in the wake of the Supreme Court's decision in *Dobbs v. Jackson Women's Health Organization*, it is hard to imagine that a state which now has the power to force a pregnant person to be a walking womb against their will would give them the 'option' of an extremely expensive, less proven way to gestate'.[182] Since abortion prohibitions in anti-abortion States are motivated by fetal-centric considerations (with little to no regard for the bodily integrity of pregnant persons), in the United States—and indeed, other jurisdictions that restrict abortion and recognize 'fetal rights'—AAPT is likely to only fuel bans on abortion, rather than to enable people to 'opt out of pregnancy'.[183]

Despite the fact that the World Health Organization and international human rights bodies (such as the Committee of the Elimination of Discrimination Against Women) have recommended against criminal regulation of abortion,[184] it remains an enduring reality across the globe. This is a contemporary problem, but as ever, looking to the future to consider possibilities like AAPT reveal the extent to which the criminal regulation of abortion—even that which is generally understood as permissive today[185]– undermines the notion of (reproductive/procreative) justice. Generally, where there are improvements in technology around pregnancy and technology—be that ultrasound (that allowed the fetus to be crystallized in images), uterus transplantation (that, for some, reifies the specialness of gestation), or AAPT (that can perform gestational work in place of persons)—there are calls to restrict abortion. A just procreative future means choices about pregnancy and gestation—this must encompass recognition of the harms of unwanted pregnancy.

[182] Patterson-Brown and Watson (n 7) 88.
[183] Romanis and Horn (n 5).
[184] World Health Organization (n 86) 24; United Nations Committee on the Elimination of Discrimination against Women (n 126).
[185] For example, because abortion is not criminal in the circumstances in which most people will seek it.

8
CONCLUSION

Novel gestations are exciting prospects. Gestation beyond bodies assigned female at birth (AFAB), and beyond bodies at all, could challenge our preconceptions about so many fundamental aspects of our social lives including our identities and our conceptions of relatedness and parenthood. However, the transformative potential of these technologies—in how they may enhance the procreative possibilities for individuals in different and new ways—are, and will be, limited by social and legal regulation that limits their emancipatory potential. Imagining the possibilities of uterus transplantation (UTx) and ectogestation facilitated by Artificial Amnion and Placenta Technology (AAPT) in contemporary contexts reveals how biological essentialism is the fault line that underpins procreative regulation in England and Wales and, as such, has created significant friction and limitation where new procreative technologies that could challenge cis-heteronormative nuclear family models come into being. Technologies enabling gestation are no exception. In this final concluding chapter, I will briefly summarize the key themes from the exploration of gestation and technologies enabling gestation in this book.

Technologies enabling gestation, and the fundamental shifts in the modalities of gestation that they make possible, require a careful conceptual analysis of procreative 'facts' that have been taken for granted, and also how we describe these 'facts'. When we consider the possibility of gestation outside of the body, we make more visible the separability of gestation and pregnancy, and of birth (being born) and birthing (as illustrated in Chapter 2). These distinctions are not just technicalities; they will materially affect individuals' experiences of procreation. Looking at technologies as a genus (as argued in Chapter 3) requires the asking of questions about the very nature of gestation and what it means—in legal, social, and political terms—since different modalities of gestation are possible. Examining what pregnancy, gestation, and birth *are* enables the subsequent investigation of what the law considers these states/processes to be and thus reveals the metaphysical assumptions underlying the law and its operation. These legal premises are under interrogated, despite the fact that these ontological orientations of the law undergird a number of legal

Biotechnology, Gestation, and the Law. Elizabeth Chloe Romanis, Oxford University Press.
 DOI: 10.1093/9780191986574.003.0008

schemas that affect procreative and pregnancy experiences in the present. I argued that the law predominantly adopts a container model of pregnancy, in which the fetus is imagined as a separate individuated entity that is merely contained by a pregnant person, which, not only negates the realities of the fetus as a part of the pregnant person but enables legal frameworks and decision-making to centre the fetus, even though it is not formally attributed any legal rights. Such an approach has harmful implications in the present but could also be exacerbated by novel technologies enabling gestation.[1] As Finn and Isaac explain, the use of devices to facilitate gestation outside the body could risk the perpetuation of the fetal container model of pregnancy.[2] In thinking about how to make space for procreative futures in which pregnant people are not constructed as containers, we must to place the metaphysical distinction between pregnancy and gestation at the forefront of our conceptualization of the technology. That ectogestation is not pregnancy needs reinforcing not least for the boundary-setting it does that could limit the policing of pregnant people that scholars have raised as a concern.[3] As Brazier has argued, 'there is little conceptual depth underpinning British law' surrounding human procreation, which has resulted in a lack of coherence in its approach.[4] Careful conceptual analyses of the processes and states of being in human procreation helps identify the right ethico-legal questions and draw critical boundaries for the protection of the rights of people who undertake generative procreative work. As we debate the next wave of procreative innovation in novel technologies enabling gestation, we have an opportunity to bring careful conceptual analyses to the fore.

The distinction between conception and gestation is critical to imagining appropriate regulatory approaches. Technologies enabling conception affect *what* entities come into being,[5] which comes with its own distinct ethico-legal and socio-political issues, like what kinds of offspring we should have.[6] Technologies enabling gestation, however, distinctly raise questions about

[1] Elizabeth Chloe Romanis and others, 'Reviewing the Womb' (2021) 47 Journal of Medical Ethics 820–29.

[2] Suki Finn and Sasha Isaac, 'Evaluating Ectogenesis via the Metaphysics of Pregnancy' in Robbie Davis-Floyd (ed), *Birthing Techno-Sapiens: Human Evolution and the Future of Reproduction* (Routledge 2021).

[3] Romanis and others (n 1); Giulia Cavaliere, 'Gestation, Equality and Freedom: Ectogenesis as a Political Perspective' (2020) 46 Journal of Medical Ethics 76–82; Claire Horn, 'Ectogenesis, Inequality, and Coercion: A Reproductive Justice-informed Analysis of the Impact of Artificial Wombs' (2023) 18 Biosocieties 523–44.

[4] Margaret Brazier, 'Regulating the Reproduction Business?' (1999) 7 Medical Law Review 166–93, 167.

[5] Elizabeth Chloe Romanis, 'Assisted Gestative Technologies' (2022) 48 Journal of Medical Ethics 439–46, 439.

[6] For example, there is considerable debate about what is termed 'procreative beneficence' (a so-called moral obligation to 'have the child that can be expected to have the best life possible'—effectively

how human entities come into being and who (and what) is responsible for the generative work involved.[7] Novel procreative technologies of both conception and gestation raise important questions about who, how, and when, people undertake or delegate gestation—who should have access to these technologies? Who are parents where these technologies are used? Because the nature of conception and gestation is so different, however, we cannot presume that rules surrounding conception, and pregnancy more generally, will translate well to ethico-legal issues arising around novel gestations, as has been illustrated throughout this book. For example, rules attributing legal parenthood in assisted conception have assumed that gestation facilitated by pregnancy is the anchor around which rules can be constructed.[8] It is unclear, however, the reasoning that underpins the legal rule is unclear, and potentially multi-faceted, which becomes difficult to understand when the anchor of gestation facilitated by pregnancy is dislodged (as demonstrated in Chapter 6). As another example, the jurisprudential discussion of procreation, protecting a negative right to have decisions about genetic parenthood respected within the right to private life[9] does not necessarily translate directly to decisions about gestation, since choices about gestation may necessarily be demanding bodily work of others of a more invasive nature (as illustrated in Chapter 4). These two examples, amongst the many others in this book, are demonstrative of reality that we cannot presume that legal frameworks that have been developed in light of technologies enabling conception can simply make space for technologies enabling gestation. Some have suggested that we make considerable amendments to the existing legal framework to make space for developments like UTx and AAPT.[10] Kendal, for example, has argued that 'Like Romanis, I also believe now is the time to start developing thoughtful policies and legislation to promote appropriate integration of these emerging technologies into the suite of existing' assisted procreative technologies.[11] My point is, however, that we should not simply incorporate these technologies into existing structures, but use these technologies as an opportunity to fundamentally rethink what is

a eugenic argument to select against disability). See a persuasive argument that there is no such moral obligation: Rebecca Bennett, 'The Fallacy of the Principle of Procreative Beneficence' (2009) 23 Bioethics 265–73.

[7] Romanis, 'Assisted Gestative Technologies' (n 5).
[8] Human Fertilisation and Embryology Act 2008, s 33(1).
[9] Per European Convention of Human Rights Art 8.
[10] Amel Alghrani, 'The Human Fertilisation and Embryology Act 2008: A Missed Opportunity?' (2009) 25 Journal of Medical Ethics 718–19; Amel Alghrani, *Regulating Assisted Reproductive Technologies: New Horizons* (CUP 2018) 272.
[11] Evie Kendal, 'Commentary on Romanis' Assisted Gestative Technologies' (2022) 48 Journal of Medical Ethics 450–51, 451.

wrong with what we have, and recognize that we cannot regulate technologies enabling gestation in the same ways we regulate technologies enabling conception because they are fundamentally different beasts.

Much like other scholars, I believe in the importance of speculative analysis—examining how future procreative technologies bring challenges to contemporary legal frameworks.[12] Speculation, to me, means making time for 'things to get messy'; for the drawing of conceptual distinctions, for us to have more questions than answers, and questioning the assumptions and the normative values that underpin existing legal frameworks. For example, in the rule that gestation facilitated by pregnancy determines legal motherhood, we need to be asking why it is that we value some procreative experiences, or some forms of generative bodily work over others, and if we are clear or comfortable with the reasoning as it stands. In the construction of abortion law, that determines that ending pregnancies where not medically necessary or the fetus is disabled, a person cannot opt out of pregnancy in favour of generative work being continued by a machine (see Chapter 4),[13] with the potential implication that bodily generative work is to be preferred (or that people who have begun pregnancy should finish it). Are we comfortable with legal rules that, even if not intended to do so, determine how gestation occurs, or that potentially perpetuates pronatalism or hierarchical thinking about gestations?

Technologies can reveal how procreation—and specifically gestation—are cultural and socio-legal artefacts as much as they are 'biological' processes. Where we have the capacity to imagine and enable new modalities of gestation, what we imagine, and what we do and do not allow, speaks to what we value. The law, even when faced with shifting social dynamics and assisted conception with transformative potential for those families, has instead reinforced notions of the 'natural' and enabled procreation within the confines of 'the binary, two-parent model of the nuclear family',[14] mirroring conceptions of 'biological' possibility. As Chadwick has argued notions of 'the natural' and 'the biological' have always been used to police procreative desires—most notably of 'nonconforming people (eg nonbinary, trans, queer)'.[15] The limits that both socially and legally reinforced biological essentialism could place on the possibilities of novel gestation in present and in the future are detrimental

[12] Alghrani (n 10); Elizabeth Chloe Romans, 'Regulating the "Brave New World": Ethico-Legal Implications of the Quest for Partial Ectogenesis' (PhD thesis, University of Manchester 2020) 25–28; Elizabeth Chloe Romanis and Alan Brown, 'Legal Parenthood, Novel Reproductive Practices, and the Disruption of Reproductive Biosex' (2024) Modern Law Review <doi.org/10.1111/1468-2230.12914> accessed 4 September 2024.

[13] Elizabeth Chloe Romanis, 'Artificial Womb Technology and the Choice to Gestate Ex Utero: Is Partial Ectogenesis the Business of the Criminal Law?' (2020) 28 Medical Law Review 342–74, 354.

[14] Alan Brown, *What is the Family of Law? The Influence of the Nuclear Family* (Hart 2019) 7.

[15] Rachelle Chadwick, 'Visceral Acts: Gestationality as Feminist Figuration' (2022) Signs 229–55, 231.

because they would dampen the equality-enhancing potential of the technology in enabling (especially marginalized) people to build their families in ways that better enable the realization of their procreative needs.

Biological essentialism could dictate who has access to technologies. The legal framework underpinning the Human and Fertilisation and Embryology Acts 1990 and 2008 has maintained a construction of parenthood that centralizes the nuclear family and, to some extent, the 'sexual' family.[16] As was discussed in Chapter 4, the Act contains provisions that limit access to novel gestations, for example, in the provision specifying who can receive fertility treatment that potentially excludes trans women from accessing in vitro fertilization (IVF) (which would be a constituent part of the UTx for procreation procedure).[17] A second example is in the provision that mandates clinics to assess people accessing procreative technologies for the 'supportive parenting' they would be able to provide,[18] which can lead to discrimination against non-traditional families.[19] This provision as it is currently constructed would necessarily mean assessing people who access UTx or complete ectogestation being assessed in this way. In questions about access, what material conditions that are in place are what we must assess—specifically whether they make space for a range of (contradictory) procreative needs on the part of different individuals. It is clear that the HFE Acts are premised with the form of gestation taken as a given which, although this is unsurprising, means that its provisions are limiting for novel gestations in themselves (in the case of UTx) or indirectly enable discrimination (in the case of welfare assessments for accessing UTx or ectogestation). There ought to be real concern about how these assessments would be conducted in respect of ectogestation as this enables a whole new degree of state or private clinic interference in who can procreate (which might have particular impact on structurally marginalized groups along the strata of migration status, class, and race). Notions of biological essentialism are evident in both of these provisions—directly in that the law can be read as suggesting that only people AFAB should gestate, and in the sense that welfare assessments are known to be problematic for how societal conceptions of traditional families can creep into these assessments.

[16] Julie McCandless and Sally Sheldon, 'Genetically Challenged: The Determination of Legal Parenthood in Assisted Reproduction' in Tabitha Freeman and others (eds), *Relatedness in Assisted Reproduction: Families, Origins, and Identities* (CUP 2014) 65.

[17] Human Fertilisation and Embryology Act 2008, s 3Z(6); Natasha Hammond-Browning, 'UK Criteria for Uterus Transplantation: A Review' (2019) 126 British Journal of Obstetrics and Gynaecology 1320–26.

[18] Human Fertilisation and Embryology Act 1990, s 13(5), as amended by Human Fertilisation and Embryology Act 2008, s 14(2).

[19] Sheelagh McGuiness and Amel Alghrani, 'Gender and Parenthood: The Case for Realignment' (2008) 16 Medical Law Review 261–83, 268.

Biological essentialism is not only evident in determining access to technologies. Some scholars have made arguments about the capacity of technologies to enable gender equality,[20] there are often considerable limiting assumptions. I do not deny that technologies enabling gestation have disruptive and transformative potential that is potentially equality-enhancing, for example, in allowing LGBTQ+ individuals to have the gestation in their procreative project facilitated in ways that better facilitate their needs. This is the case whether their needs mean people assigned male at birth are enabled to sustain a pregnancy, or machines are able to facilitate gestation affording more privacy to individuals who cannot or do not want to be pregnant themselves.[21] Scholars in the literature limit their discussion most often, however, to the question of whether ectogestation—essentially enabling machines to perform the generative function—are necessary (though not sufficient) for women's equality. I argued in Chapter 5, however, that there is significant biological essentialism in this claim—it necessarily implies the gender and sex of bodies that can gestate, implies the inferiority of bodies capable of the procreative generative function, is premised on the assimilation of bodies who can become pregnant in performing only like that those that cannot become pregnant,[22] and is defeatist about the possibilities of equality while some people choose to experience pregnancy (which could be facilitated with proper legal and social policy that values the generative work performed by individuals). Moreover, I argued that the most exciting and disruptive capacity of technologies enabling gestation was not in the possibilities of outsourcing, but instead in 'unsexing' of generative labour, and this is arguably more visible in cases of male pregnancy than ectogestation. We must ask whether the sexing of pregnancy has excluded our understanding of pregnancy as beyond the heteronormative. As Nelson asks, 'What about my pregnancy—is that inherently heteronormative?' She continues that, in some ways, the state of being pregnancy can be and feel inherently queer in itself because it 'profoundly alters' one's usual parameters of self.[23] That pregnancy is seen and discussed as hyper-feminine is a social construction and something that could become a barrier to the realization of novel 'unsexed' gestations and/or to the normalization of it.

Abortion law also propagates biological essentialism. Other scholars have made this argument in respect of abortion law in England and Wales in

[20] eg Anna Smajdor, 'The Moral Imperative for Ectogenesis' (2007) 16 Cambridge Quarterly for Healthcare Ethics 336–45.

[21] Elizabeth Chloe Romanis, 'The Equality-Enhancing Potential of Novel Forms of Assisted Gestation: Perspectives of Reproductive Rights Advocates' (2023) 37 Bioethics 637–46, 640.

[22] Giulia Cavaliere, 'Ectogenesis and Gender-based Oppression: Resisting the Ideal of Assimilation' (2020) 34 Bioethics 727–34, 728.

[23] Maggie Nelson, *The Argonauts* (Greywolf Press 2015) 16.

detail,[24] in this book I have demonstrated that the possibilities novel procreative technologies enabling gestation have led to a political resurgence in the debate about the permissibility of abortion. This is illustrative of the fact that biological essentialism about the role of bodies that can become pregnant is subsumed by political expectation. I argued in this book that technologies enabling gestation do not change the moral permissibility of abortion, since the importance of bodily integrity and of procreative rights for people who undertake pregnancy remain critical and remain in need of respect in order for individuals with the capacity to become pregnant to have any ownership over their bodily boundaries (see Chapter 7). Technologies enabling gestation do force discussion about who these rights belong to—which must always be the person undertaking generative work as part of their body. Since there are often attempts to limit abortion access we must think about how abortion law would be interpreted in light of these technologies. While abortion law *as constructed* would still enable access to abortion in early pregnancy in England and Wales, we could use the technology as a springboard for better procreative futures, which, as many scholars have argued, must encompass the decriminalization of abortion.[25] A future without decriminalization will always mean that persons who can become pregnant are plagued by the expectations placed on their bodily capacities. Abortion law does require medical justification for termination of pregnancy, and this means people would be unable to opt out of pregnancy with gestation to be continued ex utero (as explained earlier and in Chapter 4), which when there is the possibility of a procreative choice, denies that choice and propagates assumptions about procreation and the role of bodies AFAB.

Gestation[26] facilitated by pregnancy has significant implications in law. Most notably, in that it denotes legal motherhood without exception,[27] which has the effect of conscripting people who can become pregnant. I argue that the reasoning for the normative positioning of the law here is unclear, and, as I show in Chapter 6, not as historically rooted as is often claimed. Pregnancy

[24] Sheldon argues that the construction of the Abortion Act 1967 is such that pregnant people can opt out of *this* pregnancy in such a way that still reiterates that people who can become pregnant have motherhood in their destiny. Sally Sheldon, *Beyond Control: Medical Power and Abortion Law* (Pluto Press 1997).

[25] Claire Horn, 'Abortion Rights after Artificial Wombs: Why Decriminalisation is Needed Ahead of Ectogenesis' (2021) 29 Medical Law Review 80–105; Elizabeth Chloe Romanis, 'Is "Viability" Viable? Abortion, Conceptual Confusion and the Law in England and Wales and the United States' (2021) 7 Journal of Law and the Biosciences <doi:10.1093/jlb/lsaa059> accessed 4 September 2024.

[26] The law uses gestation and pregnancy as synonyms in the context of attributing parenthood, which is unsurprising given that the possibility of human gestation without pregnancy is speculative.

[27] Human Fertilisation and Embryology Act 2008, s 33(1); Zaina Mahmoud and Elizabeth Chloe Romanis, 'On Gestation and Motherhood' (2023) 31 Medical Law Review 109–40.

is a significant bodily undertaking, but this is not reason to conscript a pregnant person into motherhood after birthing as I argue in Chapter 6. It is reason to respect the work that they have done and their corresponding intentions which, more often than not, will be to parent a resulting child, but sometimes will not be. Commentators who have argued for the importance of gestation facilitating pregnancy as the determining factor in legal motherhood often explain that this is because, to do otherwise, is to preference other normative values other than bodily work. Hendricks, for example, argues that recognizing genetic progenitors as parents rather than the pregnant person is 'genetic essentialism'. However, to stipulate that pregnancy is always determinative is just another form of biological essentialism; 'gestational essentialism'. The reality is that procreative possibilities, and arrangements made as a consequence, are evolving and assuming any biological factor as determinative is hardly likely to result in a radical reimagining of procreation that respects preferences without co-opting the bodies and lives of those who can become pregnant. Moreover, the rule that gestation (facilitated by pregnancy) determines legal motherhood simply does not withstand the conceptual challenges that are raised by novel gestation. Who is the legal mother where there is no pregnant person?

Technologies enabling gestation offer an opportunity for critical reexamination of the normative determinations underpinning the law in a number of contexts surrounding procreation, such as who can procreate, and the consequences of different procreative choices. As this book has argued the opportunity should be ceased not just as a way of anticipating and preparing for future scientific developments, but also to reveal assumptions, and the implications they are having, in contemporary legal frameworks. A procreative future where there is greater choice about how new human entities are brought into being is exciting, but also brings with it the potential for growing disparities in procreative outcomes that disadvantage already structurally marginalized groups. Stratified access, notions of the nuclear family underpinning legal frameworks, and social regulation of pregnant people's choices are all challenges that already cause considerable harm, and their potential to exacerbate should serve to motivate the radical social and legal reform that might enable a future in which procreative justice is not just a pipe dream but a concrete possibility.

BIBLIOGRAPHY

Abrao Trad A and others, 'Report of an Experiment with a Fetal Ex-Utero Support System in Piglets' (2023) 15 Cureus e38223.

Adkins V, 'Impact of Ectogenesis on the Medicalisation of Pregnancy and Childbirth' (2021) 47 Journal of Medical Ethics 239–43.

Ainsworth C, 'Sex Redefined' (2015) 518 Nature 288–91.

Alghrani A, 'The Legal and Ethical Ramifications of Ectogenesis' (2007) 2 Asian Journal of WTO & International Health Law and Policy 189–212.

Alghrani A, 'The Human Fertilisation and Embryology Act 2008: A Missed Opportunity?' (2009) 25 Journal of Medical Ethics 718–19.

Alghrani A, *Regulating Assisted Reproductive Technologies: New Horizons* (CUP 2018).

Alghrani A, 'Uterus Transplantation In and Beyond Cisgender Women: Revisiting Procreative Liberty in Light of emerging Reproductive Technologies' (2018) 5 Journal of Law and the Biosciences 301–28.

Alghrani A and Brazier M, 'What is It? Whose is It? Re-positioning the Fetus in the Context of Research' (2011) 70 The Cambridge Law Journal 51–82.

Alghrani A and Griffiths D, 'The Regulation of Surrogacy in the United Kingdom: The Case for Reform' (2017) 29 Child & Family Law Quarterly 165–86.

Alkorta I, 'Surrogacy in Spain: Vindication of the *Mater Semper Certa Est* Rule' (2020) 26 The New Bioethics 298–313.

Arendt H, *The Human Condition* (2nd edn, Chicago University Press 2018).

Arni C, *Of Human Born: Fetal Lives 1800–1950* (Zone Books 2024).

Arora KS and Blake V, 'Uterus Transplantation: Ethical and Regulatory Challenges' (2013) 40 Journal of Medical Ethics 396–400.

Austin L and McGuiness S, 'Reproductive Loss and Disposal of Pregnancy Remains' (2019) 70 Northern Ireland Legal Quarterly 131–53.

Babcock Gilbert S and Polotsky A, 'Vaginal Culture for IVF Allows Two Mothers to Carry the Same Pregnancy: Is More Always Better?' (2019) 21 Case Reports in Women's Health <doi.org/10.1016/j.crwh.2019.e00099> accessed 6 September 2024.

Backes M, 'Epistemology and the Law: Why There is No Epistemic Mileage in Legal Cases' (2020) 177 Philosophical Studies 2759–78.

Bainham A, 'Arguments about Parentage' (2008) 67 Cambridge Law Journal 322–51.

Bainham A, Day Sclater S, and Richards M (eds), *What is a Parent? A Socio-Legal Analysis* (Hart Publishing 1999).

Balayla J and others, 'The Montreal Criteria and Uterine Transplants in Transgender Women' (2021) 35 Bioethics 326–30.

Baldassi C, '*Mater est quam gestatio demonstrat*: A Cautionary Tale' (2006) <https://papers.ssrn.com/sol3/papers.cfm?abstract_id=927147> accessed 6 March 2023.

Baron T, 'Pregnancy, Procreation, and Moral Parenthood' (PhD thesis, University of Southampton 2020).

Bartky S, *Femininity and Domination: Studies in the Phenomenology of Oppression* (Routledge 1990).

Bartlam B and Birch S, 'Review: A right to Parenthood' (1998) 2 Journal of Child Health Care 36–40.

Bartlett K, 'Feminist Legal Methods' (1990) 103 Harvard Law Review 829–88.

Basu R, 'Risky Inquiry: Developing an Ethics for Philosophical Practice' (2023) 38 Hypatia 275–93.

Baylis F, 'Left Out in the Cold: Arguments Against Non-medical Oocyte Cryopreservation' (2015) 37 Journal of Obstetrics and Gynaecology Canada 64–67.

de Beauvoir S, *The Second Sex* (Borde C and S Malovany-Chevallier S trs, Knopf 1949).

Begović D, 'Upholding Women's Autonomy in Pregnancy: Responding to the Challenges of New Reproductive Technologies' (PhD thesis, University of Manchester 2021).

Ber R, 'Ethical Issues in Gestational Surrogacy' (2000) 21 Theoretical Medicine and Bioethics 153–69.

Berdahl J and Moon S, 'Workplace Mistreatment of Middle Class Workers Based on Sex, Parenthood, and Caregiving' (2013) 69 Journal of Social Issues 341–66.

Berend Z, '"We Are All Carrying Someone Else's Child!": Relatedness and Relationships in Third-Party Reproduction' (2016) 118 American Anthropologist 24–36.

Bermúdez JL, 'The Moral Significance of Birth' (1996) 106 Ethics 378–403.

Bidoli A and Di Nucci E, 'Beyond Pregnancy: A Public Health Case for a Technological Alternative' (2023) 16 International Journal of Feminist Approaches to Bioethics 103–30.

Bigelow A and Power M, 'Mother–Infant Skin-to-Skin Contact: Short- and Long-Term Effects for Mothers and Their Children Born Full-Term' (2020) 11 Frontiers in Psychology <doi.org/10.3389/fpsyg.2020.01921> accessed 6 September 2024.

Birthrights, 'Systemic Racism, Not Broken Bodies: An inquiry into racial injustice and human rights in UK maternity care' (2022) <https://www.birthrights.org.uk/wp-content/uploads/2022/05/Birthrights-inquiry-systemic-racism_exec-summary_May-22-web.pdf> accessed 28 November 2023.

Blackless M and others, 'How Sexually Dimorphic Are We? Review and Synthesis' (2000) 12 American Journal of Human Biology 151–66.

Blackshaw B and Rodger D, 'Ectogenesis and the Case Against the Right to the Death of the Foetus' (2019) 33 Bioethics 76–81.

Boonin D, *A Defense of Abortion* (CUP 2003).

Bower-Brown S, 'Beyond Mum and Dad: Gendered Assumptions about Parenting and the Experiences of Trans and/or Non-Binary Parents in the UK' (2022) 18 LGBTQ+ Family: An Interdisciplinary Journal 233–40.

Brännström M, 'The Swedish Uterus Transplantation Project: The Story behind the Swedish Uterus Transplantation Project' (2015) 94 Acta Obstetricia et Gynecologica Scandinavica 675–79.

Brännström M, 'Uterus Transplantation and Beyond' (2017) 28 Journal of Materials Science: Materials in Medicine <doi.org/10.1007/s10856-017-5872-0> accessed 6 September 2024.

Brännström M, Almén Wranning C, Marcickiewicz J, and others, 'Uterus Transplantation—Substantial Progress in Research but Not Yet Ready for the Clinic' (2007) 12 Middle East Fertility Society Journal 86–95.

Brännström M, Johannesson L, Bokström H, and others, 'Livebirth after Uterus Transplantation' (2015) 385 The Lancet 607–16.

Brännström M, Racowsky C, Carbonnel M, and others, 'Uterus Transplantation: From Research, through Human Trials and into the Future' (2023) 29 Human Reproduction Update 521–44.

Brännström M, Tullius S, Brucker S, and others, 'Registry of the International Society of Uterus Transplantation: First Report' (2023) 107 Transplantation 10–17.

Brazier M, 'Regulating the Reproduction Business?' (1999) 7 Medical Law Review 166–93.

Brazier M, Farrell AM, and Griffiths D, 'Translational Bodies: Exploring the Socio-legal Contours of Human Bodies Past Present and Future' (2015) 7 Law, Innovation, and Technology 151–60.

British Pregnancy Advisory Service, 'Pills by Post—Abortion Treatment at Home: Expected Effects of Treatment' (nd) <https://www.bpas.org/abortion-care/abortion-treatments/the-abortion-pill/remote-treatment/> accessed 20 November 2023.

Brown A, *What is the Family of Law? The Influence of the Nuclear Family* (Hart 2019).

Brown A, 'Trans Parenthood and the Meaning of "Mother", "Father" and "Parent"—*R (McConnell and YY) v Registrar General for England and Wales* [2020] EWCA Civ 559' (2021) 29 Medical Law Review 157–71.

Brown A and Wade K, 'The Incoherent Role of the Child's Identity in the Construction and Allocation of Legal Parenthood' (2022) Legal Studies <doi:10.1017/lst.2022.21> accessed 6 September 2024.

Brown R and Mulligan A, '"Maternal Request" Caesarean Sections and Medical Necessity' (2023) 18 Clinical Ethics 312–20.

Browne V, *Pregnancy Without Birth: Feminist Philosophy of Miscarriage* (Bloomsbury 2023).

Butler J, *Gender Trouble* (Routledge 1990).

Campo-Engelstein L and others, 'Freezing Fertility or Freezing False Hope? A Content Analysis of Social Egg Freezing in U.S. Print Media' (2018) 9 AJOB Empirical Bioethics 181–93.

Cannold L, 'Women, Ectogenesis and Ethical Theory' (1995) 12 Journal of Applied Philosophy 55–64.

Cárdenas M, 'Pregnancy: Reproductive Futures in Trans of Color Feminism' (2016) 3 Transgender Studies Quarterly 48–57.

Carpenter H and others, 'Procreative Loss without Pregnancy Loss: The Limitations of Fetal-centric Conceptions of Pregnancy' (2024) 50 Journal of Medical Ethics 310–11.

Catsanos R, Rogers W, and Lotz M, 'The Ethics of Uterus Transplantation' (2013) 27 Bioethics 65–73.

Cavaliere G, 'Assisted Gestative Technologies, or on Treating Unlike Cases Alike' (2022) 48 Journal of Medical Ethics 452–53.

Cavaliere G, 'Ectogenesis and Gender-based Oppression: Resisting the Ideal of Assimilation' (2020) 34 Bioethics 727–34.

Cavaliere G, 'Gestation, Equality and Freedom: Ectogenesis as a Political Perspective' (2020) 46 Journal of Medical Ethics 76–82.

Cavaliere G and Palacios-González C, 'Lesbian Motherhood and Mitochondrial Replacement Techniques: Reproductive Freedom and Genetic Kinship' (2018) 44 Journal of Medical Ethics 835–42.

Cavolo A and Pizzolato D, 'Expanding the Ethical Debate on Human Artificial Placenta Trials' (2024) Research Ethics <https://doi.org/10.1177/17470161241259127> accessed 6 September 2024.

Cazorla-Ortiz G and others, 'Methods and Success Factors of Induced Lactation: A Scoping Review' (2020) 36 Journal of Human Lactation 739–49.

Chadwick R, 'Visceral Acts: Gestationality as Feminist Figuration' (2022) 48 Signs 229–55.

Chappell SG, 'Transgender: A Dialogue' *Aeon* (nd) <https://aeon.co/essays/transgender-identities-a-conversation-between-two-philosophers> accessed 2 November 2022.

Charest-Pekeski A and others, 'Achieving Sustained Extrauterine Life: Challenges of an Artificial Placenta in Fetal Pigs as a Model of the Preterm Human Fetus' (2021) 9 Physiological Reports e14742.

Cohen IG and others, 'The Regulation of Mitochondrial Replacement Techniques Around the World' (2020) 21 Annual Review of Genomics and Human Genetics 565–86.

Colgrove N, 'Artificial Wombs, Birth and "Birth": A Response to Romanis' (2020) 46 Journal of Medical Ethics 554–56.

Colgrove N, Blackshaw B, and Rodger D (eds), *Agency, Pregnancy and Persons: Essays in Defense of Human Life* (Routledge 2022).

Collier R and Sheldon S, *Fragmenting Fatherhood: A Socio-Legal Study* (Hart Publishing 2008).

Cook R and Dickens B, 'Human Rights Dynamics of Abortion Law Reform' (2003) 25 Human Rights Quarterly 1–59.

Cook R, Day Sclater S, and Kaganas F, *Surrogate Motherhood: International Perspectives* (Bloomsbury 2003).

Cooper S, *Analysis Gender in Healthcare: The Politics of Sex and Reproduction* (Palgrave Macmillan 2022).

Corea G, *The Mother Machine: Reproductive Technologies from Artificial Insemination to Artificial Wombs* (HarperCollins 1985).

Cornell D, *The Imaginary Domain: Abortion, Pornography and Sexual Harassment* (Routledge 1995).

Crenshaw K, 'Demarginalizing the Intersection of Race and Sex: A Black Feminist Critique of Antidiscrimination Doctrine, Feminist Theory and Antiracist Politics' (1989) 1 University of Chicago Legal Forum 139.

D'Alton Harrison R, '*Mater Semper Incertus Est:* Who's Your Mummy?' (2014) 22 Medical Law Review 357–83.

D'Amico G and others, 'Immunosuppression in Uterus Transplantation: From Transplant to Delivery' (2023) 29 Expert Opinion on Pharmacotherapy 29–35.

Dadlez EM and Andrews W, 'Post-Abortion Syndrome: Creating an Affliction' (2010) 24 Bioethics 445–52.

Davies M and Munro V (eds), *The Ashgate Research Companion to Feminist Legal Theory* (Ashgate Publishing 2013).

Davis A, *Women, Race and Class* (Women's Press 1982).

Davis DA, *Reproductive Injustice: Racism, Pregnancy, and Premature Birth* (New York University Press 2019).

Davis L, 'Deconstructing Tradition: Trans Reproduction and the Need to Reform Birth Registration in England and Wales' (2021) 22 International Journal of Transgender Health 179–90.

Davis-Floyd F (ed), *Birthing Techno-Sapiens: Human Evolution and the Future of Reproduction* (Routledge 2021).

De Bie F, Davey M, Larson A, and others, 'Artificial Placenta and Womb Technology: Past, Current and Future Challenges Towards Clinical Translation' (2020) 41 Prenatal Diagnosis 145–58.

De Bie F, Kim S, Bose S, and others, 'Ethics Considerations Regarding Artificial Womb Technology for the Fetonate' (2023) 23 The American Journal of Bioethics 67–78.

Department of Health and Social Security, *Report of the Committee of Inquiry into Human Fertilisation and Embryology* (Cmnd 9314, 1984).

Di Nucci E, 'Delegating Gestation or 'Assisted' Reproduction?' (2022) 48 Journal of Medical Ethics 454–55.

Dickens B, 'Reproduction Law and Medical Consent' (1985) 35 The University of Toronto Law Journal 255–86.

Diduck A and O'Donovan K (eds), *Feminist Perspectives on Family Law* (Routledge-Cavendish 2006).

Dietz C, Travis M, and Thomson M (eds), *A Jurisprudence of the Body* (Palgrave 2020).

Dimond R, 'Social and Ethical Issues in Mitochondrial Donation' (2015) 115 British Medical Bulletin 173–82.

Department of Health and Social Care, 'Abortion statistics, England and Wales: 2021' (updated July 2024) <https://www.gov.uk/government/statistics/abortion-statistics-for-england-and-wales-2021/abortion-statistics-england-and-wales-2021> accessed 14 September 2024.

Department of Health and Social Care, 'Baby loss certificate launched to recognise parents' grief' (2024) <https://www.gov.uk/government/news/baby-loss-certificate-launchedto-recognise-parents-grief> accessed 22 April 2024.

Drafting Techniques Group of the Office of the Parliamentary Counsel, 'Office of the Parliamentary Counsel: Drafting Guidance' (2020) <https://assets.publishing.service.gov.uk/media/660407d091a320001a82b06b/2024.03.19.Drafting-guidance.pdf> accessed 2 November 2022.

Drouillard J, 'The King was Pregnant: Reproductive Ethics and Transgender Pregnancy' (2021) 14 International Journal of Feminist Approaches to Bioethics 120–40.

Dunne P, 'Transgender Sterilisation Requirements in Europe' (2017) 25 Medical Law Review 554–81.

East L and others, 'Condom Negotiation: Experiences of Sexually Active Young Women' (2019) 67 Journal of Advanced Nursing 77–85.

Ebtehaj F and others (eds), *Birth Rites and Rights* (Hart Publishing 2011).

Edwards G, '1 in 3 Women Has an Abortion, and 95% Don't Regret It—So Why Are We So Afraid to Talk About It?' *The Independent* (2015) <https://www.independent.co.uk/life-style/health-and-families/features/1-in-3-women-have-an-abortion-and-95-don-t-regret-it-so-why-aren-t-we-talking-about-it-10392750.html> accessed 15 August 2023.

Eijkholt M, 'The Right to Found a Family as a Stillborn Right to Procreate?' (2010) 18 Medical Law Review 127–51.

Erin C and Ost S (eds), *The Criminal Justice System and Health Care* (OUP 2007).

Etrusco A and others, 'The Reproductive Potential of Uterus Transplantation: Future Prospects' (2022) 93 Acta Biomed e2022138.

Evans-Grubbs J, *Women and the Law in the Roman Empire: A Sourcebook on Marriage, Divorce and Widowhood* (Routledge 2002).

Falk M and others, 'Mitochondrial Replacement Techniques — Implications for the Clinical Community' (2016) 374 The New England Journal of Medicine 1103–06.

Fausto-Sterling A, *Sexing the Body: Gender Politics and the Construction of Sexuality* (Basic Books 2000).

Fausto-Sterling A, *Myths of Gender: Biological Theories about Women and Men* (Basic Books 1993).

Faye S, *The Transgender Issue: An Argument for Justice* (Allen Lane 2021).

Fenton-Glynn C, 'Deconstructing Parenthood: What Makes a Mother?' (2020) 79 The Cambridge Law Journal 34–37.

Finn S, 'Being-from-Birth: Pregnancy and Philosophy' (2023) 19 European Journal of Analytic Philosophy S7–S32.

Finn S, 'The Mereotopology of Pregnancy' (2023) 48 The Journal of Medicine and Philosophy: A Forum for Bioethics and Philosophy of Medicine 283–298.

Finn S, 'The Philosophy of Reproduction' (2021) 20 Think 49–62.

Firestone S, *The Dialectic of Sex: The Case for Feminist Revolution* (William Morrow and Company 1970).

Fischer O, 'Non-binary Reproduction: Stories of Conception, Pregnancy, and Birth' (2021) 22 International Journal of Transgender Health 77–88.

Flake A, 'A Supportive Physiologic Environment for the Extreme Premature Infant: Improving Life Outside the Womb' (2022) 57 Journal of Pediatric Surgery 167–71.

Flake A and others, 'The Artificial Placenta and EXTEND Technologies: One of These Things is Not Like the Other' (2023) 32 Journal of Perinatology 1343–48.

Flessas T and Jackson E, 'Too Expensive to Treat? Non-Treatment Decisions at the Margins of Viability?' (2019) 27 Medical Law Review 461–81.

Forman D, 'Abortion Clauses in Surrogacy Contracts: Insights from a Case Study' (2015) 49 Family Law Quarterly 29–54.

Foster C, 'Medical Law too often Doffs its Cap to the Doctor's White Coat' *The Times* (21 May 2009) <https://www.thetimes.co.uk/article/medical-law-too-often-doffs-its-cap-to-the-doctors-white-coat-z63b5xtgx93> accessed 14 May 2024.

Fovargue S and Miola J, 'The Legal Status of the Fetus' (2019) 5 Clinical Ethics 122–24.

Fox M, 'The Human Fertilisation and Embryology Act 2008: Tinkering at the Margins' (2009) 17 Feminist Legal Studies 333–44.

Freeman T and others (eds), *Relatedness in Assisted Reproduction: Families, Origins, and Identities* (CUP 2014).

Freitas R, 'Fetal Adoption' (1980) 40 The Humanist 22–23.

Gallagher J, 'First Womb-transplant Baby Born' (2014) *BBC* <https://www.bbc.co.uk/news/health-29485996> accessed 14 September 2023.

Gelfand G and Shook J (eds), *Ectogenesis: Artificial Womb Technology and the Future of Human Reproduction* (Rodopi 2006).

George J, 'Vitara Biomedical Raises $25M to Advance its Artificial Womb Technology for Premature Babies' (2022) <https://www.bizjournals.com/philadelphia/news/2022/08/09/vitara-biomedical-philadelphia-artificial-womb.html> accessed 25 June 2024.

Ginsburg F and Rapp R, *Conceiving the New World Order: The Global Politics of Reproduction* (University of California Press 1995).

Glaser E, *Motherhood: A Manifesto* (Fourth Estate 2021).

Gonzalez-Salzberg D, 'An Improved Protection for the (Mentally Ill) Trans Parent: A Queer Reading of AP, *Garçon and Nicot v France*' (2018) 81 Modern Law Review 526–38.

Goodin R (ed), *The Oxford Handbook of Political Science* (OUP 2011).

Goodwin M, *Policing the Womb: Invisible Women and the Criminalization of Motherhood* (CUP 2020).

Greasley K, *Arguments about Abortion: Personhood, Morality and Law* (OUP 2017).

Grossberg L, Nelson C, and Treichler P, *Cultural Studies* (Routledge 1991).

Gude N and others, 'Growth and Function of the Normal Human Placenta' (2004) 114 Thrombosis Research 397–407.

Haldane JBS, *Daedalus or Science and the Future: A Paper Read to the Heretics, Cambridge on February 4th, 1923* (EP Dutton & Company 1924).

Hall GA, 'Reproduction Misconceived: Why There is No Right to Reproduce and the Implications for ART Access' (2022) Journal of Medical Ethics <doi:10.1136/ jme-2022–108512> accessed 6 September 2024.

Halliday S and others, 'The (Mis)use of Fetal Viability as the Determinant of Non-criminal Abortion in the Netherlands and England and Wales' (2023) 31 Medical Law Review 538–63.

Hamidian Jahromi A, Horen S, Dorafshar A, and others, 'Uterine Transplantation and Donation in Transgender Individuals; Proof of Concept' (2021) 22 International Journal of Transgender Health 349–59.

Hammond-Browning N, 'UK Criteria for Uterus Transplantation: A Review' (2019) 126 British Journal of Obstetrics and Gynaecology 1320–26.

Hammond-Browning N, 'A New Dawn? Ectogenesis, Future Children and Reproductive Choice' (2018) 14 Contemporary Issues in Law 49–373.
Hammond-Browning N, 'Author's Reply Re: Uterine Transplantation in Transgender Women: Medical, Legal and Ethical Considerations' (2018) 126 British Journal of Obstetrics & Gynaecology 546.
Hammond-Browning N and Williams N (eds), *International Legal and Ethical Perspectives on Uterus Transplantation* (Edward Elgar 2024).
Hansen SL and Schicktanz S (eds), *Ethical Challenges of Organ Transplantation* (Transcript Publishing 2021).
Harding S, 'Rethinking Standpoint Epistemology: What Is "Strong Objectivity"?' (1992) 36 The Centennial Review 437–70.
Haraway D, *Staying with the Trouble: Making Kin in the Chthulucene* (Duke University Press 2016).
Harpwood V, *Legal Issues in Obstetrics* (1st edn, Dartmouth 1996).
Harvey P, Krohn-Hansen C and Nustad K (eds), *Anthropos and the Material* (Duke University Press 2019).
Haslanger S, 'Gender and Race: (What) Are They? (What) Do We Want Them to Be?' (2002) 34 Noûs 31–55.
Hayes S, *The Cultural Contradictions of Motherhood* (Yale University Press 1996).
Held V, 'Birth and Death' (1989) 99 Ethics 362–88.
Hellström M and others, 'Bioengineered Uterine Tissue Supports Pregnancy in a Rat Model' (2016) 106 Fertility and Sterility 487–96e.1.
Hendricks J, *Essentially a Mother: A Feminist Approach to the Law of Pregnancy and Motherhood* (University of California Press 2023).
Hendricks J, 'Not of Woman Born: A Scientific Fantasy' (2012) 62 Case Western Law Review 399–445.
Hendricks J, 'Not of Woman Born? Technology, Relationship and Right to a Human Mother' (2011) <http://trace.tennessee.edu/utk_lawpubl/45> accessed 6 March 2023.
Hendricks P, 'There is No Right to the Death of the Fetus' (2018) 32 Bioethics 395–97.
Herring J, *Family Law* (10th edn, Pearson 2021).
Herring J, *Caring and the Law* (Hart 2013).
Higgens J and Smith N, 'The Sexual Acceptability of Contraception: Reviewing the Literature and Building a New Concept' (2016) 53 The Journal of Sex Research 417–56.
Higgs E, 'A Cuckoo in the Nest? The Origins of Civil Registration and State Medical Statistics in England and Wales' (1996) 11 Continuity and Change 115–34.
Hill J, 'What Does it Mean to be a "Parent?" The Claims of Biology as the Basis for Parental Rights' (1991) 66 New York University Law Review 353–420.
hooks b, *Feminist Theory: From Margin to Center* (South End Press 1984).
Hooton V and Romanis EC, 'Artificial Womb Technology, Pregnancy, and EU Employment Rights' (2022) 9 Journal of Law and the Biosciences 1–33 <doi.org/10.1093/jlb/lsac009> accessed 6 September 2024.
Hopkins P, 'Can Technology Fix the Abortion Problem?' (2008) 22 International Journal of Applied Philosophy 311–26.
Horn C, 'Ectogenesis, Inequality, and Coercion: A Reproductive Justice-informed Analysis of the Impact of Artificial Wombs' (2023) 18 Biosocieties 523–44.
Horn C,-- 'Abortion Rights after Artificial Wombs: Why Decriminalisation is Needed Ahead of Ectogenesis' (2021) 29 Medical Law Review 80–105.
Horn C, 'Ectogenesis is for Feminists: Reclaiming Artificial Wombs from Antiabortion Discourse' (2020) 6 Catalyst: Feminism, Theory, Technoscience 1–15.

Horn C, 'Gender, Gestation and Ectogenesis: Self-determination for Pregnant People Ahead of Artificial Wombs' (2020) 46 Journal of Medical Ethics 787–88.

Horn C, 'Gestation Beyond Mother/Machine: Legal Frameworks for Artificial Wombs, Abortion and Care' (PhD thesis, Birkbeck University of London 2020).

Horsey K, 'The Future of Surrogacy: A Review of Current Global Trends and National Landscapes' (2024) 48 Reproductive Biomedicine Online <doi.org/10.1016/j.rbmo.2023.1037642> accessed 6 September 2024.

Horsey K, 'Fraying at the Edges: UK Surrogacy Law in 2015' (2016) 24 Medical Law Review 608–21.

Horsey K, 'Not Withered on the Vine: The Need for Surrogacy Law Reform' (2016) 4 Journal of Medical Law and Ethics 181–96.

Horsey K, 'Challenging Presumptions: Legal Parenthood and Surrogacy Arrangements' (2010) 22 Child and Family Law Quarterly 439–74.

Horsey K and Jackson E, 'The Human Fertilisation and Embryology Act 1990 and Non-Traditional Families' (2023) 86 Modern Law Review 1472–88.

Horsey K and others, 'UK Intended Parents' Characteristics, Experiences, and Views on Surrogacy Law Reform' (2023) 37 International Journal of Law, Policy, and the Family 3bad004 <doi.org/10.1093/lawfam/ebad004> accessed 6 September 2024.

Howard G, *The Pregnancy Police: Conceiving Crime, Arresting Personhood* (University of California Press 2024).

Human Tissue Authority, 'Guidance on the disposal of pregnancy remains following pregnancy loss or termination' (2015) <https://content.hta.gov.uk/sites/default/files/2021-06/Guidance%20on%20the%20disposal%20of%20pregnacy%20remains.pdf> accessed 22 April 2024.

Human Tissue Authority, 'Code of Practice: Guiding Principles and the Fundamental Principle of Consent' (2020) <https://content.hta.gov.uk/sites/default/files/2020-11/Code%20A.pdf> accessed 22 April 2024.

Hunt K and Gruszczynski M, 'The Ratification of CEDAW and the Liberalization of Abortion Laws' (2019) 15 Politics & Gender 722–45.

Hyun I and others, 'Embryology Policy: Revisit the 14-day Rule' (2016) 533 Nature 169–71.

International Federation of Gynecology and Obstetrics, 'FIGO Calls for the Total Decriminalisation of Safe Abortion' (nd) <https://www.figo.org/resources/figo-statements/figo-calls-total-decriminalisation-safe-abortion> accessed 14 August 2023.

Jackson E, 'Degendering Reproduction?' (2008) 16 Medical Law Review 346–68.

Jackson E, 'Conception and the Irrelevance of the Welfare Principle' (2002) 65 Modern Law Review 176–203.

Jackson E, *Regulating Reproduction: Law, Technology and Autonomy* (Hart Publishing 2001).

Jaggar A (ed), *Living with Contradictions: Controversies in Feminist Social Ethics* (Routledge 1994).

Jaggar A and Young MI (eds), *A Companion to Feminist Philosophy* (Blackwell Publishing 2017).

Janiak E and Goldberg A, 'Eliminating the Phrase "Elective Abortion": Why Language Matters' (2016) 93 Contraception 89–92.

Järvholm S and others, 'Uterus Transplantation: Joys and Frustrations of Becoming a "Complete" Woman—A Qualitative Study Regarding Self-image in the 5-year Period After Transplantation' (2020) 35 Human Reproduction 1855–63.

Jarvis G, 'Early Embryo Mortality in Natural Human Reproduction: What the Data Say, [version 2; peer review: 2 approved, 1 approved with reservations]' (2017) 5 FI000Research 2765 <doi.org/10.12688/f1000research.8937.2> accessed 6 September 2024.

Jasanoff S (ed), *Reframing Rights: Bioconstitutionalism in the Genetic Age* (MIT Press 2011).
Jenkins K, 'Ontic Injustice' (2020) 6 Journal of the American Philosophical Association 188–205.
Jenkins K, Ontology and Oppression (OUP 2023).
Johannesson L and others, 'Guidelines for Standardized Nomenclature and Reporting in Uterus Transplantation: An Opinion from the United States Uterus Transplant Consortium' (2020) 20 American Journal of Transplantation 3319–25.
Johnson T and Romanis EC, 'The Relationship between Speculation and Translation in Bioethics: Methods and Methodologies' (2023) 41 Monash Bioethics Review 1–19.
Jones Be, Ranaei-Zamani N, Vali S, and others, 'Options for Acquiring Motherhood in Absolute Uterine Factor Infertility: Adoption, Surrogacy and Uterine Transplantation' (2021) 23 The Obstetrician & Gynaecologist 138–47.
Jones Be, Rajamanoharan A, Vali S, and others, 'Perceptions and Motivations for Uterus Transplant in Transgender Women' (2021) 4 JAMA Network Open e2034561.
Jones Be, Williams N, Saso S, and others 'Uterine Transplantation in Transgender Women' (2019) 126 British Journal of Obstetrics & Gynaecology 152–56.
Jones Be, Saso S, Yazbek J, and Smith J, 'Uterine Transplantation: Past, Present and Future' (2016) 123 British Journal of Obstetrics and Gynaecology 1434–38.
Jones Bo, Peri-Toten N, and Mountford-Zimdars A, 'Geographic Opportunities for Assisted Reproduction: A Study of Regional Variations in Access to Fertility Treatment in England' (2023) 26 Human Fertility 494–503.
Jones J and others (eds), *Gender, Sexualities and Law* (Routledge 2011).
Jones R and Jerman J, 'Population Group Abortion Rates and Lifetime Incidence of Abortion: United States, 2008–2014' (2017) 112 American Journal of Public Health 1225–45.
Jones RE and Lopez K, *Human Reproductive Biology* (4th edn Elsevier 2014).
Kaczor C, 'Ectogenesis and a Right to the Death of the Prenatal Human Being: A Reply to Räsänen' (2018) 32 Bioethics 634–38.
Kaczor C, *The Ethics of Abortion: Women's Rights, Human Life, and the Question of Justice* (Taylor & Francis 2010).
Kaczor C, *The Edge of Life: Human Dignity and Contemporary Bioethics* (Springer 2005).
Kaplan D (ed), *Readings in the Philosophy of Technology* (Rowman & Littlefield Publishers 2009).
Karaian L, 'Pregnant Men: Repronormativity, Critical Trans Theory, and the Re(conceive) ing of Sex and Pregnancy in Law' (2013) 22 Social & Legal Studies 211–30.
Katz Rothman B, *The Tentative Pregnancy: Prenatal Diagnosis and the Future of Motherhood* (Viking 1986).
Katz Rothman B, 'Daddy Plants a Seed: Personhood under Patriarchy' (1996) 47 Hastings Law Journal 1241–48.
Kendal E, 'Commentary on Romanis' Assisted Gestative Technologies' (2022) 48 Journal of Medical Ethics 450–51.
Kendal E, 'Pregnant People, Inseminators and Tissues of Human Origin: How Ectogenesis Challenges the Concept of Abortion' (2020) 38 Monash Bioethics Review 197–204.
Kendal E, 'Utopian Literature and Bioethics: Exploring Reproductive Difference and Gender Equality' (2018) 36 Literature and Medicine 56–84.
Kendal E, *Equal Opportunity and the Case for State Sponsored Ectogenesis* (Palgrave 2015).
Kennedy S, 'Willing Mothers: Ectogenesis and the Role of Gestational Motherhood' (2020) 46 Journal of Medical Ethics 320–27.

Keown J, *Abortion, Doctors, and the Law: Some Aspects of the Legal Regulation of Abortion in England from 1803 to 1982* (CUP 2002).

Kilby M, Johnson A, and Oepkes D, *Fetal Therapy: Scientific Basis and Critical Appraisal of Clinical Benefits* (CUP 2020).

Kimberley L, Sutter M, and Quinn G, 'Equitable Access to Ectogenesis for Sexual and Gender Minorities' (2020) 34 Bioethics 338–45.

Kimport K and McLemore M, 'The Problem with "Justifying" Abortion: Why Real Reproductive Justice Cannot Be Achieved by Theorizing the Legitimacy of Abortion' (2022) 9 Women's Reproductive Health 27–31.

Kingma E, 'Were You a Part of Your Mother?' (2019) 128 Mind 609–46.

Kingma E, 'Lady Parts: The Metaphysics of Pregnancy' (2018) 82 Royal Institute of Philosophy Supplements 165–87.

Kingma E and Finn S, 'Neonatal Incubator or Artificial Womb? Distinguishing Ectogestation and Ectogenesis using the Metaphysics of Pregnancy' (2020) 34 Bioethics 354–63.

Kirschenheiter T, 'Responsibility Arguments in Defence of Abortion: When One is Morally Responsible for the Creation of a Fetus' (2023) 29 The New Bioethics 340–51.

Kolers A, and Bayne T, '"Are You My Mommy?" On the Genetic Basis of Parenthood' (2001) 18 Journal of Applied Philosophy 273–85.

König A, Whittaker A, Gerrits T and Rozée V, 'Shifting Surrogacies: Comparative Ethnographies' (2022) 63 International Journal of Comparative Sociology 235–46.

Koplin J, 'How Useful is the Category of "Assisted Gestative Technologies"?' 49 Journal of Medical Ethics 350–51.

Koplin J and Kendal E, 'Ethical Issues in Uterine Transplantation' (2020) 34 Korean Journal of Transplantation 78–83.

Kortsmit K and others, 'Abortion Surveillance—United States, 2020' (2022) 71 Surveillance Summaries 1–27 <https://www.cdc.gov/mmwr/volumes/71/ss/ss7110a1.htm?s_cid=ss7110a1_w.html> accessed 14 August 2023.

Lamont R (ed), *Family Law* (OUP 2022).

Lázaro R, 'Feminism and Motherhood: O'Brien vs Beauvoir' (1986) 1 Hypatia 87–102.

Lewis S, *Full Surrogacy Now: Feminist Against Family* (Verso 2019).

Langford S, 'An End to Abortion? A Feminist Critique of the "Ectogenetic Solution" to Abortion' (2008) 31 Women's Studies International Forum 263–69.

Langford S, 'Defending Intimacy against What? Limits of Antisurrogacy Feminisms' (2017) 43 Signs: Journal of Women in Culture and Society 97–125.

Law Commission of England and Wales and Scottish Law Commission, 'Building Families Through Surrogacy: a New Law: Volume II: Final Report' (Law Com No 411, Scot Law Com No 262, March 2023) <https://s3-eu-west-2.amazonaws.com/cloud-platform-e218f50a4812967ba1215eaecede923f/uploads/sites/30/2023/03/2.-Surrogacy-full-report.pdf> accessed 12 June 2024.

Lawlor M and others, 'Specific Unwillingness to Donate Eyes: The Impact of Disfigurement, Knowledge and Procurement on Corneal Donation' (2010) 10 American Journal of Transplantation 657–63.

Lee JY, 'Surrogacy: Beyond the Commercial/Altruistic Distinction' (2023) 49 Journal of Medical Ethics 196–99.

Lee JY, 'Framing Gestation: Assistance, Delegation, and Beyond' (2022) 48 Journal of Medical Ethics 448–49.

Lee JY, Bidoli A, and Di Nucci E, 'Does Ectogestation have Oppressive Potential?' (2023) Journal of Social Philosophy <doi.org/10.1111/josp.12512> accessed 6 September 2024.

Lefkowitz A, Edwards M, and Balayla J, 'The Montreal Criteria for the Ethical Feasibility of Uterine Transplantation' (2012) 25 Transplant International 439–47.

Lima D, 'Legal Parenthood in Surrogacy: Shifting the Focus to the Surrogate's Negative Intention' (2024) 46 Journal of Social Welfare and the Law 245–66.

Little M, 'Abortion, Intimacy and the Duty to Gestate' (1999) 2 Ethical Theory and Moral Practice 295–312.

Littlejohn K, *Just Get on the Pill: The Uneven Burden of Reproductive Politics* (University of California Press 2021).

Lloyd E, *The Case of the Female Orgasm: Bias in the Science of Evolution* (Harvard University Press 2005).

Loh J and Coeckelbergh M (eds), *Feminist Philosophy of Technology* (Springer 2009).

MacKay K, 'The "Tyranny of Reproduction": Could Ectogenesis Further Women's Liberation?' (2020) 34 Bioethics 346–53.

Mahmoud Z and Romanis EC, 'On Gestation and Motherhood' (2023) 31 Medical Law Review 109–40.

Mangione E, '"Recombining" Biological Motherhoods. Towards Two "Complete" Biological Mothers' (2024) Journal of Medical Ethics <doi:10.1136/jme-2023-109610> accessed 6 September 2024.

Mangione E, 'Carrying the Same Pregnancy: A Bioethical Overview on Reciprocal Effortless IVF and Similar Techniques' (2023) 18 Clinical Ethics 271–79.

Margaria A, 'Trans Men Giving Birth and Reflections on Fatherhood: What to Expect?' (2020) 34 International Journal of Law, Policy and the Family 225–46.

Margree V, *Neglected or Misunderstood: The Radical Feminism of Shulamith Firestone* (Zero Books 2017).

Marina S and others, 'Sharing Motherhood: Biological Lesbian Co-mothers, A New IVF Indication' (2010) 25 Human Reproduction 938–41.

Mason JK and McCall Smith A, *Law and Medical Ethics* (Butterworths 1983).

Mathison E and Davis J, 'Is There a Right to the Death of the Foetus?' (2017) 31 Bioethics 313–20.

Matthews M, Lal A, and Pacia D, 'The Role of Epistemic Injustice in Abortion Access Disparities' (2022) 22 American Journal of Bioethics 49–51.

Mattingly S, 'The Maternal-Fetal Dyad Exploring the Two-Patient Obstetric Model' (1992) 22 The Hastings Center Report 13–18.

Mavuso J and Chadwick R, 'Cisgender Men's Narratives about their Desires to be Pregnant: Re/constructing Reproduction, Gender, and their Entanglement' (2024) Journal of Family Studies 1–21 <doi:10.1080/13229400.2023.2301586> accessed 6 September 2024.

Mayr E and Ashlock P, *Principles of Systemic Zoology* (2nd edn, Donnelley & Sons Company 1991).

McCandless J and Sheldon S, 'The Human Fertilisation and Embryology Act (2008) and the Tenacity of the Sexual Family Form' (2010) 73 Modern Law Review 175–207.

McCann C, Kim S-k and Ergun E, *Feminist Theory Reader: Local and Global Perspectives* (5th edn Routledge 2020).

McGuiness S, 'Abortion, Criminal Law and Transgression' (2024) 105 Women's Studies International Forum 102917 <https://doi.org/10.1016/j.wsif.2024.102917> accessed 3 July 2024.

McGuiness S and Alghrani A, 'Gender and Parenthood: The Case for Realignment' (2008) 16 Medical Law Review 261–83.

Merelman R, *Language, Symbolism, and Politics* (Westview Press 1992).

Middlemiss A, *Invisible Labours: The Reproductive Politics of Second Trimester Pregnancy Loss in England* (Berghahn Books 2024).

Miglio N, *Gestational Phenomenology* (forthcoming).

Millett K, *Sexual Politics* (Granada Publishing Ltd 1971).

Mills C, 'Nuclear Families: Mitochondrial Replacement Techniques and the Regulation of Parenthood' (2021) 46 Science, Technology, & Human Values 507–27.

Milne E, 'Putting the Fetus First—Legal Regulation, Motherhood, and Pregnancy' (2020) 27 Michigan Journal of Gender & Law 149–211.

Mulligan A, 'Surrogacy and the Significance of Gestation: Implications for Law and Policy' (2024) Bioethics <doi.org/10.1111/bioe.13302> accessed 6 September 2024.

Mullock A, Romanis EC, and Begović D, 'Surrogacy and Uterus Transplantation using Live Donors: Examining the Options from the Perspective of "Womb-givers" (2021) 35 Bioethics 820–28.

Murphy T, 'Assisted Gestation and Transgender Women' (2014) 20 Bioethics 389–97.

National Health Service, 'Risks—Caesarean Section' <https://www.nhs.uk/conditions/caesarean-section/risks/> accessed 20 November 2023.

National Institute of Health and Care Excellence, 'Caesarean birth – NG192' (2023) <https://www.nice.org.uk/guidance/ng192> accessed 28 November 2023).

National Institute of Health and Care Excellence, 'Fertility Problems: Assessment and Treatment [CG156]' (2017) <https://www.nice.org.uk/guidance/cg156/chapter/Recommendations#access-criteria-for-ivf> accessed 20 May 2024.

Nelson A, 'Should Delivery by Partial Ectogenesis Be Available on Request of the Pregnant Person?' (2022) 15 International Journal of Feminist Approaches to Bioethics 1–26.

Nelson A and Romanis EC, 'The Medicalisation of Childbirth and Access to Homebirth in the UK: COVID-19 and Beyond' (2021) 29 Medical Law Review 661–87.

Nelson M, *The Argonauts* (Greywolf Press 2015).

Ngaage L and others, 'The Changing Paradigm of Ethics in Uterus Transplantation: A Systematic Review' (2020) 33 Transplant International 260–69.

NHS Imperial College Healthcare Trust, 'First womb transplant performed in the UK' (2023) <https://www.imperial.nhs.uk/about-us/news/first-womb-transplant-performed-in-the-uk> accessed 25 June 2024.

Nossiff R, 'Gendered Citizenship: Women, Equality, and Abortion Policy' (2007) 29 New Political Science 61–76.

O'Brien D, 'Fairness, Care, and Abortion' (2023) 40 Journal of Applied Philosophy 658–75.

O'Donovan L, 'Why Uterine Transplantation Requires Us to Rethink the Role of the Pre-conception Welfare Principle (2022) Journal of Law and the Biosciences <doi.org/10.1093/jlb/lsac028> 1–32 accessed 6 September 2024.

O'Donovan L, 'Gifting the Womb: A Legal and Ethical Analysis of Uterine Transplantation' (PhD thesis, University of Manchester 2021).

O'Donovan L, 'Pushing the Boundaries: Uterine Transplantation and the Limits of Reproductive Autonomy' (2018) 32 Bioethics 489–98.

O'Donovan L and others, 'Ethical and Policy Issues Raised by Uterus Transplants' (2019) 131 British Medical Bulletin 19–28.

Ongun H and others, 'Miracles of Science: Birth after Uterus Transplantation' (2024) 50 Journal of Obstetrics and Gynaecology Research 4–14.

Orentlicher D, 'Toward Acceptance of Uterus Transplants' (2012) 42 Hastings Center Report 12–13.

Orentlicher D and Hervey T, *The Oxford Handbook of Comparative Health Law* (OUP 2021).

Osbourne P, 'Problematizing Disciplinarity, Transdisciplinary Problematics' (2015) 32 Theory, Culture, & Society 3–35.

Ottley E and others, '*Dobbs v Jackson Women's Health Organization* (2022): Consequences One Year On' (2023) 31 Medical Law Review 457–68.

Overall C, *Human Reproduction: Principles, Practices, Policies* (OUP 1993).

Overall C, 'Rethinking Abortion, Ectogenesis and Foetal Death' (2015) 46 Journal of Social Philosophy 126–40.

Palacios-González C, 'Does Egg Donation for Mitochondrial Replacement Techniques Generate Parental Responsibilities?' (2018) 44 Journal of Medical Ethics 817–22.

Partridge E and others, 'An Extra-uterine System to Physiologically Support the Extreme Preterm Lamb' (2017) Nature Communications 15112 <doi:10.1038/ncomms15112> accessed 6 September 2024.

Parsons JA and Romanis EC, *Early Medical Abortion, Equality of Access, and the Telemedical Imperative* (OUP 2021).

Parsons JA and others, 'Translational or Translationable? A Call for Ethno-immersion in (Empirical) Bioethics Research' (2024) 38 Bioethics 252–61.

Paterson S, Scala F, and Sokolon M (eds), *Fertile Ground: Exploring Reproduction in Canada* (McGill-Queen's University Press 2014).

Patterson-Brown B and Watson K, 'No Substitute: The False Promise of Artificial Womb Technology as an Alternative to Abortion' (2023) 23 American Journal of Bioethics 87–89.

Pattinson S, *Law at the Frontiers of Biomedicine* (Bloomsbury Publishing 2023).

Paul E, *Taking Sides Clashing Views on Controversial Issues in Sex and Gender* (McGraw-Hill 2001).

Pearce R and others (eds), *The Emergence of Trans: Cultures, Politics and Everyday Lives* (Routledge 2019).

Petropanagos A, 'Pronatalism, Geneticism, and ART' (2017) 10 International Journal of Feminist Approaches to Bioethics 119–47.

Pew Research Center, 'Public Opinion on Abortion' (nd) <https://www.pewresearch.org/religion/fact-sheet/public-opinion-on-abortion/> accessed 14 August 2023.

Pickles C and Herring J (eds), *Childbirth, Vulnerability and Law: Exploring Issues of Violence and Control* (Routledge 2019).

Pollack Petchesky R, 'The Power of Visual Culture in the Politics of Reproductions' (1987) 13 Feminist Studies 263–92.

Poste E, *Gai Institutiones* (4th edn OUP 1904).

Power M and Schulkin J, *The Evolution of the Human Placenta* (Johns Hopkins University Press 2012).

Progress Educational Trust, '100 years of "Daedalus": The Birth of Assisted Reproductive Technology' <https://www.progress.org.uk/100-years-of-daedalus-the-birth-of-assisted-reproductive-technology/> accessed 25 June 2024.

Pruski M and Playford R, 'Artificial Wombs, Thomson and Abortion—What Might Change?' (2022) 19 Diametros 35–53.

Quintero AM and De Jaegher H, 'Pregnant Agencies: Movement and Participation in Maternal-Fetal Interactions' (2020) 11 Frontiers in Psychology <doi.org/10.3389/fpsyg.2020.01977> accessed 6 September 2024.

Raju T, 'Breastfeeding Is a Dynamic Biological Process—Not Simply a Meal at the Breast' (2011) 6 Breastfeeding Medicine 257–59.

Räsänen J, 'Who Should have Access to Assisted Gestative Technologies?' (2022) 48 Journal of Medical Ethics 447.

Räsänen J, 'Ectogenesis, Abortion and a Right to the Death of the Fetus' (2017) 31 Bioethics 697–702.

Rawls J, *A Theory of Justice* (Harvard University Press 1999).

Remez L and others, 'Global Developments in Laws on Induced Abortion: 2008–2019' (2020) 46 International Perspectives on Sexual and Reproductive Health 53–65.

Rich A, *Of Woman Born: Motherhood as Experience and Institution* (WW Norton & Company 1995).

Richards E and others, 'Uterus Transplant: State of the Art in 2021' (2021) 38 Journal of Assisted Reproduction and Genetics 2251–59.

Riggsby A, *Roman Law and the Legal World of the Romans* (CUP 2010).

Riley N and Chatterjee N, *Controlling Reproduction: Women, Society, and State Power* (Polity Press 2023).

Roberts D, *Killing the Black Body: Race, Reproduction, and the Meaning of Liberty,20th anniversary edition* (Vintage Books 2017).

Robertson J, 'Is There a Right to Gestate?' (2017) 4 Journal of Law and the Biosciences 630–36.

Robertson J, 'Other Women's Wombs: Uterus Transplants and Gestational Surrogacy' (2016) 3 Journal of Law and the Biosciences 68–86.

Robinson H, 'Pregnancy and Superior Moral Status: A Proposal for Two Thresholds of Personhood' (2024) 50 Journal of Medical Ethics 12–19.

Rodgers D, 'The Philosophy of Taxonomy' (1958) 50 Mycologia 326–32.

Romanis EC, 'Male and Nonbinary Pregnancy in the Law: Ontic Injustice and/or Invisbilisation' (forthcoming).

Romanis EC, '"The Law is Very, Very Outdated and Not Keeping Up with the Technology": Novel Forms of Assisted Gestation, Legal Challenges, and Perspectives of Reproductive Rights Advocates in England and Wales' (2023) 10 Journal of Law and the Biosciences <doi.org/10.1093/jlb/lsad027>.

Romanis EC, 'The Equality-Enhancing Potential of Novel Forms of Assisted Gestation: Perspectives of Reproductive Rights Advocates' (2023) 37 Bioethics 637–46.

Romanis EC, 'The Ethical and Legal Status of "Fetonates" or "Gestatelings"' (2023) 23 The American Journal of Bioethics 90–92.

Romanis EC, 'Abortion Access and the Benefits and Limitations of Abortion-Permissive Legal Frameworks: Lessons from the United Kingdom' (2023) 32 Cambridge Quarterly of Healthcare Ethics 378–90.

Romanis EC, 'The End of (Reproductive) Liberty as We Know It: A Note on Dobbs V. Jackson Women's Health 597 USC (2022)' (2023) 23 Medical Law International 71–87.

Romanis EC, '*R v Foster*: Exemplifying the Urgency of the Decriminalisation of Abortion' (2023) 31 Medical Law Review 606–14.

Romanis EC, 'Appropriately Framing Maternal Request Caesarean Section' (2022) 48 Journal of Medical Ethics 554–56.

Romanis EC, 'Assisted Gestative Technologies' (2022) 48 Journal of Medical Ethics 439–46.

Romanis EC, 'Abortion & "Artificial Wombs": Would "Artificial Womb" Technology Legally Empower Non-gestating Genetic Progenitors to Participate in Decisions about How to Terminate Pregnancy in England and Wales?' (2021) Journal of Law and the Biosciences <doi:10.1093/jlb/lsab011>.

Romanis EC, 'Is "Viability" Viable? Abortion, Conceptual Confusion and the Law in England and Wales and the United States' (2021) 7 Journal of Law and the Biosciences lsaa059 <doi:10.1093/jlb/lsaa059>.

Romanis EC, 'Regulating the "Brave New World": Ethico-Legal Implications of the Quest for Partial Ectogenesis' (PhD thesis, University of Manchester 2020).

Romanis EC, 'Artificial Womb Technology and the Choice to Gestate Ex Utero: Is Partial Ectogenesis the Business of the Criminal Law?' (2020) 28 Medical Law Review 342–74.

Romanis EC, 'Addressing Rising Cesarean Rates: Maternal Request Cesareans, Defensive Practice, and the Power of Choice in Childbirth' (2020) 13 International Journal of Feminist Approaches to Bioethics 1–26.

Romanis EC, 'Partial Ectogenesis: Freedom, Equality, and Political Perspective' (2020) 46 Journal of Medical Ethics 89–90.

Romanis EC, 'Artificial Womb Technology and Clinical Translation: Innovative Treatment or Medical Research?' (2020) 34 Bioethics 392–402.

Romanis EC, 'Artificial Womb Technology and the Significance of Birth: Why Gestatelings are Not Newborns (or Fetuses)' (2019) 45 Journal of Medical Ethics 728–31.

Romanis EC, 'Challenging the "Born Alive" Threshold: Fetal Surgery, Artificial Wombs, and the English Approach to Legal Personhood' (2020) 28 Medical Law Review 93–123.

Romanis EC, 'Artificial Womb Technology and the Frontiers of Human Reproduction: Conceptual Differences and Potential Implications' (2018) 44 Journal of Medical Ethics 751–55.

Romanis EC and Adkins V, 'Artificial Placentas, Pregnancy Loss and Loss-sensitive Care' (2024) 50 Journal of Medical Ethics 299–307.

Romanis EC and others, 'Reviewing the Womb' (2021) 47 Journal of Medical Ethics 820–29.

Romanis EC and Brown, 'Legal Parenthood, Novel Reproductive Practices, and the Disruption of Reproductive Biosex' (2024) Modern Law Review <doi.org/10.1111/1468-2230.12914> accessed 1 September 2024.

Romanis EC and Horn C, 'Artificial Wombs and the Ectogenesis Conversation: A Misplaced Focus? Technology, Abortion, and Reproductive Freedom' (2020) 13 International Journal of Feminist Approaches to Bioethics 174–94.

Romanis EC, Mullock A, and Parsons J, 'The Excessive Regulation of Early Abortion Medication in the UK: The Case for Reform' (2022) 30 Medical Law Review 4–32.

Romanis EC and Parsons J, 'Directed and Conditional Uterus Donation' (2022) 48 Journal of Medical Ethics 810–15.

Romanis EC, Segers S, and de Jong B, 'Value Sensitive Design and the Artificial Placenta' (2024) <https://doi.org/10.1136/jme-2024-110066> accessed 18 September 2024.

Rosenblum D, 'Unsex Mothering: Toward a New Culture of Parenting' (2012) 35 Harvard Journal of Law and Gender 57–116.

Ross E, 'Gestating Bodies: Sensing Foetal Movement in First Time Pregnancy' (2019) 41 Sociology of Health & Illness 95–111.

Ross L and Solinger R, *Reproductive Justice: An Introduction* (University of California Press 2017).

Rosser S, *Teaching Science and Health from a Feminist Perspective* (Pergamon Press 1986).

Ruddick S, *Maternal Thinking: Towards a Politics of Peace* (Beacon Press 1989).

Savell K, 'Is the Born Alive Rule Out-dated and Indefensible?' (2006) 28 Sydney Law Review 625–64.

Schick A, 'Whereto Speculative Bioethics? Technological Visions and Future Simulations in A Science Fictional Culture' (2016) 42 Medical Humanities 225.

Schouten G, 'Fetuses, Orphans, and a Famous Violinist: On the Ethics and Politics of Abortion' (2017) 43 Social Theory and Practice 637–65.

Segers S and Romanis EC, 'Ethical, Translational, and Legal Issues Surrounding the Novel Adoption of Ectogestative Technologies' (2022) 15 Risk Management and Healthcare Policy 2207–20.

Segers S and others, 'The Ethics of Ectogenesis-aided Foetal Treatment' (2020) 34 Bioethics 264–370.

Segers S and Accoe D, 'Telling "Science" from "Science-Fiction": The Ethics of Ectogestative Technology' (2023) 177 JAMA Pediatrics 1110.

Seneviratne M, 'Pre-Natal Injury and Transferred Malice: The Invented Other' (1996) 59 Modern Law Review 884–92.

Shalev C, *Birth Power: The Case for Surrogacy* (Yale University Press 1989).

Shanley ML, *Making Babies, Making Families: What Matters Most in an Age of Reproductive Technologies, Surrogacy, Adoption, and Same-sex and Unwed Parents* (Beacon Press 2001).

Shahvisi A, 'Towards Responsible Ejaculations: The Moral Imperative for Male Contraceptive Responsibility' (2020) 46 Journal of Medical Ethics 328–36.

Sheldon S, 'British Abortion Law: Speaking from the Past to Govern the Future' (2016) 79 Medical Law Review 283–316.

Sheldon S, 'Fragmenting Fatherhood: The Regulation of Reproductive Technologies' (2005) 68 Modern Law Review 523–53.

Sheldon S, *Beyond Control: Medical Power and Abortion Law* (Pluto Press 1997).

Sheldon S and Jonathan Lord, 'Care not Criminalisation; Reform of British Abortion Law is Long Overdue' (2023) 49 Journal of Medical Ethics 523–24.

Sheldon S and Kaye Wellings (eds), *Decriminalising Abortion in the UK: What Would it Mean?* (Policy Press 2020).

Sheldon S and others, '"Supportive Parenting", Responsibility and Regulation: The Welfare Assessment under the Reformed Human Fertilisation and Embryology Act (1990)' (2015) 78 Modern Law Review 461–92.

Shenfield F and others, 'ESHRE Task Force on Ethics and Law 10: Surrogacy' (2005) 20 Human Reproduction 2705–07.

Sifferlin A, 'Exclusive: First U.S. Baby Born After a Uterus Transplant' (2017) *Time* <https://time.com/5044565/exclusive-first-u-s-baby-born-after-a-uterus-transplant/> accessed 14 September 2021.

Simonstein F (ed), *Reprogen-Ethics and the Future of Gender* (Springer 2009).

Simkulet W. 'Abortion and Ectogenesis: Moral Compromise' (2020) 46 Journal of Medical Ethics 93–98.

Singer P, *Practical Ethics* (CUP 1979).

Singer P and Wells D, *The Reproduction Revolution: New Ways of Making Babies* (OUP 1984).

Singh P, 'Fetuses, Newborns & Parental Responsibility' (2020) 46 Journal of Medical Ethics 188–93.

Smajdor A, 'In Defence of Ectogenesis' (2012) 21 Cambridge Quarterly of Healthcare Ethics 90–103.

Smajdor A, 'The Moral Imperative for Ectogenesis' (2007) 16 Cambridge Quarterly for Healthcare Ethics 336–45.

Smith B and Brogaard B, 'Sixteen Days' (2003) 1 Journal of Medicine and Philosophy 45–78.

Sparrow R, 'Is it Every Man's Right to Have Babies if He Wants Them? Male Pregnancy and the Limits of Procreative Liberty (2008) 18 Kennedy Institute of Ethics Journal 275–99.

Spencer B and Mychaliska G, 'Updates in Neonatal Extracorporeal Membrane Oxygenation and the Artificial Placenta' (2022) 49 Clinics in Perinatology 873–91.

Stratman C, 'Ectogestation and the Good Samaritan Argument' (2023) Journal of Law and the Biosciences <doi.org/10.1093/jlb/lsad012>.

Stratman C, Ectogestation and the Problem of Abortion' (2021) 34 Philosophy & Technology 683–700.

Stuvøy I, 'Troublesome Reproduction: Surrogacy under Scrutiny' (2018) 7 Reproductive Biomedicine and Society Online 33–43.

Swennen F and Croce M, 'The Symbolic Power of Legal Kinship Terminology: An Analysis of "Co-motherhood" and "Duo-motherhood" in Belgium and the Netherlands' (2016) 25 Social & Legal Studies 181–203.

Thomson JJ, 'A Defense of Abortion' (1971) 1 Philosophy & Public Affairs 47–66.

Thomson M, 'Legislating for the Monstrous: Access to Reproductive Services and the Monstrous Feminine' (1997) 6 Social & Legal Studies 401–24.

Thomas T, '"A Giant Step"': Charities Welcome Plan to Widen Access to IVF on NHS' *The Guardian* <https://www.theguardian.com/society/2022/jul/20/a-giant-step-charities-welcome-plan-to-widen-access-to-ivf-on-nhs> accessed 6 November 2022.

Tongue Z, 'Locating Abortion and Contraception on the Obstetric Violence Continuum' (2024) 17 International Journal of Feminist Approaches to Bioethics 1–24.

Union of Physically Impaired Against Segregation (1974) <https://disability-studies.leeds.ac.uk/wp-content/uploads/sites/40/library/UPIAS-UPIAS.pdf> accessed 1 September 2024.

US Food and Drug Administration, 'Breakthrough Devices Program' (nd) <https://www.fda.gov/medical-devices/how-study-and-market-your-device/breakthrough-devices-program> accessed 25 June 2024.

US Food and Drug Administration, 'Pediatric Advisory Committee Meeting Announcement' (2023) <https://www.fda.gov/advisory-committees/advisory-committee-calendar/pediatric-advisory-committee-meeting-announcement-09192023> accessed 25 June 2024.

US Food and Drug Administration, 'Pediatric Advisory Committee Meeting about Artificial Wombs on 19 and 20 September 2023' (2023) <https://www.fda.gov/advisory-committees/pediatric-advisory-committee/2023-meeting-materials-pediatric-advisory-committee> accessed 16 November 2023.

Usuda H, Watanabe S, Miura Y, and others, 'Successful Maintenance of Key Physiological Parameters in Preterm Lambs Treated with Ex Vivo Uterine Environment Therapy for A Period of 1 Week' (2017) 217 American Journal of Obstetrics and Gynecology 457.e1–457.e13.

Usuda H, Watanabe S, Saito M, and others, 'Successful Use of An Artificial Placenta to Support Extremely Preterm Ovine Fetuses at the Border of Viability (2019) 221 American Journal of Obstetrics and Gynecology 69.e1–69.e17.

van de Hout-van der Jagt B and others, 'Interprofessional Consensus Regarding Design Requirements for Liquid-Based Perinatal Life Support (PLS) Technology' (2022) 9 Frontiers in Pediatrics <doi.org/10.3389/fped.2021.793531>.

van Willigen B and others, 'A Review Study of Fetal Circulatory Models to Develop a Digital Twin of a Fetus in a Perinatal Life Support System' (2022) 10 Frontiers in Pediatrics 915846.

Verweij EJ and Elselijn Kingma, 'Artificial Placenta—Imminent Ethical Considerations for Research Trials and Clinical Translation' (2023) 23 The American Journal of Bioethics 87–89.

Warren MA, 'The Moral Significance of Birth' (1989) 4 Hypatia 45–65.

Warren MA, 'On the Moral and Legal Status of Abortion' (1973) 57 The Monist 43–61.

Watt H and McCarthy A, 'Targeting the Fetal Body and/or the Mother-Child Connection: Vital Conflicts and Abortion' (2019) 87 The Linacre Quarterly 147–60.

Welin S, 'Reproductive Ectogenesis: The Third Era of Human Reproduction and Some Moral Consequences' (2004) 10 Science and Engineering Ethics 615–26.

Weller C, 'What You Need to Know about Egg-freezing, The Hot New Perk at Google, Apple, and Facebook' The Insider (2017) <https://www.businessinsider.com/egg-freezing-at-facebook-apple-google-hot-new-perk-2017-9> accessed 6 November 2022.

West R, 'Jurisprudence and Gender' (1988) 55 The University of Chicago Law Review 1–72.

Wilkinson S and Williams N, 'Should Uterus Transplants be Publicly Funded?' (2016) 42 Journal of Medical Ethics 559–65.

Willekens H and others (eds), *Motherhood and the Law* (Universitätsverlag Göttingen 2019).

Williams N, 'Amel Alghrani, *Regulating Assisted Reproductive Technologies—New Horizons*' (2020) 38 Medical Law Review 431–36.

Williams N, 'Should Deceased Donation be Morally Preferred in Uterine Transplantation' (2016) 30 Bioethics 415–24.

Williams N, O'Donovan L, and Wilkinson S, 'Presumed Dissent? Opt-out Organ Donation and the Exclusion of Organs and Tissues' (2022) 30 Medical Law Review 268–98.

Williams P, *The Alchemy of Race and Rights* (Harvard University Press 1991).

Woollard F. 'Mother Knows Best: Pregnancy, Applied Ethics, and Epistemically Transformative Experiences' (2020) 38 Journal of Applied Philosophy 155–71.

World Health Organization, 'Abortion Care Guideline' (2022) <https://www.who.int/publications/i/item/9789240039483> accessed 6 November 2023.

World Health Organization, 'Fact Sheet: Infertility' (nd) <https://www.who.int/news-room/fact-sheets/detail/infertility> accessed 21 June 2024.

YouGov, 'Should Women Have the Right to An Abortion?' (nd) <https://yougov.co.uk/topics/politics/trackers/should-women-have-the-right-to-an-abortion> accessed 14 August 2023.

Young IM, *Throwing Like a Girl and Other Essays in Feminist Philosophy and Social Theory* (Indiana University Press 1990).

de Ziegler D and others, 'Assisted Reproductive Technology Strategies in Uterus Transplantation' (2019) 112 Fertility and Sterility 19–23.

INDEX

For the benefit of digital users, indexed terms that span two pages (e.g., 52–53) may, on occasion, appear on only one of those pages.

Figures are indicated by an italic *f* following the page number.